Naturalism, Evolution and Mind

ROYAL INSTITUTE OF PHILOSOPHY SUPPLEMENT: 49

EDITED BY

D. M. Walsh

CAMBRIDGE
UNIVERSITY PRESS

PUBLISHED BY THE PRESS SYNDICATE OF THE UNIVERSITY OF CAMBRIDGE
The Pitt Building, Trumpington Street, Cambridge, CB2 1RP,
United Kingdom

CAMBRIDGE UNIVERSITY PRESS
The Edinburgh Building, Cambridge CB2 2RU, United Kingdom
40 West 20th Street, New York, NY 10011–4211, USA
10 Stamford Road, Oakleigh, Melbourne 3166, Australia

Printed in the United Kingdom at the University Press, Cambridge
Typeset by Michael Heath Ltd, Reigate, Surrey

*A catalogue record for this book is available
from the British Library*

Naturalism, evolution and mind/edited by D.M. Walsh.
    p. cm.—(Royal Institute of Philosophy supplement,
    ISSN 1358-2461; 49)
    Proceedings of the 1999 Royal Institute of Philosophy Conference,
    held in Edinburgh, Scotland.
    Includes bibliographical references and index.
    ISBN 0-521-00373-3 (pbk.)
    1. Philosophy of mind—Congresses. 2. Naturalism—Congresses.
I. Walsh, D. M. II. Series.

    BD418.3 .N36 2001
    128´.5—dc21

                                                              2001025817

ISBN 0 521 00373-3 paperback
ISSN 1358-2461

Contents

Contents

Preface

The papers collected in this volume are the proceedings of the 1999 Royal Institute of Philosophy Conference, held in Edinburgh, Scotland. All of the papers included here, except two, were invited as original contributions. The papers by Thomas Bontly and Michael Wheeler and Anthony Atkinson are expanded versions of shorter papers submitted in response to a general call for papers. I would like to thank the speakers/contributors for their many efforts and for their outstanding patience.

There are many people and organisations to be thanked both for assistance in the organisation of the conference and for assistance in the preparation of the proceedings for publication. I would like to express my gratitude to The Royal Institute of Philosophy for encouragement and help throughout all phases of the project. It is particularly a pleasure to acknowledge the assistance of Professor Anthony O'Hear and Ms Ingrid Purkiss. The Faculty of Arts, Divinity and Music at the University of Edinburgh provided funding, without which the conference could not have happened. The Scots Philosophical Club also provided financial support. Many of the graduate students of the Department of Philosophy, University of Edinburgh provided invaluable logistical support, as did many members of staff. I thank them for their contribution.

A few, special acknowledgements are in order. I would like to thank Timothy Williamson for the initial suggestion to propose a conference of this sort. David Papineau and Elliott Sober provided moral support and enthusiasm during the crucial early stages of development of the conference. Their support helped to attract such an impressive array of contributors. José Bermudez and Michael Wheeler provided particular help in reading and commenting upon various submitted papers. I reserve special thanks to Julian Kiverstein for assistance with the preparation of the manuscript.

D.M. Walsh
Kitleyknowe, Scotland

Notes on Contributors

Anthony Atkinson is Lecturer in Psychology at King Alfred's College, Winchester, U.K.

Thomas Bontly is Assistant Professor of Philosophy at The University of Connecticut, Storrs.

Peter Carruthers is Professor of Philosophy and Chair of the Philosophy Department at the University of Maryland, College Park.

Fred Dretske is Professor Emeritus at Stanford University and the University of Wisconsin and presently a Senior Research Scholar at Duke University.

Frank Jackson is Professor of Philosophy in the Research School of Social Sciences, The Australian National University, Canberra.

Allan Millar is Professor of Philosophy at The University of Stirling.

Ruth Garrett Millikan is a Board of Trustees Distinguished Professor and the Alumni Association Distinguished Professor 2000–2003 at the University of Connecticut.

David Papineau is Professor of Philosophy at King's College, University of London.

Henry Plotkin is Professor of Psychobiology in the Department of Psychology at University College London and is Scientific Director of the Economic and Social Research Council Research Centre on Economic Learning and Social Evolution.

Lawrence Shapiro is Associate Professor of Philosophy at The University of Wisconsin-Madison.

Elliott Sober is Hans Reichenbach Professor of Philosophy and Henry Vilas Research Professor at The University of Wisconsin-Madison.

Denis Walsh is Lecturer in Philosophy at The University of Edinburgh.

Michael Wheeler is Lecturer in Philosophy at the University of Dundee.

Andrew Whiten is Professor of Evolutionary and Developmental Psychology and Bishop Wardlaw Professor of Psychology at the University of St Andrews.

Editor's Introduction

D.M. WALSH

The papers collected in this volume are the proceedings of the 1999 Royal Institute of Philosophy conference: the theme of the conference, the same as the title of this collection, *Naturalism, Evolution and Mind*. The essays collected here cover a wide array of disparate themes in philosophy, psychology, evolutionary biology and the philosophy of science. They range in subject matter from the mind/body problem and the nature of philosophical naturalism, to the naturalization of psychological norms to the naturalization of phenomenal and intentional content, from the methodology cognitive ethology to issues in evolutionary psychology. They are united by the simple thought that the great promise of current naturalism in philosophy of mind resides in its potential to reveal mental phenomena as continuous with other phenomena of the natural world, particularly with other biological phenomena.

The study of the mind is undergoing something of a revolution. Advances in a number of disparate disciplines have given new impetus to the study of long-standing problems in the philosophy of mind. The essays collected in this volume give an overview of some of the ways in which developments in cognitive ethology, the philosophy of biology, evolutionary psychology, cognitive science and other fields have impacted upon the philosophy of mind.

Given the diversity of approaches and points of view on display it is something of a vain hope that a synoptic introduction might extract a single, overarching theme from this collection. To impose one would be artificial, not to say unilluminating. These papers may not present a single point of view or even cluster around a single, relatively well circumscribed issue, but that is not say that they constitute only a gerrymandered collection. It is fascinating to see the way in which various disparate themes emerge, recur and intertwine among the papers: the significance of the concept of adaptation to the study of mind, the importance of higher-order intentionality, the role of the concept of function in naturalizing intentionality and phenomenal character, the significance of normativity to the understanding of mental phenomena. These themes and others appear repeatedly in the essays which follow.

The collection begins with an object lesson in the ways in which thinking of the mind as a biological category illuminates traditional

1

D. M. Walsh

philosophical problems. Larry Shapiro's *Mind The Adaptation* applies evolutionary thinking to the mind/body problem. Shapiro offers us a simple proposal: the mind is an adaptation. This proposal is contrasted with two existing conceptions of the mental: type-identity physicalism and functionalism. To its credit the mind-as-adaptation thesis steers a course between the 'baseless chauvinism' of type-identity physicalism and the promiscuity of functionalism. It is a commonplace that type-identity materialism constrains the domain of the mental too narrowly. If pain is identical to a certain kind of neurological state then creatures who are not endowed with the sort of physical machinery capable of realizing that state are also incapable of feeling pain. Functionalisms of various sorts have often been thought of as the antidote to the parochiality of type identity theory. According to functionalism, mental states are defined in terms of inputs and outputs *irrespective* of the sort of machinery that realizes them. But, so the usual rejoinder goes, if anything that realizes the set of inputs and outputs which characterizes a mental state *has* that mental state we may find ourselves, implausibly, counting systems like the economy of Bolivia and the nation of China among the bearers of mental states.

Shapiro argues that construing minds as adaptations captures our intuitions about the sorts of things capable of having minds with greater fidelity. Furthermore the concept of an adaptation may well serve to regiment or refine these largely pre-theoretic intuitions. The concept of an adaptation plays an especially significant part in modern systematics. We may find ourselves with a more tractable conception of the nature of mind if we are able to replace a set of largely pre-theoretic intuitions with one which has earned its keep within evolutionary biology.

An adaptation, according to Shapiro, 'is a structure plus a function', where the function of a biological trait is simply the effect that it has been selected for. Because being an adaptation of a certain sort requires that a trait has both a particular structure *and* a particular history, the individuation of mental categories is externalistic. Traits with the same structure may not count as being traits of the same kind. Contrary to physicalism then, sameness of physical realization is not sufficient for sameness of mental state. Of course, the usual objection to physicalism is that the conditions it sets on an entity's having a mind are already too restrictive. So far all we have from the mind-as-adaptation proposal is that these conditions are insufficient. Mind as adaptation has yet to demonstrate that they are unnecessary too. After all, the intuition that type physicalism violates is that mind ought to accommodate at least some form of multiple realizability. This issue is addressed in Shapiro's comparison of functionalism with the mind-as-adaptation view.

The problem with functionalism seems to be that it opens the up the prospect of untrammelled multiple realizability. 'It is only when one chooses to individuate kinds on the basis of function alone that one can remain neutral about the nature of the stuff that fills the functional role. However, it is just this neutrality that also seems to reduce functionalism to absurdity...' (p. 33) Mind-as-adaptation permits a certain amount of multiple realizability—anything that is structured like a brain can be a mind so long as it has the right selectional (that is *not* to say, phylogenetic) history. But how much multiple realizability is allowed? Shapiro here invokes a principle from functional morphology: that function constrains structure. There are only a certain few ways to build a functioning eye. As it turns out, traits which have been selected independently for subserving the function of eyes show remarkable structural similarities. Shapiro conjectures that the same sort of constraints apply with minds. The intuitions upon which claims of the wild multiple realizability of minds are based are in conflict with empirical facts about the ways in which function constrains structure. Something which subserves the function of a mind could not be structured like whatever it is that physically realizes the economy of Bolivia.

'Mind-as-adaptation is...shorthand. It's a slogan that invites us to conceive of the various cognitive capacities that we typically associate with the mind as structures with functions' (Shapiro p. 36). This issue arises again in later essays. Shapiro clearly presents rationale for the evolutionary psychology discussed by Wheeler and Atkinson and Plotkin. It is also interesting to note the tension between Shapiro's justification for the use of history in individuating mental categories and Jackson's claim that the mental categories with which we are most familiar are functional and not historical.

Thomas Bontly's (*Should Intentionality be Naturalized?*) discussion of naturalism raises another set of issues related to the realization of mental states by physical states. Naturalism is both a constraint upon, and a goal of, much of current philosophy of mind, but Bontly's discussion elegantly reminds us that few if any of us are able to say what naturalism is. For some, naturalism is simply a methodological thesis (a position reflected in Sober's contribution)—to be natural is to subject to investigation by a battery of methods recognizable as scientific. Bontly's claim is that naturalism, if it is a substantive thesis at all, is a thesis about the way in which mental states are realized in the world described by physics. After

D. M. Walsh

all, a central tenet of naturalism seems to be that the respective ontologies of the various branches of science comprise a unity.

One common way to cash out the presumed unity implicit in naturalism is to appeal to causal closure. Everything that is natural, it is commonly supposed, comprises a domain which is causally closed and complete. To make a case that putative entities of a certain kind constitute part of the natural world one simply has to show their role in the causal structure of the world. The way to demonstrate that intentional states are natural is to show how they are realized in the world by states susceptible of strictly physical description. The way to demonstrate the autonomy of the intentional sciences seems to require that intentional states play some irreducible causal role in the closed causal structure of the physical world. But the rub is that the causal closure of the physical world is incompatible with the causal efficacy of mental states. If we insist that the mental must be realized in the physical we risk either the causal exclusion of the mental *or* causal overdetermination in the sense that every event with a mental cause also has a sufficient physical cause.

Bontly is dubious of this sort exclusion argument. It threatens to introduce either exclusion or overdetermination for every cause which supervenes on some physical state or other. Supervenient properties are not in general excluded by their subvening physical realizers. So the fact that mental states supervene on physical states should not exclude them from being independently causally efficacious. Nor, in general, is it the case that demonstrating the causal efficacy of a property of a given kind requires demonstrating the manner of its physical realization. There is little reason to suppose that the overly stringent naturalistic standards that have been applied in the realm of intentional psychology are any more appropriate there than in any other field of the natural sciences.

After the discussion of mind/body matters in the first two papers, attention turns to three long-standing problems posed to naturalism by the nature of mental states: phenomenal content, normativity and intentionality. In each of these cases, recent work in higher-order intentionality and teleosemantics offer distinctive, sometimes conflicting perspectives on these issues. Peter Carruthers (*Consciousness: explaining the phenomena*) asks whether phenomenal consciousness is susceptible of reductive, naturalistic explanation. It is thought by many that such a reductive project is bootless on account of the distinctive feature of phenomenal consciousness which puts it beyond the ambit of naturalism. Phenomenal conscious states are, well, phenomenal; there is something it is like to undergo them. This what it is like, it seems, is ineffable, at least it

4

evades capture in the descriptive physicalist vocabulary. Phenomenal states are also, evidently, subjective. These features open an 'explanatory gap' which the physical sciences evidently cannot breach.

Carruthers acknowledges a significant aspect of the explanatory gap; we have a capacity to recognize phenomenal properties of experience 'non-inferentially or "straight-off"'. Our concepts of what constitute phenomenal experience are bare recognitional ones. He demurs at the claim that the phenomenal properties by which we recognize phenomenal states must be, as many mysterians insist, *instrinsic* properties. According to Carruthers, what needs to be *explained* by the naturalist is the *subjective feel* of phenomenal states; what needs to be explained *away* is the apparent intrinsicness of their properties. The explanatory gap exists because of competing ways in which we conceptualize the mental, from the scientific or introspective perspectives, but the fact that we have distinctive ways of conceptualizing the phenomenal doesn't entail that these conceptualizations do not pick out the same features of the world. Naturalizing phenomenal consciousness involves giving a scientifically acceptable account of those features of the natural world that fall under our bare recognitional concepts.

Carruthers offers a dispositionalist Higher Order Thought theory of phenomenal consciousness. In Carruthers' scheme conscious experiences are '*analog intentional contents*' (p. 70). They are perceptual states whose contents represent states of the world, which in turn are apt (disposed) to form the contents of higher-order thoughts. The contents of phenomenal states are 'analog' (or analog-like) in virtue of the fact they are more fine-grained than any of our descriptive concepts. The content of phenomenal experiences outstrips our capacity to subsume it entirely under the battery of descriptive concepts at our disposal—hence the famous ineffability of phenomenal experience.

Controversially, Carruthers supposes that the Higher Order Thoughts which constitute phenomenal experiences require a full-blown theory of mind system sufficiently sophisticated to understand the is/seems distinction. This level of sophistication, it is thought is generally not attained in children until the age of at least 3.

The dispositionalist HOT theory can explain away the apparent existence of qualia (the distinctive, apparently intrinsic properties of experience). Perceptual states represent objects as having intrinsic properties (Carruthers uses the example *redness*). The higher order *seemings* of redness, will then be '... *seemings* of the presence of a certain *intrinsic* property' (p. 75). Yet the contents of these states will be representational and not intrinsic. The

D. M. Walsh

subjectivity of phenomenal feel can also be accounted for. It is here that Carruthers appeals to teleosemantics. According to consumer semantics variants of teleosemantics, the representational content of a state depends upon the consumer systems which use that state. Because conscious perceptual states are used by the mind-reading HOT device, the contents of these states have a dual-nature. They represent the world to us as being in such and such a state *and* by dint of being the contents of HOTs represent *that* the world is being perceived by us to be in such and such a state: '… each perceptual state with the content *red* is already a state with the higher-order analog content *seems red* or *experience of red*. Each such state then has, as part of its content, a dimension of *seeming* or *subjectivity*.' (p. 76).

Carruthers points to the significant role of consumer semantics in naturalizing the phenomenal content of experience. The theme of consumer semantics surfaces in each of the following two papers. It is implicitly denied in Dretske's account of the respective roles of history and norms in naturalizing intentionality. It is explicitly recommended in Millikan's discussion of the significance of natural information to the nature of intentional content.

Dretske (*Norms, History and the Mental*) addresses a problem seen by many as the scourge of naturalism, the norm-ladenness of the mental. Mental concepts, it is often supposed, are imbued with normativity. Normativity enters into considerations of the mental in a number of ways. Psychological states—beliefs and desires—are individuated, it is often supposed, by their norm-governed roles in cognitive affairs. The goal of beliefs and judgments is truth. As such psychological states are subject to normative evaluation. There is something undesirable, or to be avoided, about false beliefs. If the natural world is norm-free then naturalism cannot sustain an account of mental states and the norm-governed relations they enter into. One common way to naturalize the normativity inherent in the mental is to suppose that norms are introduced by selectional (or learning) history—a trait is supposed to do *f* if it has been selected to do *f*. If the mental is essentially normative, and norms come from history, then the mental is essentially historical. Thoughts, like fossils, require a certain kind of history.

Dretske is dubious of the attempt to ground the normativity inherent in cognition in the putative norms of biology. Rather he simply repudiates the entire problem of naturalizing the norms of the mental. Neither the concepts of mental states, like *belief* and *judgment* nor the truth they aim at are norm-laden, argues Dretske. Truth and falsity are not normative categories: truth is merely correspondence. Nor is belief a normative category. It is not part of the essence of belief to aim at truth; a belief which serves its purpose only when it is false is no less a belief.

Dretske uses the analogy of a road sign. 'An arrow … can point to Chicago or away from Chicago. There is a difference here, yes, but the difference is not normative. Aside from our purpose in putting the sign there or in using it as a guide…, there is nothing right or wrong, nothing that is supposed-to-be or supposed-not-to-be, about an arrow pointing to Chicago' (p. 92). The normativity often thought to be inherent in beliefs, truth, meanings etc. resides not in these things but in the intentions we have in deploying them. We avoid false beliefs because, by and large, they do not serve our purposes. 'The normativity of perceptual beliefs and experiences thus derives from the teleofunctions of the mechanisms producing them, and these teleofunctions emerge from the historical (selectional) process that shaped those mechanisms' (p. 98). But, Dretske goes on to argue, this isn't sufficient to establish the point that perceptual concepts are norm-laden. The norms inherent in our purposes are historical ones. Dretske concludes that '… although we may need history to explain norms, we do not need history to explain mentality because mentality, though subject to norms…, isn't constituted by them' (p. 99).

But, Dretske surmises, normativity may work its way into the determination of the mental by another route. If intentionality— the aboutness of mental states—is essentially historical, and norms devolve from history, intentionality may also be essentially norm-laden. Dretske resists the conclusion; intentional contents are history-laden, but they are not, on account of that, norm-laden.

Dretske's themes are taken up in various other places in this collection. Alan Millar presents a strikingly different account of the ways in which normativity might be thought to be integral to the mental. Furthermore, Dretske's distinctive conception of the roles of history and natural information in the determination of intentional content present the ideal platform for the discussions of teleosemantics offered by Millikan and Jackson which follow. Millikan challenges the notion of natural information implicit in Dretske's account of content. Jackson addresses the presumed significance of history. Millikan and Jackson do not however offer a unified front. Indeed they appear to take diametrically opposed views on an issue of central importance. Millikan believes that it is a requirement on any naturalized account of content that it countenance the possibility that a creature may have a concept that applies to Xs and not Ys even though that creature cannot distinguish between Xs and Ys. Jackson, in contrast, cites with approval, Locke's claim that 'Words being voluntary signs, they cannot be voluntary signs imposed on [a man] by things he knows not' (quoted in Jackson p. 127). These two positions look to be in tension.

Millikan (*What Has Natural Information to do with Intentional Representation?*) outlines the conception of 'natural information' which figures in many informational accounts of intentional content, most particularly those advocated by Dretske. According to Dretske, for an intentional state to represent a state of affairs that s is F, it must carry information that s is F. The relation between a signal, r, and the information it carries is cashed out in terms of probabilities. 'A signal r carries the information that s is F = The conditional probability of s's being F, given r (and [background knowledge] k is 1 (but, given k alone, less than 1)' (quoted in Millikan p. 105). The probability of 1 between the signal and the occurrence of the state of affairs about which it carries information here is explicitly intended to convey the idea that there is a law of nature which determines that r is tokened only when s is F. Of course a signal r is capable of carrying information of the correct sort only if certain enabling conditions are met. Dretske calls these channel conditions. So, by the definition of natural information, r carries natural information that s is F only if the conditional probability that s is F given r is 1, given that a set of appropriate channel conditions obtains and that this probability is underwritten by natural law. The official definition of information makes no mention of the frequency with which the channel conditions are met. Millikan dubs this form of information 'InformationL'

Millikan asks what good it does for an animal to receive informationL about its environment. Here she diagnoses a problem for accounts of intentionality based on informationL. 'InformationL depends upon a channel between the information source and the signal producing a correspondence between the two in accordance with natural necessity. But unfortunately, relatively few things that an animal needs to know about figure as sources for this kind of information.' (p. 114). A mouse may need to know of the presence of a hawk overhead. However, it is not a matter of natural necessity that only hawks produce the sort of effects by which mice detect them. Millikan concludes that '[I]t is the *properties* of hawks...that enter into natural laws, not the hawks ... themselves, and it is never a matter of natural law that only hawks ... have these properties.' (p. 115).

Millikan asks whether some corrective can be applied to the notion of natural information to suit the purposes of a naturalized theory of intentional representation. It is a requirement on an adequate theory of intentional representation that it demonstrate how representations can be false or represent non-existent entities. Dretske's solution to this challenge, according to Millikan, is to overlay a theory of teleological function onto a conception of natural information. Indeed we saw this strategy at work in the preceding chapter. The representational content of a state is determined by the natural information it carries. The possibility of error is introduced by the claim that the apparatus in question—the animal's cognitive system—has been designed by evolution to convey informationL and sometimes that apparatus fails to operate as it was designed to do. The problem here is that it introduces the error at the wrong place. Most cases of misrepresentation are not the result of breakdown of the animal's perceptual or cognitive systems. They are the result of uncooperative environment. Nothing has gone wrong, for example, with an organism which represents its own reflection in a mirror as a potential mate. It simply finds itself in an environment which systematically undermines the design of its perceptual system.

Millikan insists that error is introduced in the wrong place because teleology has been introduced in the wrong place. She recommends, to borrow Carruthers' phrase, 'a dose of consumer semantics'. What determines whether a signal represents a state of affairs is not some nomic relation between the signal and the state of affairs but how the signal is *used* by a downstream consumer device. What determines how the signal is used, in turn, is fixed by the conditions under which the downstream device has produced outputs which, in the past, have been selectively beneficial. To be sure, there must be some correlation between the state represented (that s is F) and the representation, r, but this correlation does not need to be nomic covariation. So long as the signal r correlates sufficiently closely to the conditions under which the outputs of the consumer device are beneficial (s's being F) then r can be said to represent that s is F. In these circumstance r carries information, of a sort, that s is F. Millikan calls this informationC. InformationC differs from informationL insofar as the latter but not the former involves conditional probabilities of 1. If informationC is to count as a form of natural information, it follows that a signal r could carry information about, that is to say represent, X even if r does, or would, also correlate with Y. Even if a creature could not discriminate X's from Y's it may be capable of having a representation of X which is not also a representation of Y. Millikan's contention is that only a 'softer' notion of information, such as informationC, resists the verificationist implication that creature cannot have a representation whose content is X and not Y if it cannot distinguish X's from Ys.

It is another question whether the verificationist implication is one that should be resisted. This question is usually answered in the affirmative. But Jackson isn't so sure. Jackson (*Locke-ing onto Content*) cites Locke to the effect that '...language ... rests on voluntary, if largely implicit, agreements to use words and sentences to stand for how we take things to be.' Jackson contends that this Lockean point raises a significant problem for precisely the sort of teleological account of semantics that Millikan endorses. Teleological theories of content typically rely on history. Jackson, citing Papineau, gives a rough sketch: '...the belief that P is the state selected to co-vary with P, and the desire that P is the state selected to bring about P' (p. 130). But, one does not need to know the history of a particular intentional state in order to know its content. When we communicate the contents of our beliefs to one another, we communicate something about the way we take the world to be; we typically do not communicate the historical determinants of the state. We exploit what Jackson calls the 'folk' or 'functional' roles of our beliefs. There are two aspects to intentional content: current functional role, which is easily accessible and selectional history which isn't. Jackson argues that 'Locke's point tells us that the way we acquired language and its evident utility depend upon the contents of very many of our beliefs and desires being pretty much common knowledge; but if content is given by selectional history, these contents will be very far from common knowledge' (p. 131).

The teleosemanticist can choose either of two options. The first is to acknowledge that intentional states have two kinds of content, functional role (informational) content and selectional content. The second is to propose that specification of a state's history and its current functional role are merely two ways of latching onto the same intentional content. Jackson does not recommend the former. It makes teleosemantics a much less interesting theory. Teleosemantics is, after all, proffered as an account of *the* content of intentional states. The second option is more congenial to the teleosemanticist. It holds that intentional content is selectional content and that in turn is for the most part also consonant with current functional role. So to understand what the selectional content of an intentional state is, you only need to look at its current role. In much the same way, functional anatomists latch onto the function of an anatomical trait by studying its current functional role and this procedure is justified even if function is determined by selectional history.

But even this strategy has its disadvantages. Jackson points out that '[t]o meet Locke's point, teleologists must hold that it is common knowledge that the folk roles pick out the contents of intentional states.' (p. 134). We should expect, then, that teleological theories of content provide a satisfactory answer to the question why current functional roles are such reliable guides to intentional states. The proposal from some advocates of teleosemantics (Jackson cites Papineau) is that the folk roles reference-fix on contents in just the way that the macro-properties of natural kinds, say of water, reference-fix on, but do not determine, those kinds. But if folk-roles are such a good way to fix on selectional roles, it is obscure why it is that selectional role and not folk role is the real determinant of content. Why is it not the case that contents just happen to have been selected in virtue of the folk roles they play? After all, what is important to us is the utility of the *current* roles of our thoughts. If the current role of a thought and its selected role should peel apart, why should we suppose that content is fixed wholly by its historical role? Observance of Locke's point strongly suggests that what fixes intentional content is current folk role and not selectional role.

Jackson generalizes his claim about the significance of Locke's point. It tends to favour causal descriptivist views of reference over causal theories of reference. Causal descriptivists, like causal theorists, hold that the reference of a term is that entity which has certain requisite causal properties. They also hold that what makes it the case that a term attaches to its referent is that users of the term have in mind certain properties that distinguish the referent. These may be the very causal properties that causal theorists appeal to. Applying the name 'Sydney' to Sydney '... requires associating properties with Sydney, including the ones the namers were attaching to the name 'Sydney' instead of the name 'Melbourne'. There is no way of knowing which thing Sydney is independently of knowing its properties.' (p. 139). Applying a name to a term as part of a shared language involves undertaking an agreement to use the name to pick out the bearer of such and such a set of properties and that involves being able to distinguish that object from others.

Alan Millar and David Papineau both undertake discussions of the ways in which human psychology is distinguished from that of non-human animals. Papineau's concern is to develop an understanding of the nature of means-end reasoning that at once sets human cognition apart from other animals and can be shown to be an adaptation. Millar's concern is to demonstrate the link between the capacity for rational deliberation that is characteristic of means-end reasoning and the possession of propositional attitudes.

Papineau begins his characterization of means-end reasoning by

D. M. Walsh

listing a variety of increasingly sophisticated ways by which organisms could tailor their responses to various environmental conditions. Many organisms are capable of regulating their behaviour in accordance with conditions of their environment in such a way as to bring abut the fulfilment of their goals. Some are capable of learning these conditional strategies. These capacities do not yet guarantee full-blown means-end reasoning. Means-ends reasoning requires at least that organisms are capable of explicitly representing general information, of the sort that all *F*s are *G*, in the motivation of action; 'It is one thing to be able to represent the whereabouts of a particular pond, or apple, or lion. It is another to represent that ponds contain water, or that apples are a source of food, or that lions are bad for your health' (p. 153). Means-end reasoning, Papineau suggests, '… requires 'explicit' representation of general information in the specific sense that *such information can be processed to deliver new items of general information*'. (p. 156). 'In effect, then', Papineau claims, 'I have now defined means-end reasoning as the ability to perform novel actions' (p. 156). Papineau proposes that means-end reasoning, construed in this way, is a biological adaptation peculiar to humans.

Taken together, the claim that means-end reasoning is an adaptation and the claim that it is peculiar to humans raise two prima facie objections. The first that means-ends reasoning is *too easy*, the second that it is *too hard*. If means-end reasoning is an adaptation, why suppose that it is not also to be found in other animals? On the other hand, if it is distinctive to humans what reason is there to suppose that it is an adaptation?

Along the first line of objection it may be pointed out that there are apparently many examples to be drawn from non-human animals in which the production of novel behaviour results from the explicit representation of generalizations. Organisms navigate from *A* to *C* by reconstructing the routes from *A* to *B* and from *B* to *C*. Classical conditioning can teach an animal to associate conditions of type *A* with conditions of type *C* simply by the association of *A*s with *B*s and *B*s with *C*s. None of these counts as full-blown means-end reasoning of the sort that distinguishes humans, according to Papineau. He refines his conception of means-end reasoning to include an element of 'causal non-egocentricity'. The explicitly represented information must involve the representation of objective causal relations. Papineau continues: 'Let me now require that [full-fledged means-end reasoning] involve, not just any use of general information to infer new general conclusions, but specifically that it allow animals to infer new causal facts of the form 'R will

12

lead to **O**' from other causal facts which are not embodied in the form of behavioural dispositions.' (p. 168). It seems that non-human animals exhibit no (or little) capacity to generate novel behaviours based upon the explicit representation of general, objective causal relations.

There is, then, a contentful notion of means-end reasoning which, it seems, does set humans apart. But this is such a specialized capacity that it is difficult to see how it could have been selected for. One suggestion is that means-ends reasoning is a spandrel, a by-product of selection for a capacity such as mind-reading or language use. Papineau contends that means-end reasoning cannot be an offshoot of selection for the capacity to ascribe mental states to others precisely because the latter capacity presupposes means-end reasoning. In fact, Papineau argues, however means-end reasoning arose, there must have been *some* selection for its role in the regulation of actions. These considerations lead Papineau to conclude that means-end reasoning is a module whose specific purpose is to regulate, calibrate and reset our standing behavioural dispositions.

Alan Millar proposes, for reasons somewhat similar to those invoked by Papineau, that among animals only humans possess propositional attitudes. Millar draws a connection between the possession of higher-order intentionality, the capacity to act for reasons, and the possession of propositional attitudes. The connection is that only rational agents are capable of entertaining propositional attitudes. Only individuals capable of deliberative thinking are rational agents. And only individuals endowed with higher-order intentionality can be deliberative thinkers. He argues for this position by establishing first that if one has propositional attitudes one must, to some degree, satisfy certain requirements on rationality, for example that one by and large avoids inconsistency in one's beliefs, that one avoids acquiring new beliefs without reason and that one is prepared to perform actions which are necessary for the fulfilment of one's goals. The question is whether evaluative rationality of this sort is beyond the ken of non-human animals.

It is an appealing idea that to be a rational animal is to be the type of thing that is capable of believing or acting for a reason. Believing or acting for a reason, in turn, requires deliberative thinking, the capacity to consider whether a given consideration is a reason or to be motivated by it *because* it is a reason. Non-human animals, generally lack this capacity for deliberative thinking.

It may *appear* that an animal capable of only first-order intentionality is capable of deliberative thinking. Many animals clearly

have goals and are prepared to do what is necessary to bring these
goals about. These dispositions conform to the requirements of
rationality. But merely conforming to the requirements of rationality is not sufficient for deliberative thinking. Acting in accordance
with the requirements of rationality is not the same as acting
because you recognize that rationality requires you to do so. Millar
makes this distinction vivid by contrasting two conceptions of acting (or believing) for a reason. According to one, the *Motivation
Principle*, to act (or believe) for a reason one must have some
motivating reason to act or believe in this way *and* believe that this
motivating reason is a normative (good) reason. This conception of
acting (believing) for a reason clearly requires higher-order
intentionality. Millar contrasts this notion of having a reason with
another he calls the *Mental State theory*, according to which for an
individual to perform action y or to believe p for a reason it must act
or believe *because* it has some other intentional state q such that q
constitutes a normative reason to perform y or to believe p. This
conception of acting or believing for a reason requires no higher-
order thought. It does not require that the putative agent *takes* the
normative reason *as* a normative reason. There are a number of
deficiencies of the mental state theory as an account of acting (or
believing) for a reason, not least of which is its inability to account
for an agent's acting for a reason when those reasons are bad ones.
The upshot is that '[r]ationalizing explanation, and the notion of
believing for a reason, make tolerably clear sense only in relation to
a psychological economy such that the subject can misjudge the
normative force of a consideration.' (p. 192) This capacity, in turn,
requires higher-order intentionality. Millar's conclusion, then, is
that the possession of genuine propositional attitude psychology, constrained as it is by rationality, requires higher-order intentionality.

Millar further bolsters the claim that genuine propositional attitude psychology requires higher-order intentionality by considering
two fundamental categories of propositional attitudes: intention
and autobiographical memory. An intention to y, Millar argues, is
only motivating if the agent believes that she has the intention to y.
Similar considerations apply for recalling in memory. Recalling
some past experience is not merely believing that you had the experience, but having the experience presented to you as something you
recall. Intention and memory are, arguably, required for propositional attitude psychology and if they are second-order
intentionality is too. Millar concludes that animals that lack higher-
order intentionality may well have intentional states, but they do not
possess full-blown propositional attitude psychology.

Higher-order intentionality in non-human animals is the topic of Andrew Whiten's excursion through some recent empirical work on non-human primate cognition. Attributing propositional attitudes to others is of course an important component of our capacity to explain, predict and manipulate the activities of others. It has been noticed that non-human primates interact in the wild in surprisingly sophisticated ways which suggest that they too have the capacity to attribute propositional attitudes to others. The question whether monkeys and apes possess a theory of mind—the capacity to interpret behaviours of others as the manifestation of mental states—has become an issue of central importance both in primate ethology and in more general considerations concerning the nature and origin of propositional attitude psychology. Sober, in the paper immediately following Whiten's, discusses some of the methodological implications that arise from this question.

Whiten (*Theory of Mind in Non-Verbal Apes: Conceptual issues and the critical experiments*) asks: 'Are non-human primates mind-readers?' and 'What considerations are relevant to determining whether they are?'. The central problem for the empirical study of 'mind-reading', as Whiten sees it, is to devise tests which adequately distinguish mind reading from a cognitively less demanding alternative, *behaviour reading*. The cues to an organism's state of mind are its observable patterns of behaviour. Whiten asks: 'How shall we distinguish the chimp who truly perceives the other as *wanting* [a] banana from one who is simply sensitive to the external signs that her mindreading counterpart would presumably need to discriminate in any case?' (pp. 201–2). Whiten distinguishes four different potential ways of differentiating mind reading from mere behaviour reading. These are: counterdeception, implicit mind, recognizing intervening variables and experience projection.

Counterdeception is the capacity to detect a would-be deceiver's intention to deceive. Primate ethologists have observed an impressive collection of behaviours which can be construed as counterdeception. In each of these cases, the putative mindreader relies upon memory of previous behavioural tendencies of the counterdeceiver. Detection of deception, then, may merely involve responding to behavioural cues rather than ascribing devious intentions. Whiten concludes that counterdeception is suggestive of mindreading, but is not definitive evidence. *Implicit mind* involves the supposition that understanding behaviours correctly involves implicitly ascribing mental states. One cannot, for instance, understand an animal as searching for some object without attributing to it the intention of finding that object. Whiten finds the ascription of an implicit theory of mind an intriguing, but nevertheless a '…weak basis for diagnosing mindreading over and above behaviour reading' (p. 205). *Recognizing 'intervening variables'*: a behaviour interpreter might seek to classify and explain an array of inputs and behavioural outputs as connected in some systematic way. For example, the amount of water that a rat is disposed to drink, the amount of quinine it is prepared to tolerate in its water supply, the effort it is willing to expend in order to drink, may all be outputs which are correlated with an array of inputs e.g. time since last drinking, the dryness of its food etc. Rather than supposing that each of these input factors is independently associated with each of the output factors, it is in some sense simpler and more explanatorily effective to suppose that there is a single intervening variable which is affected by each the inputs and in turn affects the outputs. In this simple (non-psychological) example the intervening variable is obviously *thirst*. Whiten finds this a much more promising avenue for distinguishing mind reading from mere behaviour reading. Evidence that non-human primates recognized psychological states as intervening variables would constitute strong evidence that they possess theory of mind. *Experience projection* involves the capacity to use one's own experiences to understand the nature of experiences of others. Evidence of experience projection, Whiten claims, would certainly constitute strong evidence of mindreading. One might have good evidence for experience projection by observing, for instance, whether an individual who had been blindfolded had the ability to take into account the effect of blindfolding on other individuals. Would, for example, a subordinate individual act more boldly in the presence of a blindfolded dominant than in the presence of that same individual lacking the blindfold?

Having laid out what might count as a definitive test of mindreading capacity, Whiten surveys recent experimental work in non-human primate ethology. There is evidence for the capacity of chimpanzees to attribute mental states as intervening variables between inputs and behavioural outputs. Chimpanzees appear to respond to another's ignorance of the presence of a predator by increasing the rate of alarm calls. There is little evidence that non-human primates have the capacity to project experiences.

Elliott Sober (*The Principle of Conservatism in Cognitive Ethology*) finds much to applaud in the cognitive ethologists' approach to mindreading. One particularly beneficial outcome is that it redresses a deplorable anti-epistemological bias in recent philosophy of mind. 'Philosophy of mind' he says 'is, and for a long while has been 99% metaphysics and 1% epistemology. Attention is lavished on the question of the nature of mind, but questions concerning how we know about minds are discussed much less thoroughly' (p. 225). Sober sees the question of whether primates are mind readers as an extension of (or a better way into) the problem of other minds and he welcomes the attention this avenue of enquiry brings to the problem. Sober echoes Whiten in stating that the fundamental question faced by cognitive ethologists studying non-human primate cognition is an epistemological one: '...what counts as good evidence that that a creature has a mind?...'.

The principal methodological constraint on cognitive ethology is conservatism. That is the view that one is entitled to attribute a mental state in the explanation of a behaviour only if the behaviour cannot be explained without doing so. If Whiten's careful prescription for a methodology appropriate to the study of mindreading is anything to go by this certainly appears to be a constraint that cognitive ethologists accept. 'Mindless' explanations of behaviour are preferred to 'minded' ones. Similarly, explanations involving first-order intentionality are preferred to those invoking higher-order intentionality. Sober's question is what justifies this conservatism. His answer seems to be 'not much'. Why should there be a 'special stigma' attached to the positing of mental states? After all, one might suppose that the Type 2 error of mistakenly withholding the attribution of a mental state is as much an error as the Type 1 error of mistakenly ascribing one. Yet the principle of conservatism seems to counsel only against making the Type 1 error.

One possible justification for conservatism is parsimony. Mindless explanations may well be simpler than those which invoke no mental states. Sober cites with approval Whiten's discussion of intervening variables. Positing mental states as intervening variables between inputs and behavioural outputs is appealing and justified in the circumstances precisely because it is *simpler* to suppose that a single mental state controls the systematic relation between inputs a range of inputs and a related range of outputs. Mindless explanations of the same relations would need to posit multiple independent relations between the various inputs and each of the outputs. This would leave unexplained the systematic relations between these factors. While simplicity may be a consideration in choosing between competing hypotheses, it does not univocally favour 'mindless' explanations of behaviour over 'minded' ones. There is nothing inherently less simple about mindless explanations. The same point applies to the preference for first-order intentionality over higher-order. One cannot appeal to the principle of parsimony to justify this bias either.

D. M. Walsh

Sober draws an analogy between adaptationism in evolutionary biology and cognitivism in ethology. It has been supposed that one may invoke the process of adaptation to explain the presence or prevalence of a trait *only if* the same phenomenon cannot be explained as the result of phylogenetic inertia. The preference for phylogeny over adaptation is also a form of methodological conservatism. Sober contends that neither kind of hypothesis is simpler or more easily supported by evidence. 'They are on an epistemic par.' There are ways to decide between hypotheses which invoke adaptation and those which invoke phylogenetic inertia which simply involve gathering data. These hypotheses make different predictions. For example, the adaptationist hypothesis predicts optimality; the inertia hypothesis does not. Similar considerations apply to cognitive conservatism. Sober outlines a test based on Reichnbach's principle of the common cause for distinguishing first-order from higher-order intentionality in certain experimental set-ups. The point is merely that what justifies the ascription of one or the other form of intentionality is not the principle of parsimony. It is simply the fact that they predict different observable outcomes, and the data decide.

Sober advocates a form of naturalism about the mind which is methodological. It holds that the study of mental phenomena is subject to the same sorts of methods as any other domain of the natural sciences. The explanatory models he has been discussing are justified not by their content, but by their form. It doesn't matter to the justification of the experimental set-up whether what is being tested is first-order versus higher-order intentionality or adaptationism versus phylogenetic inertia. It is the *form* of the model which is justified and not its content.

Our final two papers concern the expanding field of evolutionary psychology. Evolutionary psychology, broadly construed, is the view that the mind is a suite of adaptations, a set of adaptive solutions to specific problems raised by the environment of our human ancestors. As such the mind can be studied in the same way that we study any morphological or behavioural adaptations. In many ways this issue brings us back to the considerations raised by Shapiro in Chapter 1. Wheeler and Atkinson discuss some methodological concerns which arise form evolutionary psychology. Henry Plotkin, one of evolutionary psychology's most prominent proponents, surveys some significant work in this discipline to date and assesses its future prospects.

The Massive Modularity Thesis has been one of the central pillars of orthodox evolutionary psychology. It is, roughly, the view that the human mind is an assemblage of discrete tools designed to address specific problems posed by our ancestral environment (The Environment of Evolutionary Adaptedness), rather than a general all-purpose apparatus. The adaptations which constitute the mind are domain-specific, special-purpose devices rather than domain-general all-purpose devices. The Massive Modularity Hypothesis has been the subject of a considerable amount of discussion. Yet there are a number of confusions concerning the content of this hypothesis. Michael Wheeler and Anthony Atkinson (*Domains, Brains and Evolution*) propose to do some much needed 'conceptual spring-cleaning' on precisely this issue.

Their first order of business is to clarify the concept of a domain in order to ascertain what precisely the domain-specificity claim amounts to. Evolutionary Psychology has at its disposal the resources needed to generate a workable definition of a domain: A domain is a suitably related set of adaptive problems. An adaptive problem, in turn, is a set of environmental conditions which together can exert selection pressure. An adaptive problem is domain specific. Our various cognitive apparatus can be expected to be adaptive responses to various domain-specific adaptive problems. A central question which now confronts evolutionary psychologists is whether we should expect the adaptive solutions to these specific selective pressures to take the form of special purpose devices or general-purposes devices. Evolutionary psychologists have plumped strongly for the former on almost a priori grounds.

Wheeler and Atkinson discuss a dissenting opinion raised by Shapiro and Epstein who claim that general purpose devices may evolve by exaptation. They claim that Shapiro and Epstein's argument misses the point. The exapted mechanisms discussed by Shapiro and Epstein are themselves domain-specific responses to certain domain-specific problems which are subsequently co-opted to solve *other* domain-specific problems. The general-purpose mechanisms which evolutionary psychologists argue against are those which are always, as it were, general-purpose. Wheeler and Atkinson offer some reasons to suppose that special-purpose solutions might well be more likely to evolve than general ones. In doing so they invoke two general requirements on demonstrating that a structure of any sort is an adaptation. These they call the *Minimal Requirement* and the *Darwinian Requirement*. The first of these states that '... for some postulated design even to be a reasonable candidate for [a solution to a set of adaptive problems] ... that design... must, in principle, be able to solve all and each of those adaptive problems' (p. 253). The *Darwinian Requirement* states that

D. M. Walsh

the proposed solution must have been superior to any of the available alternatives. The thrust of the evolutionary psychologists' case for specific-purpose devices is that general-purpose devices meet neither of these requirements. Atkinson and Wheeler argue that in principle a general-purpose device might well meet the Minimal Requirement. But what of the Darwinian requirement? Recent work on AI-oriented robots suggests that robots which employ special-purpose mechanisms in association with domain-specific information are typically superior to those employing general-purpose mechanisms. This suggests that faced with competition from a special-purpose device, a general-purpose device will be at a selective disadvantage.

Wheeler and Atkinson consider a set of selective regimes in which general-purpose devices might be expected to evolve. Diffuse co-evolution occurs when a trait in one population encounters selective pressures imposed by a number of traits in other populations. Wheeler and Atkinson propose that 'where multiple, simultaneous, systematically related selection pressures are in operation, the adaptive response may well be a general-purpose mechanism' (p. 259). But here there is trouble looming for the very distinction between special-purpose and general-purpose devices. A domain has been defined as a suitably related set of adaptive problems. But what constitutes a suitable relation just might be that the relevant selection pressures are 'systematically related'. The judgement whether a piece of psychological architecture is domain-general or domain-specific can only be made against the background of some specification of the domains in question. There may be no fact of the matter whether a given set of selection pressures constitutes a domain. The authors conclude that '[t]o the extent that this is so, and to the extent that such troublesome cases are widespread, the idea that there is a robust and principled distinction between domain-specific and domain-general features of an evolved cognitive architecture threatens simply to evaporate...' (pp. 262–263).

The final paper is a transcript of a presentation by Henry Plotkin (*Evolution and the Human Mind: how far can we go?*) intended for public consumption. Its brief is to introduce a non-specialist audience to the central tenets of the evolutionary approach to the study of mind and to point toward future directions. As such I think it provides an appropriate afterword to this comprehensive survey of the concerns of those interested in the ways in which evolutionary considerations may inform our understanding of the place of mind in the natural world.

Plotkin begins by pointing out the curious *absence* of

Editor's Introduction

evolutionary theory from psychology despite the fact that the two sciences made their first appearance at almost the same time. Despite interest in the implications of evolution to the study of the mind outside academic psychology (particularly by philosophers) evolutionary theory made few inroads into the study of psychology until very recently.

'The fundamental tenet of evolutionary psychology is that the human mind is a product of evolution, and has characteristics consistent with its evolutionary origins.' (p. 269) But apart from this shared principle, there is little agreement on the ways in which evolutionary thinking is to guide or constrain the study of human psychology. Plotkin draws upon two examples of the study of the evolution of the human mind in order to illustrate the diversity of possible approaches. Despite their differences each of these demonstrates the enormous potential for evolutionary psychology.

Plotkin describes research on birth-order effects pioneered by Sulloway. Drawing upon selfish gene theory, Sulloway surmised that siblings within a family must compete for parental care and in doing so each must adopt a slightly different strategy. The surest strategies for firstborn children will be those which secure parental resources by identifying with parental values. Younger siblings must exploit other less conventional niches. The adoption of a niche available to a child, it is presumed, should manifest itself in personality type. The prediction, then, is that first born children will, on average, be more conventional than their younger siblings. Sulloway finds, consistent with predictions, that '... firstborns are more dominating, assertive, status-conscious and defensive. Younger sibs are less self-assured, more open to ideas, questioning, flexible, easygoing' (p. 271).

The second example of the impact of evolution on the study of human psychology comes in its potential for enhancing our understanding of the origin of human culture. Culture is considered a supertrait by many psychologists and biologists, not the result of direct selection but a consequence of selection for more specific cognitive capacities. One can only speculate at this point how far the evolutionary study of human culture might go, but Plotkin sees this as the central challenge for our understanding of the evolution of the human mind.

Mind the Adaptation

LAWRENCE A. SHAPIRO

By now, even the kid down the street must be familiar with the functionalist's response to type-identity physicalism. Mental kinds like pain, love, the belief that Madison sits on an isthmus, etc., are not identical to physical kinds because it's conceptually (if not empirically) possible that entities physically distinct in kind from human beings experience pain, love, beliefs that Madison sits on an isthmus, etc. Type-identity physicalism, in short, is baselessly chauvinistic in its rejection of the possibility of nonhuman minds.

Perhaps less familiar, but still widely acknowledged, is the following Trouble with Functionalism. Functional characterizations of mental kinds are hopelessly unconstrained. If mental kinds are defined simply in terms of relations between inputs, other states, and outputs, then such obviously mindless things as the nation of China and the Bolivian economy (Block, 1978; 1980) might end up having minds.

It's worth noting that the points both in favour of and against functionalism depend substantially on unfettered intuition. Why believe that something without a brain like ours can have a mind? To date, no artificial intelligences have come close to matching a human being's mental abilities and no extraterrestrial intelligences have been discovered. Robots like Commander Data and alien geniuses like Spock remain nothing more than an intuitively plausible challenge to physicalism. Similarly, it's nothing but intuition that makes us believe that the nation of China or the Bolivian economy cannot have minds. How could we know whether the nation of China could have a mind unless we actually organized its population so that it mirrored the organization of the brain?

Personally, I agree with the intuitions that make functionalism preferable to physicalism and I also agree with the intuitions that cause trouble for functionalism. However, because these *are* just intuitions, they're of little value when trying to convince others whose intuitions differ from our own that they are wrong. That's the problem with intuitions: we all like the ones we have but we don't all have the same ones. For this reason, we ought to pounce hungrily upon a framework that promises to justify our intuitions without itself appealing (directly, at least) to other intuitions. Indeed, if such a framework were available, we ought to be willing

23

Lawrence A. Shapiro

to sacrifice a few recalcitrant intuitions if the framework did a good job justifying the rest.

So, here's where we stand. Intuitively, physicalism is wrong. It ought to be possible to realize minds in different kinds of physical substances. Intuitively also, there are troubles with functionalism. There ought to be some constraint on the kinds of things that can have minds—minds ought to be more than merely an abstract relation between inputs, other states, and outputs. If only there were a third choice: a theory of mind that aligned more closely with our intuitions about minds. We could then say to the physicalist, 'you're wrong that minds are identical to brains, because there is a principled and defensible way to characterize minds according to which minds are not identical to brains.' Turning then to the functionalist, we could say 'you're wrong that minds are simply functional roles, because here's a principled and defensible way to characterize minds according to which they are not.'

Below I develop a conception of *mind as adaptation*. Evolutionary theory, in particular that branch of evolutionary theory concerned with classification, justifies an analysis of mind that resonates more harmoniously with our intuitions about minds than does either physicalism or functionalism. It's because minds are adaptations, I shall argue, that it is wrong to identify minds with physical kinds. Similarly, it's because minds are adaptations that there exist constraints on the kinds of things that can realize minds. Spelling all this out will take some work, but I hope that the appeal of the project is immediately evident. Whether something is an adaptation is not a matter for intuition to settle. The criteria for something's being an adaptation are clear, if not always easy to apply, and receive their justification from principles derived from evolutionary theory. I mention these virtues now, because it shall turn out that defining minds as adaptations carries a small cost. In particular, it requires that we give up *some* ordinary ways of talking about minds. However, all things considered, this cost is minimal when weighed against the solid foundation that the mind-as-adaptation doctrine provides for some of our central intuitions about minds.

Adaptations

'Adaptation' is a term that receives wide use in biology and it would be presumptuous to assume that biologists assign to it a single or even a predominant meaning (West-Eberhard, 1992; Moore and Willmer, 1997). Moreover, apparent consensus about the meaning

24

of 'adaptation' may in fact give way to disagreement when reflecting on related concepts like *function*. Given this state of affairs, I must assume some modesty about the analysis of adaptation that I develop in this section. My goal now is to defend an analysis of adaptation that, I claim, plays a very important role in evolutionary theory. I shall be clear about what this role is, but I shall not spend any time considering whether it serves other roles in the biological sciences as well. My sights are set on the implications of *this* analysis of adaptation for justifying certain intuitions we have about minds.

The analysis of adaptation I offer is rooted in cladistics—the prevailing theory of systematics in evolutionary biology. The goal of cladistics is to capture the phylogenetic relationships between species. In its aim to map phylogeny, cladistics can lay claim to an objectivity that other systems of classification, like phenetics, lack (Hull, 1970; Ridley, 1986; Ridley, 1996; Sober, 1993). While there may be no fact of the matter about whether bats are more similar to mice than they are to birds, there is a fact about whether bats and mice share a less distant ancestor than do bats and birds. Cladistics systematizes species on the basis of these facts about relatedness. Similarities between species, as far as the cladist is concerned, might serve as evidence for shared ancestry, but it is of interest *only* insofar as it serves this function.

Cladistic analysis starts with the identification of characters and character states. It is convenient to think of characters as determinable properties and character states as determinates of a determinable property. Just about any feature of an organism qualifies as a character, from molar features like hair length and eye colour, to molecular features like the sequence of DNA on a gene or the size of a protein. Characters may also be determinable *behaviours*, like bird song melody or duration. For cladistic purposes it is essential that the character state under examination is heritable, for otherwise it can provide no evidence about descent, but other than this requirement the cladist's choice about which characters to study is decided on pragmatic grounds. The cladist focuses on whichever character promises to shed the most light on phylogenetic relationships between species. Usually, the cladist is safer working with selectively neutral traits, because when two species share the same selectively neutral character it is more likely that the shared character is evidence of homology than would be true if the trait were selectively advantageous (Darwin, 1859, ch. 13; Ridley, 1986, p. 21). Similarly, if choosing to study a character for which there has been selection, the cladist will select one that is broadly adaptive over one that adapts an organism to a very idiosyncratic environment. The reason for this preference is that broadly adaptive characters are conservative—they tend to change more slowly than characters that have evolved as adaptations to unusual environmental conditions. Thus, broadly adaptive characters will tend to reveal more about ancestry than specialized adaptations (Ridley, 1986, p. 24).

With a set of characters in hand, cladistic analysis proceeds through the discovery of derived homologies between species. Homologies are characters that species share as a result of inheritance from a common ancestor. To illustrate the importance of *derived* homologies for purposes of phylogenetic inference, imagine we are faced with the task of describing the phylogenetic relationship between three species of bears. Species A and B have long hair and species C has short hair. Is B more closely related to A than it is to C? It need not be. On the assumption that long hair is a derived homology then B *is* more closely related to A than it is to C (see Figure 1).

However, two other possibilities remain. It may be the case that the long hair in A and B is not a derived homology, but an ancestral homology. In contrast to a derived homology, which all descendants of a common ancestor share, an ancestral homology will be present in some, but not all descendants of a common ancestor. Thus, if long hair is an ancestral homology in A and B, then B is more closely related to C than it is to A (see Figure 2).

Finally, the long hair in A and B may not be a homology at all but, rather, a homoplasy. Homoplasies are characters that species share in virtue of convergent evolution. Thus, if A and B evolved long hair independently of each other then it is possible that B is more closely related to C than it is to A (see Figure 3).

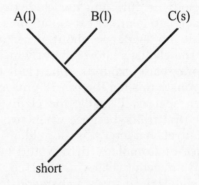

A(l)   B(l)   C(s)

short

Figure 1.

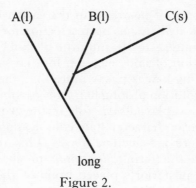

long

Figure 2.

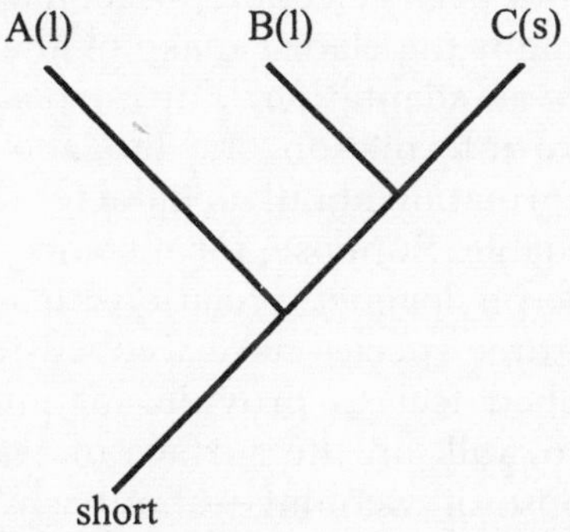

A(l)   B(l)   C(s)

short

Figure 3.

As simplified as this discussion of phylogenetic inference is, it should be apparent that cladistics is only as possible as are judgments of similarity between character states. The claim that two species share a character state rests on the assumption that the state of the character in the first species is very similar to the state of the character in the second. Having made this judgment of similarity it then becomes necessary to determine whether the similarity is a result of shared ancestry or convergent evolution.

In speaking of characters and judgments of similarity between states of a character I have not yet said anything about that which distinguishes characters that are adaptations from characters that are not. Quite simply, adaptations are those character states for which there has been selection. Thus, I propose that we reserve the word 'adaptation' for those character states and only those character states for which there has been selection. On this analysis, the

Lawrence A. Shapiro

increase in length of bear hair in the earlier example is an adaptation if and only if there has been selection for long hair. It is important in this context to be mindful of Sober's (1984) distinction between selection of and selection for. To say that there has been selection for long hair is to say more than that selection has played a role in the evolution of long hair. It's possible—indeed plausible—that selection has played *some* role in the evolution of all character states. However, a character state counts as an adaptation when and only when there is selection *for* it. This requirement precludes application of the term *adaptation* to character states like the deformed and posteriorly placed brain of the salamander *Thorius*, which owes its condition to the selection for large eyes (Wake, 1991). Selection may be a cause *of* the deformity in *Thorius* brains, but there has not been selection *for* such a deformity.

What use might the cladist make of the fact that the trait under investigation is an adaptation? For purposes of phylogenetic inference, the more information one has about a given character the better, and information about a character's history of selection may well prove valuable. Suppose, for instance, that a cladist is attempting to map the phylogenetic relationships of three species of salamanders. All three species have webbed feet, but two of the three use their webbed feet to provide suction and the third uses its webbed feet to walk on the surface of water. This fact about the adaptive purpose of webbing—about why, in each case, there has been selection for webbing—may bear on the cladist's decision about how to classify the three species of salamander. The first two species of salamander share a selection history that the third does not, suggesting that they also share a nearer ancestor with each other than either does with the third species. Thus, for purposes of phylogenetic inference, the use to which a trait is put—the reason for its selection—can count as a character.

I now wish to introduce some new vocabulary that will aid in future discussion. Instead of talking about characters and character states, which, as we have just seen, might be either physical features of an organism or uses to which an organism puts these features, I will talk about structures and functions. By 'structure' I shall mean a physical feature of the organism—its hair, its webbed feet, its coloration, etc. I will use the term *function* to name the effect of a structure that explains, if the structure is an adaptation, why that type of structure was selected. Thus, if long hair is an adaptation, and if there has been selection for long hair because it is warmer than short hair, then it is the function of long hair to provide warmth.

28

With these remarks in mind, my analysis of adaptation can be stated like this: an adaptation is a structure plus a function. Because adaptations consist in both a structure and a function, comparisons of adaptations for purposes of cladistic analysis demand judgments of similarity along two dimensions. Table 1 describes the relationships that can exist between two kinds of adaptations:

| | | Structure | |
		similar	different
Function	similar	1	2
	different	3	4

Table 1

Note that because the table assumes that the structures in question are adaptations, it is a given that there has been selection for the structures. The table illustrates simply the kinds of relationships that adaptations may bear to each other. Consideration of some examples will make these relationships clear.

Type 4 relationships are the easiest to see. Naturally we are dealing with different adaptations when we have different structures with different functions. Hands and eyes are different structures with different functions. It's no surprise then that hands and eyes are distinct adaptations. Likewise, long hair and short hair, assuming there has been selection for these things, are different structures that, suppose, have evolved for different reasons. Hence they are different adaptations.

Type 1 relationships are very often the result of common ancestry, and so it is these that provide confirming evidence of shared ancestry. Chimp thumbs and human thumbs are very similar structures and, let's assume, have very similar functions. Thus they are very similar adaptations. In addition to adaptations that owe their similarity to homology are adaptations that owe their similarity to convergence. These are homoplastic adaptations. Thus, the cephalopod eye and the vertebrate eye are similar in both structure and function, and accordingly qualify as being similar kinds of adaptation, despite having evolved independently of each other. Likewise, the saber teeth of the placental saber-toothed tiger and the marsupial saber-toothed tiger appear to be identical structures and plausibly have identical functions. Therefore, the saber teeth of these animals are very similar adaptations.

Lawrence A. Shapiro

Examples of adaptations that bear the type 3 relationship to each other, i.e. that have the same structure but differ in function, are surprisingly easy to come by. Cases of mimicry provide obvious examples. In some cases of mimicry, a mimic will evolve the coloration of an undigestible model so that predators that have previously encountered the model will avoid the mimic. Mimicry like this is common among species of butterflies. If we suppose the model's coloration was originally selected for because it provided the capacity for conspecific identification then the structurally similar coloration of the mimic will be a different kind of adaptation. Similarly, there exist instances of aggressive mimicry, where a predatory mimic comes to resemble a non-aggressive model. The saber-toothed blenny manages to approach and nibble portions of other fish because it has evolved the shape, coloration, and behaviour of the parasite-removing cleaner wrasse (Futuyma, 1998, p. 82). Perhaps these structures of the cleaner wrasse are adaptations for camouflage or locomotion or sexual attraction, or perhaps they are not adaptations at all. Nevertheless, these same structural properties in the blenny have the function of helping the fish to obtain food.

In some cases, convergence in structure is common not because of mimicry, but because a structure is well-suited for various functions. Thus, the salamander species *Bolitoglossa salvinii* and *Chiropterotriton magnipes* both have increased webbing between the digits of their feet, resulting in feet that, to all appearances, are structurally identical. However, in the former case the increased webbing has been selected for its suction effects and in the latter case the webbing has the function of preventing the foot from breaking the surface tension of water (Wake, 1991, p. 558). Webbed feet, then, are an example of a single kind of structure that, in different species, may have distinct functions. Thus, on my analysis of adaptation, the webbed feet of *B. salvinii* and *C. magnipes* must count as different adaptations.

Finally, we come to adaptations that bear the type 2 relationship to each other—those that share a function but that differ in structure. Here we might point to the different kinds of structures that various species use to attract mates. The function of the peacock's tail is similar to that of the cricket's song, but the structures of these things are quite distinct. Were they not, we would expect to find crickets and peacocks attracted to each other. Similarly, the sonar equipment of many bats seems to have been selected for roughly the same reason as the eyes of many organisms. Bat sonar, in other words, has the same function as many kinds of eyes. Nevertheless, bat sonar counts as a different kind of adaptation than eyes, on my analysis, because sonar differs in structure from eyes.

To summarize the above results, cladistic methods invite an analysis of adaptation as a combination of structure and function. Accordingly, adaptations count as being similar in kind when they are similar structures with similar functions. Sometimes this similarity of adaptive type may be the result of homology, but it is also possible that similar adaptations have evolved independently more than once. Adaptations differ from each other when they differ in structure, function, or both. I hope I have said enough about what, for the cladist, adaptations are. It's now time to consider some implications of the thesis that minds are adaptations. As I remarked earlier, my goal is a theory of mind that rejects both physicalism and rampant functionalism. I agree with the intuitions that create difficulties for physicalism and functionalism, but I don't think that intuitions ought to be allowed to carry the day. Let's now see whether the analysis of adaptation that I have developed above provides principled and defensible reasons to be critical of physicalism and functionalism.

Physicalism from the Mind-as-Adaptation Perspective

If minds are adaptations then a theory of mind that identifies minds with types of physical structures cannot be right. However, the reason for this does not derive from functionalist intuitions about the plausibility of robot or alien minds, but from principles about how to individuate adaptations. Adaptations are structures with functions. But, a structure has a function only as a result of a particular sort of history—one in which selection is involved. To this extent, the individuation of adaptations is externalist. Thus, two molecule for molecule identical structures could nevertheless be distinct kinds of adaptations if their histories differ. Indeed, in my discussion of adaptations that bear a type 3 relationship to each other—similarity of structure but difference in function—I presented several examples of kinds that physicalists might type-identify but that cladists would distinguish. In short, physicalism is an incorrect theory of mind if minds are conceived as adaptations.

I am aware that this criticism of physicalism does not justify the intuitive point that functionalists make against physicalism. If minds are adaptations then physicalism is wrong not because minds might be realized in non-brain substances, but because the individuation of minds contains an historical element that physicalists neglect. However, as I will argue below, the mind-as-adaptation perspective accommodates the intuitive point. In fact, it provides an explanation for the intuition that non-brains appear to have or be minds.

Functionalism from the Mind-as-Adaptation Perspective

To appreciate the shift from thinking of minds as functional kinds to thinking of them as adaptations, it is necessary to be more explicit about functional characterizations of minds. Functionalism is not a univocal theory of mind. Within functionalism are those, to use Block's (1980b) labels, who are *functional state identity theorists* and those who are *functional specifiers*. The distinction captures a division over how to answer a question like the following: With what are we to identify pain? There seem to be two options:

(1) Pain is a functional state defined by inputs, e.g. paper cuts; outputs, e.g. cursing; relations to other states, e.g. anger.
(2) Pain is that type of physical state that fulfils the role described in (1).

Whereas (2) identifies pain with that type of thing which is caused by paper cuts, causes cursing, etc., (1) makes no attempt to wed the concept of pain to any particular kind of realization. Claim (1) identifies pain simply with a functional role. Functionalists who prefer the first way of identifying pain are functional state identity theorists and those who favour the second are functional specifiers.

Putnam is a prominent advocate of functional state identity theory. For this reason it is possible to make sense of his remark that functionalism is consistent with dualism (Putnam, 1967/80, p. 228). Pain, to use Putnam's example, is nothing more than a particular kind of functional role—one defined as an interaction between certain inputs, other states, and outputs. But this identification of pain with a kind of functional role implies nothing about that which assumes the role. It is consistent with this definition of pain that the role-playing be done by C-fibres or by soul-stuff. David Lewis, on the other hand, identifies pain with a functionally specified type of physical state (Lewis 1969/80, p. 233). Those kinds of physical states that assume the functional role of pain are identical to pain, and so pain can be at once a physical and functional state. Moreover, because in different organisms different kinds of physical states may play the functional role of pain, pain has multiple realizations.

In what follows I will use the term 'functionalism' to refer to functional state identity theory. This is because the functional specifier's view seems incoherent (see Block 1980b). Functional specifiers want, on the one hand, to allow for the possibility of multiply realizable kinds; on other hand, they want to identify functional kinds with types of physical structures. One cannot have it both ways. Interestingly, functional specification, although incoherent when proposed as a functionalist theory of mind, bears a close resemblance to the view I advocate here—mind as adaptation. Just as the functional specifier identifies a mental state with a physical kind that fills a particular functional role, the mind-as-adaptation view identifies the mind with a structure/function combination. It is only when one chooses to individuate kinds on the basis of function alone that one can remain neutral about the nature of the stuff that fills the functional role. However, it is just this neutrality that also seems to reduce functionalism to absurdity, for it opens the possibility that the nation of China and the Bolivian economy might constitute minds.

It is for this reason that the mind-as-adaptation perspective is clearly preferable to functionalism. In order to individuate adaptations one must attend to both function *and* structure. As we saw above, characters that share a function but that differ in structure are distinct adaptations. Thus, when conceived as an adaptation, minds with structures that differ from our own are not minds. Nothing but a brain can be a mind. It is for this reason that the nation of China and the Bolivian economy cannot be minds.

So, conceiving of mind as an adaptation provides a principled and defensible reason to deny that the nation of China and the Bolivian economy might realize minds, just as it provides a principled and defensible reason to reject physicalism. However, the mind-as-adaptation view might, at this point, seem to have thrown the baby out with the bath water. It avoids what's unattractive about physicalism and functionalism only by renouncing what's very attractive about functionalism—the intuitive possibility of robot and alien minds.

Minds as Adaptations

Having defended an analysis of adaptation and used it to respond to the physicalist and the functionalist, it is now time to examine more fully what it means to call the mind an adaptation. I am particularly concerned to defuse the problem that the discussions of physicalism and functionalism above uncovered. The problem is this: intuitively,

Lawrence A. Shapiro

it ought to be possible for Commander Data and Spock to have minds. However, the mind-as-adaptation view forbids the possibility of robot and alien minds unless robots and aliens are equipped with structures like our own brains and with selection histories that provide these brains with functions similar to the functions of our own brains. Suppose Data and Spock exist. How can we reasonably deny that they have minds?

I have two responses to this worry. The first makes an empirical point and the second a conceptual one. The empirical point is this. Consider that roughly 96% of known species have relatively good eyes (Barnes, 1987). This suggests that eyes have evolved independently many times. Land (1991) estimates that the spherical lens in fish eyes, for instance, has evolved eight times in four distinct phyla. There is, in short, massive convergence in the evolution of eyes. Why should this be? Why should we find in nature the same design repeated over and over again? A plausible answer to this question is that there are only a handful of structures that can function as an eye. Indeed, Land remarks that 'the number of fundamentally different ways of producing an image in an eye is relatively small, somewhere between eight and ten.' (Land, 1991, p. 118). If there are only eight to ten ways of building an eye, and eyes are tremendously adaptive, then we're likely to see the same kinds of structures arising independently of each other in many lineages.

In the same spirit as the eye example, Conway Morris says :

> ... the point I wish to stress is that again and again we have evidence of biological form stumbling on the same solution to a problem. Consider animals that swim in water. It turns out that there are only a few fundamental methods of propulsion. It hardly matters if we choose to illustrate the method of swimming by reference to water beetles, palagic snails, squid, fish, newts, ichthyosaurs, snakes, lizards, turtles, dugongs, or whales; we shall find that the style in which the given animal moves through the water will fall into one of only a few basic categories. (Conway Morris, 1998, pp. 204–5).

The point Land and Conway Morris make can be generalized in the following way: function constrains structure. It's simply false that any function can be multiply realized in numerous ways.

Applied to the matter at hand, this moral suggests the following response to the worry that if minds are adaptations then Data and Spock cannot have minds. The response is this: if Data and Spock appear able to do all the things that we attribute to organisms with minds, then it is likely that Data and Spock have structures in their heads like our brain. Indeed, if we grant as a reasonable extension to the generalization above that the more complex a function the more it constrains structure then we might see as *very* likely that Data and Spock have brain-like structures in their heads. In any event, I hope it is clear that we are now dealing with an empirical issue. The functionalist says that minds can be multiply realized, but if this is barely true for eyes or for aquatic propulsion systems then why should it be true for minds, which, presumably, are far more complex than these? The intuitions to which functionalists appeal are in this case misleading. They are intuitions that conflict with the empirical facts about functional constraints on structure and so they should not be trusted.

The conceptual point I wish to make in response to the worry about robot and alien minds is this. Two adaptations differ, on my analysis of adaptation, when they differ in either structure *or* function. However, this means that different adaptations may, nevertheless, share the same function. In discussing adaptations that bear the type 2 relationship to each other I gave some examples of different adaptations with identical functions. Let's now suppose that Data and Spock do not have anything resembling a brain in their heads. If minds are adaptations then they do not have minds. However, this does not imply that they do not have structures that can do many of the same things that our brain does. It's conceivable (though, as I have argued above, empirically unlikely) that Data and Spock have structures in their heads that differ radically from brains but that, nonetheless, are able to do everything our brains can do. This means that while they do not have minds—if minds are adaptations—they may still have things that function *like* minds. Similarly, we say of the dialysis patient that she does not have a kidney although she is attached to a machine that functions *like* a kidney. This conceptual point licenses a very sensible response to Block's criticism of functionalism. What we would like to say about the nation of China or the Bolivian economy, I suspect, is that whereas these things might function like minds, they are not minds. This we cannot say if minds are functional kinds. But, if we construe minds as adaptations, then this is just the response to which we are committed.

Looming Questions

In this final section I will try to respond to questions that the mind-as-adaptation view raises. It's worth emphasizing at this point that

Lawrence A. Shapiro

I am offering the mind-as-adaptation view as a theory of mind, in the same sense that physicalism and functionalism are theories of mind. The physicalist says that minds are brains, the functionalist says that minds are functional roles, and the theory I offer says that minds are a specific kind of structure that, over time, has evolved a particular sort of function. I like to think that my theory of mind is more defensible than physicalism and functionalism because rather than resting on intuitions about what kinds of things can have minds, it draws its motivation from a theory of systematics that has proven to be successful in its quest to uncover objective facts about phylogeny. The categories of cladistics have earned their keep through the knowledge about phylogeny that they have provided, and it is these very same categories to which I appeal in my characterization of minds. So, while functionalists have little more than intuition on their side when they dismiss physicalism as implausibly chauvinistic, I have cladistics to justify my claim that minds are structures with functions. Why are they structures with functions? Because they are adaptations, and for purposes of discovering the branching pattern of evolution we ought to construe adaptations as structures with functions. Why ought we to construe minds as adaptations? Because doing so gives us a principled theory of mind that aligns better with our intuitions than does either physicalism or functionalism.

The first question is this: what are minds? I have been speaking in the loose manner that physicalists and functionalists also deploy. Of course minds are not simple things. 'Mind', as I use the term, refers to a collection of cognitive capacities: memory, attention, language, perception, etc. Stated more precisely then, the suggestion I am defending is that each of these capacities ought to be conceived as particular kinds of structures with particular functions. To claim that memory, for instance, is an adaptation is to commit oneself to the claim that memory is to be identified with that physical structure that performs the function we associate with memory. 'Mind-as-adaptation' is, accordingly, shorthand. It's a slogan that invites us to conceive of the various cognitive capacities that we typically associate with the mind as kinds of structures with functions.

This more precise statement of the view that minds are adaptations bears on my argument that if Data and Spock have mental-like capacities then they are likely to have structures in their heads similar to our brains. This argument depended on the principle that function constrains structure. But, also plausible is that structure constrains structure. By this I mean that if one structure is to cooperate successfully with another, the two must both have properties that facilitate their interaction. For instance, while there may be many ways to build something that keeps time, once one has settled on a gear with a certain radius and a certain number of cogs, the other gears that one places in the clock must be made to fit with this first one. The structure of the first gear constrains the structures of the others, relative to the function of keeping time. Similarly, if memory is to interact with other cognitive capacities then the structures of these other capacities must complement that of memory. The point of this observation is this: stated more precisely, the mind-as-adaptation view makes even clearer the improbability of unfettered multiple-realization. Not only does function constrain structure, but when various functional components work together their realizations place constraints on each other. Together, these two principles strengthen the likelihood that if Data and Spock have mental-capacities just like our own then they have brains very similar to our own.

The next two questions concern the dependence of the mind-as-adaptation theory on similarity judgments. On my analysis of adaptation, similarity and difference in kinds of adaptations depends on similarity and difference in kinds of structures and kinds of functions. But, one may object, how is it possible to determine similarity and difference in kinds of structures and functions? In responding to these questions I shall assume that some answer is possible. However dire the difficulty may seem, the fact remains that cladists do make judgments of similarity and these judgments are effective. Thus, when despairing that similarity judgments are impossible, one should whistle a happy tune and take solace in cladism's success.

The example of the bears with differing hair lengths helps to make vivid the problem of judging similarity in structures. In this example I imagined that there were three species of bears with either long or short hair. Between the three species, the character of hair length had just two states. But now imagine that we are faced with systematizing five species of bear and that their hair is not simply either long or short. Perhaps A and B have hair that is six inches long, C and D have hair that is two inches long, but E has hair that is four inches long. Is E's hair length more similar to A&B's or to C&D's?

There are several points to make in response to this kind of worry. The first is that cladists are unlikely to examine characters that have not evolved into clearly distinct states. The second is that my focus is upon adaptations. Thus, one need not get tangled up in questions about similarities in structures if the functions of the

Lawrence A. Shapiro

structures clearly differ. Perhaps A, B, and E live in cold climates and C and D live in tropical climates. If further investigation leads us to believe that the longer hair of A, B, and E insulates them from the cold, then the four inch hair of E is an adaptation more similar to the adaptations of A and B then it is of C and D.

But how are we to determine similarity in structure when we confront structures that are similar in function? Suppose we are wondering whether the 4 inch hair on bears of species E constitutes the same kind of adaptation as the 5 inch hair on some species of wolf. Suppose further that the hair on both species has an insulating function. Do we have a case of sameness in adaptation? The question seems important, because similar issues may arise in discussion of mental capacities. Do chimpanzees and humans share any mental capacities if their brains differ in slight ways? It is in an effort to subdue these worries that I have so far spoken of *similarity and difference* in adaptations, rather than identity or sameness of adaptations.[1] We are here dealing with an issue of grain. At an extremely coarse level of grain, hair of any length is the same structure; at an extremely fine level of grain, hairs that differ in length by a single millimetre are different structures. The choice in grain must be decided relative to some purpose, and for cladistic purposes the grain at which one classifies structures will be that which most benefits phylogenetic inference. If one is trying to decide whether one species is more closely related to a second than it is to a third within the same genus then one will presumably be working with a finer grain of analysis than one would if trying to decide whether a given species is more closely related to a second or a third of different genera.

These remarks about similarity in structure, vague as they may be, suffice to distinguish the mind-as-adaptation view from functionalism. The functionalist never concerns himself with questions about whether the realizers of two 'minds' are similar enough to justify the claim that the two are indeed of a kind. Indeed, it is an axiom of functionalism that considerations of constitution are irrelevant to the individuation of functional kinds. Thus, for instance, Fodor remarks that 'because it is (roughly) a sufficient condition for being a mousetrap that a mechanism be customarily *used* in a certain way, there is nothing in principle that requires that a pair of

[1] Certainly there are cases of molecular adaptations that are undeniably similar in structure. Thus, the lysozymes in the stomachs of species with foregut fermentation (e.g. langur monkeys and cows) have converged on identical amino-acid sequences (Stewart, Schilling and Wilson, 1987). Surely molecular identity suffices for structural identity.

38

mousetraps *have* any shared mechanical properties.' (Fodor, 1968, pp. 115–6). The moral, Fodor believes, holds good for minds as well. Yet, it is just this axiom of functionalism that leads to the Troubles that Block makes so plain. On the mind-as-adaptation view, in contrast, function is *not* a sufficient condition for being the member of a certain kind. If, given some grain of analysis, two organs with similar functions are distinct structures, they are not of a kind. These judgments of similarity, like all judgments of similarity, are relative, but this is not cause for concern in the present context. Indeed, it is because functionalism cannot avail itself of such judgments as applied to structure that Block is able to reduce it to absurdity.

Judgments of similarity and difference when applied to functions face their own questions. It may seem that function attribution is at best difficult and at worst hopelessly indeterminate (see Enç, forthcoming). Consider, for instance, the notorious mechanism in the frog that responds to moving black dots. Should one describe the function of this mechanism as a black dot detector, a fly detector, a food detector, an energy provider, or, most basically, a fitness enhancer? All of these effects are simultaneous: it does one at the same time that it does all the others. However, depending on which assignment one chooses, the frog's mechanism will have the same function as, respectively, a lizard's black dot detector (assuming they have them), a fly's mate detector (assuming they have them), a bee's pollen detector, chlorophyll, and every other adaptation.

However, as with the case of judgments of similarity between structures, these difficulties are not fatal to the mind-as-adaptation theory. Because my focus is on adaptations and not simply functional kinds, a response to which I availed myself in discussing structural similarity is available here as well: one can ignore questions about functional similarity when the structures involved clearly differ. Moreover, it may be possible to assuage worries about functional similarity judgments fairly directly. After all, there are facts of the matter about which selection pressures explain the evolution of a given adaptive structure. Thus, while it is true that both the frog's black dot detector and the human's epiglottis were both selected for their fitness enhancing effects, it is false of the latter that it was selected for providing energy. Because the epiglottis cannot provide energy, it cannot be this capacity that explains why it was selected. Similarly, while it is true of both the black dot detector and chlorophyll that is for the acquisition of energy that each evolved, it is false that chlorophyll's ability to detect food explains its origin. Likewise, the need for food (nutrients) might explain the evolution

Lawrence A. Shapiro

of both the black dot detector and the bee's pollen detector, but it cannot be the ability to detect flies that explains the evolution of the pollen detector. As we seek the causes that help to explain the evolution of a given kind of structure, the specification of the structure's function becomes more exclusive.

Applied to minds, this route to function determination would bid us to distinguish structures that have evolved for very different reasons. But, this ought not to be controversial. Surely part of what it is to be a mind is to function in a certain way. When viewing minds as adaptations, the surprise—and windfall—is not that functions don't contribute to a definition of mind, but that structure does.

Bibliography

Barnes, R. (1987). *Invertebrate Zoology* (Philadelphia: Saunders).

Block, N. 1978/1980. 'Troubles with Functionalism', in N. Block (ed.) (Cambridge: Harvard University Press), pp. 268–305.

Block, N. (ed.) 1980a. *Readings in Philosophy of Psychology, vol. 1.* (Cambridge: Harvard University Press).

Block, N. 1980b. 'Introduction: What is Functionalism?', in N. Block (ed.) (Cambridge: Harvard University Press), pp. 171–84.

Conley-Dillon, J and Gregory, R. (eds) 1991. *Evolution of the Eye and Visual System* (New York: Macmillan).

Conway Morris, S. 1998. *The Crucible of Creation* (Oxford: Oxford University Press).

Cummins, R., Ariew, A. and Perelman, W. M. forthcoming: *Functional Explanation in Psychology and Biology* (Oxford: Oxford University Press)

Darwin, C. 1859. *The Origin of Species* (London: Penguin Books).

Enç, B. forthcoming: 'Indeterminacy of Function Attributions', in R. Cummins, A. Ariew and W. M. Perelman (ed).

Fodor, J. 1968. *Psychological Explanation* (New York: Random House)

Futuyma, D. 1998. *Evolutionary Biology*, 3rd edition. (Sunderland: Sinauer).

Hull, D. 1970. 'Contemporary Systematic Philosophies', *Annual Review of Ecology and Systematics,* **1**, 19–53.

Land, M. 1991. 'Optics of the Animal Kingdom', in J. Conley-Dillon and R. Gregory (eds.), (New York: Macmillan), pp. 118–135.

Lewis, D. 1969/1980. 'Review of Putnam', in N. Block (ed.) (Cambridge: Harvard University Press), pp. 232–33.

Moore, J. and Willmer, P. 1997. 'Convergent Evolution in Invertebrates', *Biological Review,* **72**, 1–60.

Putnam, H. 1967/1980. 'The Nature of Mental States', in N. Block (ed.) (Cambridge: Harvard University Press), pp. 223–31.

Ridley, M. 1986. *Evolution and Classification: The Reformation of Cladism* (New York: Longman).

Ridley, M. 1996. *Evolution*, 2nd edition (Cambridge: Basil Blackwell Science).

Sober, E. 1984. *The Nature of Selection* (Cambridge: MIT Press).

Sober, E. 1993. *Philosophy of Biology* (Boulder: Westview Press).

Stewart, C., Schilling, J. and Wilson, A. 1987. 'Adaptive Evolution in the Stomach Lysozymes of Foregut Fermenters', *Nature*, **330**, 401–4.

Wake, D. 1991. 'Homoplasy: The Result of Natural Selection, or Evidence of Design Limitations?', *The American Naturalist*, **138**, 543–67.

West-Eberhard, M. 1992. 'Adaptation: Current Usages', in E. Keller and E. Lloyd (eds) *Keywords in Evolutionary Biology* (Cambridge: Harvard University Press), pp. 13–18.

Should Intentionality be Naturalized?

THOMAS BONTLY[1]

One goal of recent philosophy of mind has been to 'naturalize' intentionality by showing how a purely physical system could have states that represent or are about items (objects, properties, facts) in the world. The project is reductionist in spirit, the aim being to explain intentional relations—to say what they really are—and to do so in terms that do not themselves utilize intentional or semantic concepts. In this vein there are attempts to explain intentional relations in terms of causal relations, informational relations, teleological or functional relations, relations involving abstract similarity or isomorphism, and various combinations thereof.[2] What makes these accounts naturalistic is the presumed objectivity and scientific respectability of the properties appealed to in the explanans. What makes them all reductive is their shared presumption that intentionality can be explained in terms that have a wider application to intentional systems as well as to systems that have no mental properties at all.

I emphasize the reductionism implicit in the naturalizing project because it the source of an ongoing debate amongst naturalist sympathizers. Some, like Fodor, see a successful reduction of intentional relations as necessary for a naturalistic world-view. As he puts it:

> The worry about representation is above all that the semantic (and/or intentional) will prove permanently recalcitrant to integration in the natural order. ... What is required to relieve this worry is therefore, at a minimum, the framing of naturalistic conditions for representation ... of the form 'R represents S' is true iff C. ... (Fodor, 1984, p. 32).

[1] This is an expanded and revised version of my 'In Defense of Naturalizing,' presented at the Royal Institute of Philosophy conference Naturalism, Evolution, and Mind in Edinburgh, UK, July 1999. An earlier version was presented at the University of Connecticut, and I thank both audiences for helpful discussion. Special thanks to Larry Shapiro, Elliott Sober, Dennis Stampe, and Denis Walsh for comments and discussion.
[2] Such approaches are found in Stampe, 1977; Dretske, 1981; Millikan, 1984; and Cummins, 1996.

Thomas Bontly

Notice, Fodor says that only a reductive account will calm fears about the status of intentionality—that reductionism is not only sufficient but also necessary for naturalism. And if it turns out that intentionality is not reducible, then there will be many (call them 'global naturalists') who will doubt that it is real at all. As Fodor says elsewhere: 'It's hard to see ... how one can be a Realist about intentionality without being, to some extent or other, a Reductionist. ... If intentionality is real, it must really be something else' (Fodor, 1987, p. 97).

Other friends of naturalism have taken to questioning the need for naturalizing. Why, they ask, should we seek a reductive account of intentional relations? What significance could such projects hold? The present paper attempts to find an answer. The first section presents one plausible conception of naturalism in terms of physical realization and argues that it has reductive consequences for intentionality. In the second part, I consider whether physical realization goes to the heart of what it means to be 'natural.' The third section, finally, takes up the notorious 'exclusion problem,' asking whether mental causation in a physical world might require the physical realization of mental properties.[3]

1. The Reductive Consequences of Naturalism

What is naturalism? It would probably be impossible to provide a definition satisfactory to all. Philosophical '-ism' words typically mean different things to different people, and there is no guarantee that the various theses so-labelled bear so much as a family resemblance to each other. Rather than trying to analyse the doctrine, therefore, I will begin with a formulation that seems to capture its intended spirit and work from there. As Michael Tye puts it, 'The key idea in naturalism is that the mental is a part of nature in the same way as the chemical, biological, and geological' (Tye, 1992, p. 437). Since chemical, biological, and geological kinds participate in causal interactions falling under scientific laws, Tye infers that mentality is natural only if it likewise participates in lawful causal interactions. Does the converse also hold? Would it be sufficient for the truth of naturalism if the mental were to engage in lawful causal interactions? Not according to Tye. Dualists hold that mental states participate in causal interactions, and a non-Cartesian

---

[3] For ease of exposition, I will sometimes speak interchangeably of intentional properties and mental properties, but I do not mean to suggest that all mental properties are intentional.

dualist could grant that these interactions fall under psychological laws. Substance dualism may well turn out to be untenable, but certainly it is a logical possibility. It is, however, a possibility that Tye says is inconsistent with the spirit of naturalism, so we haven't yet a sufficient condition for the mind to be a part of nature.

What's missing, Tye says, is that mental states must 'also bear the same general ontic relationship to lower level physical items as do the physical entities quantified over and referred to in higher level physical laws' like those of biology and chemistry. Tye describes that ontic relationship in terms of constitution and realization. Chemical tokens (like a token water molecule) are wholly constituted of physical parts, and chemical properties (like the property of being an acid) are realized by underlying physical properties. Presumably, the same holds for the tokens and types of other 'special' sciences, and, Tye says, the same must hold for mind if it is a part of nature. In his view, then, mentality is natural if and only if (a) mental states participate in lawful causal interactions, (b) mental state tokens are physically constituted, and (c) mental state types (that is, mental properties) are physically realized.

Tye's explication of naturalism is not at all unusual; most 'naturalizers' seem to have some view like this in mind when they say that the mind is part of nature. However, Tye draws a surprising conclusion from his account of naturalism. The mind stands in no need of naturalizing, he says, because the conditions just reviewed are obviously satisfied! The argument is simply this:

[T]he mental is studied by psychology. Psychology is a science no different in its procedures and laws from other sciences. So, of course, the mental is part of nature in the ways I have described. To suppose otherwise is to suppose that there is something peculiar about the mental which prevents it from having the features adumbrated above. And there just is no good reason for any such supposition. So ... naturalism with respect to the mental, once properly explicated, is really beyond question. (Tye, 1992, p. 437).

According to Tye, then, (a)–(c) follow directly from the scientific status of psychology, so we needn't identify mental properties with anything else in order to vindicate naturalism.

Now, Tye's premise is surely open to debate. Some might question whether psychological theories are falsifiable or testable—whether they have what it takes to qualify as science rather than pseudo-science. Others might argue that psychology cannot be science precisely because there can be no psychological laws.[4] A thorough discussion of these issues would take us too far astray, however, and anyway naturalists will surely grant that psychology is a genuine science involving causal laws. But how are (b) psychophysical constitution and (c) realization supposed to follow from this premise? Perhaps Tye thinks that (b) and (c) follow from (a), but Tye has already granted (p. 432) that the causal potency of the mental is consistent with substance dualism, a position that rejects both (b) and (c). Likewise, condition (a) looks to be consistent with emergentist views that affirm the physical constitution of mental particulars but deny that mental properties are physically realized. Unlike dualists, emergentists generally hold that all particulars are physical entities, composed entirely of physical parts. However, they also insist that at certain levels of complexity, entirely new properties 'emerge,' and neither their emergence nor their causal powers can be given any physical explanation[5]. In citing dualism and emergentism, I do not mean to endorse the views. My point is simply that, without significant further assumptions, they look to be consistent with the thesis that mental properties fall under causal laws discoverable by science.[6] And this means that Tye's argument gives us no reason to believe that the mind is already natural in the sense he has spelled out.

In fact, Tye's explication of naturalism shows us exactly why naturalists are invested in reductionism. First of all, the physical realization thesis is really quite demanding, a good deal stronger than the idea that mental properties are dependent or 'supervenient.' Supervenience is a sort of necessary correlation or covariation between two sets of properties. Psychophysical supervenience says that any two items with the same physical properties must have the same mental properties—'no mental difference without a physical difference'—but it is silent as to why. Realization, on the other hand, is a fairly strong and specific dependency relation that carries with it definite metaphysical commitments. As Jaegwon Kim puts it, talk of realization suggests 'that when we look at concrete reality there is nothing over and beyond instantiations of physical properties and relations, and that the instantiation on a given occasion of an appropriate physical property in the right contextual (often causal) setting simply counts as, or constitutes, an instantiation of a

---

[4] The first question might be pressed by the Popperian, the second by a Davidsonian.

[5] These facets of emergentism are discussed in McLaughlin (1992).

[6] In section 3, I discuss other assumptions that might lead to (c) psychophysical realization.

mental property on that occasion' (Kim, 1992, pp. 313–14). So the realization thesis says that an organism's mental properties are really implicit in a complete physical description of it.

For well-known reasons, however, it seems prima facie implausible that intentional and other mental properties are 'nothing over and above' physical properties, since the former have a variety of features that physical properties seem to lack. To take first a weary example, suppose that Fred is thinking about unicorns. It seems that he stands in an intentional relation to things that do not exist. Or suppose that Clyde believes that the Vikings won the Superbowl; he thereby stands in an intentional relation to a state of affairs that has never obtained and (one hopes) never will. But physical relations hold only between real existents: you can't ride a unicorn, and you can't stand on the football field where the Vikings won the Superbowl. Or consider the fact that the attitudes we have to intentional contents appear to have a sort of normativity not possessed by physical properties. If, for example, Martha believes that the faculty meeting starts at 3pm, then she ought not to believe also that it will be over before noon, nor should she be seen in the hallway at 2:59 if she wishes not to attend. An intentional description of her present mental state therefore has normative implications, but a description of her physical state seems to have no such implications, so once again it is hard to see how subjects could have their intentional properties simply in virtue of their physical properties.

The moral is that the realization thesis cannot be taken for granted, even if intentional explanations are scientifically respectable. There are aspects of intentionality that require explanation, and if they cannot be explained (or explained away) physicalistically, then the realization thesis is false—either intentional properties are real but not natural (in Tye's sense) or else they are not real at all. Naturalists must therefore shoulder the explanatory burden of showing that, first impressions to the contrary, intentional properties can be identified with something that objects do have simply in virtue of their physical properties. And some progress has been made on this front. Consider, for example, Stampe's (1977) idea that a state's representational content is determined by the state of affairs that would cause it under ideal conditions—i.e., conditions of well-functioning for the mechanism producing the state. If the teleological notion of function can be explained in causal-historical terms (Millikan, 1984), and if further the physical properties of a system determine its causal properties, then we have given a physicalistic explanation of the capacity for intentional states to misrepresent the world, putting us one step closer to vindicating the realization thesis.

Thomas Bontly

In fact, it is hard to see what else besides a causal or functional account of mental properties would do. Realization is not a general-purpose dependency relation that can hold between any two properties whatsoever. As it is usually understood, only 'higher-order' properties are properly said to be 'realized.' A higher-order property is just the property of having a (first or lower-order) property that meets some requirement R.[7] Ordinarily, we think of R as a causal requirement, from which we get orthodox functionalism: to be in pain, for example, just is to have the property of having a property that fills a characteristic causal role (causing winces and being caused by flesh wounds and the like). Or, less verbosely, we say that pain just is this causal role. Now, orthodox functionalism is not the only possibility here (there being other sorts of higher-order properties besides causal roles—e.g. Millikan's proper functions), but the important point for our purposes is that talk of realization is only appropriate—it's only meaningful—against the assumption that mental properties are indeed higher-order. Since that is exactly what reductive naturalists typically seek to show, it follows that Tye's explication of naturalism, and his condition (c) in particular, commits us to a sort of reductionism: it obligates us to identify mental properties with higher-order properties of some sort.[8]

2. Which Naturalism?

Is Tye's version of naturalism satisfactory? In particular, it was condition (c) that was found to have reductionist consequences, but why suppose that naturalists are committed to the physical realization of mental properties? Along these lines, Shapiro questions whether reductive (he calls them 'lego') naturalists have 'hit upon

[7] Cf. Kim, 1992, pp. 313–14 & 1998, pp. 23–24; Papineau, 1993, p. 25.
[8] My argument that Tye's naturalism entails a type of reductionism assumes a standard (functionalist) conception of realization. Tye could object that he had some weaker notion of realization in mind, however; perhaps all he means is that mental properties are determined by or supervenient upon physical properties. The weaker idea is suggested by his comment that '[t]he realization relation is, at least in part, one of determination: the lower level property synchronically fixes the higher level one, so that the tokening of the former at any time t necessitates the token of the latter at t but not conversely' (Tye, 1992, p. 436). The text leaves it unclear whether synchronic necessitation is sufficient or only necessary for realization, but even taking necessitation to be sufficient, this weaker realization thesis does not follow from the fact that psychology is genuine science.

48

the correct characterization of what it means to be natural' (Shapiro, 1997, pp. 309–10), and he provides three reasons to think that they have not. First, reductive naturalism is 'inconsistent with the functionalist framework on which cognitive science and other special sciences rest' (Shapiro, 1997, p. 314). The presumption in cognitive science is that psychological kinds are functional kinds that can be realized in different ways in different structures. In David Lewis's (1980) famous example, pain could be realized by C-fibre firing in humans and by the inflation of hydraulic cavities in the feet of Martians. As long as the function subserved by these physically different structures is the same, they realize the same psychological state despite the obvious physical difference. Since classical reductionism requires the identity of psychological types with physical types, multiple realizability speaks in favour of functionalism and against reductionism.

It is certainly true that functionalism is in and psychophysical reductionism out, but two points deserve emphasis. First, the sort of reductive naturalism considered here is not old-fashioned psychophysical reductionism or the type-identity theory. The reductive naturalist proposes to identify intentional (or other mental) properties, not with first order physical properties, but with higher-order properties like functional properties. A theory of mental representation that identifies a state's semantic content with the state of affairs that would cause it under ideal conditions is not type-physicalism, and it is perfectly consistent with multiple realizability. The second point, which follows from the first, is that functionalism is itself a reductive doctrine; it identifies mental properties with, or reduces them to, functional properties of one sort or another. For these reasons, multiple realizability is a red herring in the present context. There is nothing anti-functionalist in the sort of reductive naturalism considered here.

Shapiro's second objection to reductive naturalism is that it 'cannot support a contrast between the natural and the non-natural,' which he says any acceptable account of naturalism ought to do. An account of naturalism should explain (to use Shapiro's examples) why oxygen, fingernails, and elephants are natural while fast-food containers, televisions, and poker chips are not. But the sort of reductive naturalism I have been considering fails to draw these distinctions. Token fast-food containers are all made entirely of physical stuff, and the property of being a fast-food container— itself a functional property—can be realized by the appropriate physical properties. The same goes for televisions and poker chips, so all of these things turn out natural on the present account.

Thomas Bontly

Shapiro concludes that, given the present conception of naturalism, everything seems to be natural, so an important desideratum for an account of naturalism goes unsatisfied (Shapiro, 1997, p. 317).

Now, I confess that I am unsure whether Shapiro's objection is that reductive naturalism draws no natural/non-natural distinction, or that it draws one but in the wrong place. Three distinctions are implicit in Tye's account: between those properties that are physically realized and those that are not, between those token events that are physically constituted and those that are not, and between those things that fall under causal laws and those that do not. And the contrasting classes may not be empty. Numbers do not fall under causal laws, and according to the Cartesian mental states cannot be realized in physical stuff with only physical properties. Of course, the Cartesian may be wrong about these things; perhaps every property ever instantiated in the world of experience is physically realized, in which case some of the contrasting classes may turn up empty. But that is hardly an objection to naturalism, for that is exactly the way thoroughgoing naturalists take the world to be.

Perhaps then it would be better to understand Shapiro as objecting to the place where reductive naturalism draws the line between natural and non-natural; it should be drawn so as to exclude fast-food containers, televisions, and poker chips from the natural realm, but reductive naturalism includes them. However, I question the presupposition that there is a correct place to draw the line in question, for there is no single distinction that naturalism must capture. The word 'natural' can be used to introduce many different contrasts: with the artificial ('natural flavouring'), the conventional ('natural meaning' or 'natural law'), the acquired or learned ('natural proclivities'), the unusual ('natural habitat'), the unsavoury ('natural causes'), and so on. Shapiro evidently prefers to contrast the natural with the conventionally or culturally defined, so he places fast-food containers in the non-natural category. But this is just one contrast marked with the word 'natural,' and another is the distinction emphasized by materialists between the physical realm and the realm of immaterial minds. I see no reason to think that an account of naturalism should be built on one contrast rather than the other. If either, the latter contrast—between the physical and the spiritual or supernatural—has a prima facie claim to be the contrast for naturalism about the mind, having figured in discussions of the mind-body problem for centuries.

Shapiro's final objection to reductive conceptions of naturalism is related to though better motivated than the one just considered. Reductive naturalists, he says, effectively 'beg the question about what is natural.' He suggests that we look at the matter from the standpoint of the workaday cognitive psychologist:

> How would such a scientist respond if told that the phenomenon she studies, e.g. memory, is natural only if it can be explicated in the explanatory vocabulary of some other nonintentional 'natural' science, like physics or chemistry? ... The assumption the cognitive scientist might reasonably adopt is that mental phenomena, even if irreducibly intentional, are nevertheless natural: On this view, cognitive science ought to be placed alongside, rather than beneath, other so-called natural sciences, for its subject matter, the cognitive scientist might insist, is no less natural than the nonintentional subject matters of physics and chemistry. (Shapiro, 1997, p. 315)

Instead of a relatively demanding conception of naturalism like Tye's, Shapiro urges that we adopt (what he calls) methodological naturalism, according to which 'intentionality belongs in the natural category if it can be the subject of a scientifically rigorous investigation' (Shapiro, 1997, p. 320). Since intentional phenomena are investigated by cognitive science, he says, intentionality again winds up natural whether it can be reduced or not.

This is certainly a legitimate complaint, there being no obvious reason why a 'naturalist' has to take a particular view of the relation between psychology and other domains. For example, Arthur Danto (1967) once defined 'naturalism' as the doctrine that 'whatever exists or happens is ... susceptible to methods ... exemplified in the natural sciences.' Naturalism doesn't entail any particular ontology, he said, and in particular it doesn't entail materialism or physicalism. Indeed, earlier this century one W. D. Oliver (1949) even argued that naturalism is incompatible with materialism. So haven't we, in accepting Tye's account of naturalism, simply conflated two very different doctrines? Haven't we appropriated a very attractive word ('natural' having a positive connotation) and attached it to a much stronger thesis that we should probably call 'realization physicalism' or 'token materialism' instead?

The present debate will likely end in a stalemate. 'Fine,' we say, 'let's call it 'physicalizing intentionality' rather than 'naturalizing intentionality' and just get on with our work. The name is ugly, but what's in a name?' Disputes about the meaning of philosophical '-ism' words are seldom fruitful, and I see no way to determine which specific theses really capture the essence of 'naturalism' (or, for that matter, of 'empiricism,' 'feminism,' or any other '-ism'). One would like to begin by analysing the meaning of the word

Thomas Bontly

'naturalism,' but as it lacks the corpus of well-established ordinary-language uses that can be studied through intuition, conceptual analysis does not seem appropriate. Perhaps the best we can do when attempting to clarify a philosophical doctrine is to be relatively true to its historical roots, and certainly naturalists do have a long history of reductive proclivities. On the other hand, there are historical precedents for Shapiro's methodological account of naturalism as well: e.g., Danto's definition (above), or Quine's (1969) naturalized epistemology with its emphasis on the scientific investigation of the knower. Without a method to determine which bent—ontological or methodological—is closer to the heart of naturalism, we are at an impasse. Perhaps reductionist assumptions cannot be justified in the name of naturalism after all.

If there is a victory here for the critics of reductionism, it is a hollow victory however, and the worst the reductive naturalist can be accused of is a bit of false advertising. What is at issue in attempts to 'naturalize the mind' is the doctrine known as physicalism—i.e., the idea that everything at bottom is physical—and what we care about, when evaluating this or any other philosophical thesis, is not what to call it, but whether it is true. By focusing on the meaning of the word 'natural,' we miss an important question: namely, what is the relationship between intentional mental properties and the physical properties that occur at the same time? One view says that the relationship is one of realization, and in the final section we shall submit the thesis to closer examination.

3. Psychophysical Realization and the Exclusion Problem

Worries about mental causation probably provide the most common motivation for the psychophysical realization thesis. The problem, originally Descartes', can be given a contemporary spin as follows: on the one hand, common sense or 'folk' psychology is predictively and explanatorily successful. Attributing beliefs, desires, and other mental states to people helps greatly in predicting what they will think and do, which success would be quite surprising if what they believe and desire did not affect their actions. On the other hand, the contemporary scientific image seems to have no room for non-physical causes of behaviour. In principle, every movement a person makes can be explained by appeal to physical states and processes occurring within him. The easiest solution would be to identify mental properties with the physical properties that cause behaviour, but the so-called 'multiple realizability' of the mental

52

seems to rule out psychophysical type-identities[9]. The physical realization thesis then presents itself as a way to have our cake and eat it too—to have casual interaction without full-blown type-materialism.

But how exactly does the realization thesis constitute a solution to the problem of mental causation? To illustrate the difficulties, consider a recent discussion of the issue by Antony and Levine:

> The domain of physical phenomena, according to current physical theory, is causally closed. Nothing can affect the distribution of matter and energy in space-time except the instantiation of basic physical properties in the basic objects that occupy space-time. Mental states/events are both caused by and cause changes in the distribution of matter and energy in space-time. So, the mechanisms by which these changes are brought about must be physical mechanisms. Hence, mental events must be realized in physical properties. (Antony and Levine, 1997, p. 100).

The passage identifies two assumptions alleged to argue for physical realization:

> The Principle of Causal Interaction (CI): mental events cause and are caused by physical events.
> The Causal Closure of the Physical (CCP): nothing can cause a physical event except another physical event (that is, the exemplification of a physical property).

The trouble comes when we try to link these assumptions to the realization thesis. Taken together, the two principles actually seem to entail that there are token psychophysical identities; if the only thing that can cause a physical event is another physical event, then each mental event must actually be some physical event. But there could be token identities even if the realization thesis is false, as Davidson's (1970) anomalous monism takes to be the case. Since anomalous monism rejects psychophysical laws, it is inconsistent with the realization thesis. If token event identities are sufficient to solve the problem of mental causation, then, why do mental properties have to be physically realized?

According to Davidson, one event causes another only if they can be brought together under a strict law. Anomalous monism denies that there are strict laws involving mental events as such, so

[9] To avoid begging the question, we should take the multiple realizability of the mental to be merely the claim that beings with no physical states in common can still undergo the same mental states. So understood, multiple realizability does not entail that the mental is physically realized.

Thomas Bontly

it is only in virtue of their physical descriptions that mental events can be subsumed under strict laws. Consequently, it is often objected that anomalous monism preserves the causal interaction thesis, but only by sacrificing the causal efficacy of mental properties.[10] Perhaps, then, we should understand Antony and Levine to be arguing for the realization thesis from this stronger premise:

The Causal Efficacy of Mental Properties (CEMP): At least some mental events cause physical events in virtue of the mental properties of those mental events.

CEMP entails CI but not vice versa, and I assume that anomalous monism fails to satisfy this stronger constraint.[11] But CEMP actually seems to contradict Antony and Levine's other premises. Antony and Levine's version of CCP says that only physical properties make a difference as to what physical events occur, and we are assuming that mental and physical properties cannot be identified. Thus, CEMP is true only if CCP is false, and it seems to matter not at all whether mental properties are physically realized.

So we have the makings of a nasty dilemma: the realization thesis is either unnecessary or insufficient to solve the problems of mental causation. If CI is all we care about, then a token identity thesis will suffice; if we want to preserve CEMP in addition to CI, then type identities seem be necessary. Part of the problem comes from Antony and Levine's statement of the completeness of physics. Their claim that '[n]othing can affect the distribution of matter and energy in spacetime except the instantiation of basic properties in the basic objects that occupy spacetime' effectively precludes any solution to the problem of mental causation short of identifying mental properties with the aforementioned basic properties. However, their version of the completeness of physics is almost certainly stronger than any statement we are entitled to make on the basis of current physical theory.[12] A weaker claim would be that the specification of prior physical conditions is sufficient to explain any

---

[10] This is argued by Kim, 1984, among others.

[11] The assumption may be controversial. Davidson (1993) attempts to rebut the charge of mental property epiphenomenalism.

[12] This is not to say that Antony and Levine's principle is false. How the completeness of physics is to be understood is a difficult question, not to be separated from the reasons for thinking it true. Since CCP is intended as an empirical thesis, we would have to examine current physical theory to see how it should be formulated. Papineau (forthcoming) explains the theoretical justification, but these matters extend well beyond the scope of my paper.

physical event, that mental (or other nonphysical) properties are not needed to give a complete causal explanation of physical happenings. We might thus preserve the spirit of Antony and Levine's argument with the following assumption:

(CCP) Any physical event can be given a complete causal explanation in terms of physical laws and prior physical events.

What does it mean to say that a causal explanation is (or is not) complete? Here we should defer to a general theory of the causal relation. Suppose, for instance, that causes are prior conditions that nomologically suffice for their effects. What we single out as 'the' cause is ordinarily, perhaps always, just a part of such a sufficient condition, but it is always a necessary part of a sufficient condition, without which the remaining parts of the condition would not have been sufficient for the effect (Mackie, 1965; Bennett, 1988). On this view, the completeness of physics would be the claim that every physical event (that has any explanation at all) has a nomologically sufficient condition of which no nonphysical event is a necessary part. If we follow Kim in thinking of events as property exemplifications, the claim is that for every exemplification of a physical property, there is a set of physical properties, all of which were exemplified at a prior time, and which together are sufficient for the effect property to be exemplified at the time that it was.

Now, the existence of one sufficient condition does not logically preclude the existence of others, so the reformulated CCP looks to be compatible with CEMP. That is, for some physical events, there could be a second set of properties, also exemplified earlier and also jointly sufficient for the physical effect, a necessary part of which is the exemplification of one or more mental properties. The problem with this scenario, however, is that it appears to mean that mental causation invariably involves overdetermination. Whenever there is a mental cause M of some physical effect E, there is also a physical cause P. Both M and P are sufficient (in the circumstances) to bring about E, so E would have occurred even if P hadn't—indeed, even if no physical condition sufficient for E had occurred. Not only is this hard to believe, but it seems also to conflict with the completeness of physics. Evaluating the above counterfactual in the standard way, it means that in the closest possible world where no physical event sufficient for E took place, E occurred nonetheless. This would be acceptable if E had no explanation in that world, but by hypothesis E finds a nonphysical explanation in M, so CCP is violated in that world. If CCP is violated in close possible worlds, then the fact that it is not violated in the actual world is just an accident,

Thomas Bontly

and surely this is unacceptable. As a claim about the laws of physics, CCP should be taken to have modal implications—to describe not only how the world is but also how it could be. If the laws of physics together with antecedent physical conditions suffice to explain every possible physical event, these events cannot be overdetermined by mental causes.[13]

However, the conclusion that mental causation need involve overdetermination rests on the assumption that a mental cause sufficient (in the circumstances) for E is nomologically independent of whatever physical condition is sufficient for E. To call an effect overdetermined is to say that it has two causes such that if either one had not occurred, the effect still had to occur. If mental properties strongly supervene on physical properties, this counterfactual will generally be false: in the closest possible world where P doesn't occur, M doesn't either, and so neither does E. Of course, M might have an alternative supervenience base P*, and so perhaps M could have occurred without P. But if M is sufficient for E, then so too is every property in M's supervenience base. It follows that whenever M occurs, it occurs together with a physical event sufficient for E. Strong supervenience, therefore, saves mental causation from the overdetermination problem.

The point is important in the present context because it shows that psychophysical realization does not follow from CCP together with CEMP. As discussed earlier, supervenience is consistent with realization but does not entail it. Mental properties can properly be said to be realized only if they are higher-order properties like functional properties, while supervenience means only that an object's physical properties necessitate or determine its mental properties. Physical properties might necessitate mental properties if the latter are functional properties realized by the underlying physical structure, but it could also be that mental properties are unanalysable first-order properties that just do lawfully supervene on the physical.[14]

This conclusion is especially significant, I think, for it threatens to undermine Kim's (1989 & 1998) 'exclusion argument' against mental causation. The exclusion argument assumes a kind of causal

[13] Kim, 1998, p. 45 suggests a similar argument.
[14] Horgan, 1993 and Kim, 1998 both argue that physicalists should be committed to the realization thesis because unexplained supervenience relations violate the spirit of physicalism. Like 'naturalism,' I suspect that 'physicalism' means different things to different people. Anyway, our question is whether the realization thesis is true, not whether it follows from physicalism.

incompatibilism, where one complete causal explanation of an event excludes any other causal explanation of that same event (except, perhaps, in genuine cases of overdetermination). A physical event, for example my arm's going up, has a complete physical cause (we can assume), so any mental cause is thereby excluded. As Kim (1998, p. 37) asks, 'what causal work is left for [the mental cause] to contribute?'

At one time, Kim (1984 & 1989) had hoped to solve the exclusion problem with a general model of 'supervenient causation.' On this account, mental properties (and macroscopic properties in general) are causally efficacious in virtue of their (strong) supervenience upon microphysical properties that are themselves causally efficacious; my having mental property M causes some physical effect by supervening on a physical property P that itself causes the effect. But Kim has since abandoned that position: 'So long as M remains a distinct property not to be identified with P, we must, it would seem, still contend with two purported causes of a single event. ... We must conclude then that the supervenience of M on P does not by itself remove M as a competitor of P as a cause, and the threat of its being excluded by P seems to remain' (Kim, 1993b, p. 361).

Does Kim's exclusionary reasoning show that mental properties must be physically realized if they are causally efficacious? I think not, and for two reasons. First of all, if mental properties are physically realized, then by definition they are functional properties distinct from their physical realizers. We can still ask 'what causal work is left' for the functional property to contribute, and the exclusion problem remains. This drives Kim (1998) to deny that mental properties are real properties at all, and he now holds that mental predicates express functional concepts but designate the physical property(s) that satisfies the associated concepts. In other words, mental predicates are disguised definite descriptions that nonrigidly designate physical properties.[15] In Kim's opinion, then, the only solution to the exclusion problem is to embrace a form of the psychophysical identity theory; physical realization is not enough.

But second, we should question the extreme causal incompatibilism that underlies the exclusion argument. The reason is this: no matter what account of the causal relation you prefer, it still seems that merely supervenient mental properties could be causally efficacious, consistent with the completeness of physics. We have already seen this to follow from the account of causes as nomologically

---

[15] This is essentially Lewis's (1980) hybrid of functionalism and the identity theory.

Thomas Bontly

sufficient conditions. The exemplification of one condition sufficient for some effect is perfectly consistent with the exemplification
of another condition sufficient for that same effect, and the effect
will only be overdetermined if neither of these conditions depends
or supervenes on the other. We reach the same conclusion if we
relax the requirement that causes be nomologically sufficient for
their effects and require instead some form of positive statistical
relevance (Sober, 1999), and arguably, the same result follows from
a counterfactual treatment of causation. The main ingredient
Lewis's (1973) counterfactual theory is the idea of counterfactual
dependence: an event e is counterfactually dependent on another
event c just in case it is true that if c hadn't occurred, e wouldn't
have occurred. Then c caused e just in case c and e both occurred
and either (i) e is counterfactually dependent on c or (ii) there is a
sequence of events x1, x2,...xn such that x1 is counterfactually
dependent on c, x2 is counterfactually dependent on x1,..., and e is
counterfactually dependent on xn. Now, let's suppose that S's
having P* at one time is counterfactually dependent on, and so
caused by, S's having P at an earlier time. If M supervenes on P,
then it is also true that if S hadn't had M, S wouldn't have had P.[16]
Thus we have a series of counterfactual dependence between S's
having M and S's having P*, and it follows that S's having M
caused S to have P*.[17]

The metaphysics of causation and the counterfactual approach in
particular require far more careful and lengthy treatment than I can
give them here. For now, however, it appears unlikely that any
theory of causation will support Kim's extreme causal incompatibilism, and if that is right, then we can conclude on the one hand
that supervenient properties needn't be excluded by their physical
bases. On the other hand, psychophysical supervenience does not
entail psychophysical realization, so we have not found herein a reason to think that mental properties must be 'naturalized' in order to
be causally efficacious. Perhaps the best rationale for attempting to

[16] Backtracking counterfactuals, where the antecedent event occurs after
the consequent event, are not allowed by Lewis's theory. Since supervenience is a synchronic necessitation relation, however, the counterfactual
'if M hadn't occurred, P wouldn't have occurred' does not backtrack.
[17] This result is not entirely happy for Lewis's theory of causation, since
it seems to show that every property supervening on a causally efficacious
property is itself causally efficacious. In fact, supervenient
events/properties seem to cause several problems for Lewis's account of
causation, but that discussion must wait.

naturalize intentionality is simply we'll never know whether it can be done unless we try. Perhaps that is reason enough.

Bibliography

Antony, L. and J. Levine 1997. 'Reduction with Autonomy', in J. Tomberlin (ed.) *Philosophical Perspectives 11: Mind, Causation, and World* (Malden, MA: Blackwell Publishers), pp. 83–105.

Beckerman, A., Flohr, H. and Kim, J. (eds) 1992. *Emergence or Reduction?* (Berlin: de Gruyter).

Bennett, J. 1988. *Events and Their Names* (Indianapolis: Hackett Publishing Co.).

Block, N. (ed.) 1980. *Readings in the Philosophy of Psychology* I (Cambridge, MA: Harvard University Press).

Brown, S. (ed.) 1974. *Philosophy of Psychology* (New York: The Macmillan Press).

Cummins, R. 1996. *Representations, Targets, and Attitudes* (Cambridge, MA: MIT Press).

Danto, A. 1967. 'Naturalism', in P. Edwards (ed.) *The Encyclopedia of Philosophy*, Vol. 5, pp. 448–50.

Davidson, D. 1970. 'Mental Events', in L. Foster and J. Swanson (eds.) (Amherst, MA: The University of Massachusetts Press), pp. 79–101.

Davidson, D. 1974. 'Psychology as Philosophy', in S. Brown (ed.) (New York: The Macmillan Press), pp. 41–52.

Davidson, D. 1993. 'Thinking Causes', in J. Heil and A. Mele (eds) (Oxford: Clarendon Press), pp. 3–17.

Dretske, F. 1981. *Knowledge and the Flow of Information* (Cambridge, MA: MIT Press).

Dretske, F. 1988. *Explaining Behavior: Reasons in a World of Causes* (Cambridge, MA: MIT Press).

Eells, E. 1991. *Probabilistic Causality* (Cambridge: Cambridge University Press).

Fodor, J. 1984. 'Semantics, Wisconsin Style', *Synthese*, **59**, 231–50.

Fodor, J. 1987. *Psychosemantics.* (Cambridge, MA: MIT Press).

Foster, L. and Swanson, J. (eds) 1970. *Experience and Theory* (Amherst, MA: The University of Massachusetts Press).

Heil, J. and Mele, A. (eds) 1993. *Mental Causation* (Oxford: Clarendon Press).

Horgan, T. 1993. 'From Supervenience to Superdupervenience: Meeting the Demands of a Material World', *Mind*, **102**, 555–86.

Kim, J. 1971. 'Causes and Events: Mackie on Causation', *Journal of Philosophy*, **68**, 426–41.

Kim, J. 1984. 'Epiphenomenal and Supervenient Causation', *Midwest Studies in Philosophy*, **9**, 257–70. Reprinted in Kim (1993a).

Kim, J. 1989. 'The Myth of Nonreductive Materialism', *Proceedings and*

Thomas Bontly

Addresses of the American Philosophical Association, **63**, 31–47. Reprinted in Kim (1993a).

Kim, J. 1992. 'Multiple Realizability and the Metaphysics of Reduction', *Philosophy and Phenomenological Research*, **52**, 1–26. Reprinted in Kim (1993a).

Kim, J. 1993a. *Supervenience and Mind* (Cambridge: Cambridge University Press).

Kim, J. 1993b. 'Postscripts on Mental Causation', in Kim (1993a), pp. 358–67.

Kim, J. 1998. *Mind in a Physical World* (Cambridge, MA: MIT Press).

Lewis, D. 1973. 'Causation', *Journal of Philosophy*, **70**, 556–67.

Lewis, D. 1980. 'Mad Pain and Martian Pain', in N. Block (ed.) (Cambridge, MA: Harvard University Press), pp. 216–22.

Mackie, J. 1965. 'Causes and Conditions', *American Philosophical Quarterly*, **2/4**, 245–55 and 261–4.

McLaughlin, B. 1992. 'The Rise and Fall of British Emergentism', in A. Beckerman, H. Flohr, and J. Kim (eds) (Berlin: de Gruyter), pp. 49–93.

Millikan, R. 1984. *Language, Thought, and Other Biological Categories* (Cambridge, MA: MIT Press).

Moore, G. E. 1922. 'The Conception of Intrinsic Value', in *Philosophical Studies*. (New York: Harcourt, Brace, and Co.), pp. 243–75.

Moore, G. E. 1942. 'A Reply to My Critics', in P. Schilpp (ed.) *The Philosophy of G. E. Moore* (Evanston: Northwestern University Press), pp. 533–677.

Oliver, W. 1949. 'Can Naturalism Be Materialistic?', *Journal of Philosophy* **46**, 608–15.

Papineau, D. 1993. *Philosophical Naturalism* (Oxford: Blackwell).

Papineau, D. (forthcoming). 'The Rise of Physicalism'.

Quine, W. V. 1969. 'Epistemology Naturalized', in *Ontological Relativity and Other Essays* (New York: Columbia University Press), pp. 69–90.

Shapiro, L. 1997. 'The Nature of Nature: Rethinking Naturalistic Theories of Intentionality', *Philosophical Psychology*, **10**, 309–22.

Shoemaker, S. 1981. 'Some Varieties of Functionalism', *Philosophical Topics*, **12**, 93–119.

Sober, E. 1999. 'Physicalism from a Probabilistic Point of View', *Philosophical Studies*, **95**, 135–74.

Stampe, D. 1977. 'Towards a Causal Theory of Linguistic Representation', *Midwest Studies in Philosophy*, **2**, 42–63.

Stich, S. 1992. 'What Is a Theory of Mental Representation?', *Mind*, **101**, 242–61.

Stich, S. and S. Laurence 1994. 'Intentionality and Naturalism', *Midwest Studies in Philosophy*, **19**, 159–82.

Tye, M. 1992. 'Naturalism and the Mental', *Mind*, **101**, 421–41.

Consciousness: Explaining the Phenomena

PETER CARRUTHERS

My topic in this chapter is whether phenomenal consciousness can be given a reductive natural explanation. I shall first say something about phenomenal—as opposed to other forms of—consciousness, and highlight what needs explaining. I shall then turn to issues concerning explanation in general, and the explanation of phenomenal consciousness in particular.

1. Phenomenal consciousness.

Phenomenal consciousness is a form of *state*-consciousness: it is a property which some, but not other, mental states possess. More specifically, it is a property which mental states have when it is *like something* to undergo them (Nagel's famous phrase, 1974). Put differently, phenomenally conscious states have distinctive subjective *feels*; and some would say: they have *qualia* (I shall return to this terminology in a moment). Phenomenal consciousness is to be distinguished from *creature*-consciousness, on the one hand (this is the property which creatures have when they are awake, or when they are aware *of* properties of their environment or body); and also from other varieties of state-consciousness, on the other hand (including a number of forms of functionally definable *access*-consciousness, where states may be said to be conscious by virtue of their accessibility to reasoning, or to verbal report, say). (See Rosenthal, 1986; Block, 1995; Lycan, 1996; and my 2000, ch. 1 for elaboration of these and other distinctions.)

Most people think that the notion of phenomenal consciousness can only really be explained by example. So we might be asked to reflect on the unique quality of the experience we enjoy when we hear the timbre of a trumpet blast, or drink-in the pink and orange hues of a sunset, or sniff the heady sweet smell of a rose. In all of these cases there is something distinctive which it is *like* to undergo the experience in question; and these are all cases of states which are phenomenally conscious. As Block (1995) puts it: phenomenal consciousness *is* experience.

Peter Carruthers

Explanations by example look somewhat less satisfactory, how- ever, once it is allowed—as I think it has to be—that there are a good many types of *non*-conscious experience. A variety of kinds of neurophysiological and psychological evidence suggests that we possess at least two (perhaps more) functionally distinct visual systems, for example—a conceptualizing system whose contents are conscious (realized in the temporal lobes of the brain), and a sensorimotor system charged with the detailed on-line control of movement, whose contents are not conscious (and which is realized in the parietal lobes). Thus movement control is possible for those who are blindsighted, or whose temporal lobes are damaged and who are otherwise blind; such control can take place more swiftly than conscious experience in the normally sighted; and sensorimotor control is not subject to the various distinctive illusions which effect our conscious experience. (See Marcel, 1983 & 1998; Weiskrantz, 1986 & 1997; Baars, 1988 & 1997; Castiello *et al.*, 1991; Bridgeman *et al.*, 1991 & 1997; Milner and Goodale, 1993 & 1995; Aglioti *et al.*, 1995 and my 2000, ch. 6. for a review.) And while it might be *possible* for someone to claim that *both* sets of experiences are phenomenally conscious (although only the products of the conceptualizing system are access-conscious), this is a very unattractive option. It is very hard to believe that within blindsight subjects, for example, there are phenomenally conscious visual experiences which the subject cannot be aware of. At any rate, for the purposes of the discussion here I shall assume that only states which are access-conscious can be phenomenally conscious.[1]

If there can be experiences which are not conscious ones, then plainly we cannot explain the idea of phenomenal consciousness by identifying it with experience. Perhaps what we *can* say, however, is that phenomenally conscious events are those for whose properties we can possess introspective recognitional capacities. And then the citing of examples should best be understood as drawing our atten- tion, introspectively, to these properties. Phenomenally conscious states and events are ones which we can recognize in ourselves, non- inferentially or 'straight-off', in virtue of the ways in which they feel to us, or the ways in which they present themselves to us subjectively.

Note that this proposal need not be construed in such a way as to imply that phenomenally conscious properties depend for their existence upon our recognitional capacities for them—that is, it need not imply any form of higher-order thought (HOT) account of

[1] For defence of this assumption see my 2000, ch. 6.

phenomenal consciousness. For it is the *properties recognized* which are phenomenally conscious; and these need not be thought to depend upon HOT. So this characterization of the nature of *feel* does not beg any question in favour of the sort of dispositionalist HOT theory to be sketched here and defended in detail in my 2000. First-order theorists such as Dretske (1995) and Tye (1995), as well as mysterians like McGinn (1991) and Chalmers (1996), can equally say that phenomenally conscious properties (feels) include those properties for which we possess introspective (second-order) recognitional capacities. For they can maintain that, although we do in fact possess recognitional concepts for these properties, the properties in question can exist in the absence of those concepts and are not in any sense created or constituted by them in the way that (as we shall see later) dispositionalist HOT theory maintains.

Note, too, that this talk of what an experience *is like* is not really intended to imply anything relational or comparative. Knowing what a sensation of red *is like* is not supposed to mean knowing that it is like, or resembles, some other experience or property X. Rather, what the experience is *like* is supposed to be an intrinsic property of it—or at least, it is a property which *strikes us* as intrinsic (see below), for which we possess an immediate recognitional capacity. Here the point converges with that made in the previous paragraph: the non-metaphorical substance behind the claim that our phenomenally conscious states are ones which are *like something* to possess, is that such states possess properties for which we have recognitional concepts

An important word about terminology before we proceed any further: many philosophers use the term 'qualia' liberally, to refer to those properties of mental states (whatever they may be) in virtue of which the states in question are phenomenally conscious. On this usage 'qualia', 'subjective feel' and 'what-it-is-likeness' are all just notational variants of one another. And on this usage, it is beyond dispute that there are such things as qualia. I propose, myself, to use the term 'qualia' much more restrictedly (as some other writers use it), to refer to those putative *intrinsic and non-representational* properties of mental states in virtue of which the latter are phenomenally conscious. On this usage, it is not beyond dispute that there are such things as qualia. On the contrary, it will be possible to be a qualia-irrealist (denying that there exist any intrinsic and non-representational properties of phenomenally conscious states) without, of course, denying that there is something it is *like* to smell a rose, or to undergo a sensation of red or of pain.

What primarily needs to be explained, then, are the *subjective*

Peter Carruthers

feels of phenomenally conscious states. Indeed, this is the defining feature of phenomenal consciousness. Since there is, by definition, something which it is *like* to undergo a phenomenally conscious state, anything which doesn't explain this isn't really an explanation of phenomenal consciousness, but will be (at best) an explanation of something else—some form of access consciousness, perhaps. Second, phenomenally conscious states at least *seem* to their subjects to possess the properties of *qualia*—seeming to have properties which are intrinsic and non-relational. I shall argue that this feature of phenomenal consciousness is best *explained away* by a would-be naturalizer. We should—if we can—claim that *there are no qualia,* while explaining how people can easily come to believe that there are.

The reason why anyone wishing to provide a naturalistic explanation of phenomenal consciousness should seek to explain away our temptation to believe in qualia, rather than accepting and directly explaining their existence, is that otherwise we shall be forced to look for some sort of neural identity, or neural realization, by way of an explanation. For there is no question but that intentional contents, causal roles, and computational processes are all relational in nature. So if there were any intrinsic non-relational, properties of conscious experience, our only option would be to seek an explanation at the level of neurology. But this would make the problem of phenomenal consciousness well nigh insoluble. For it is very hard to see how, even in principle, further facts about the neurological events in our brains could explain why those very events have a subjective *feel* or a *what-it-is-likeness* to them (McGinn, 1991).

Unfortunately, word has gotten around the philosophical and scientific communities that the problem of phenomenal consciousness is the problem of explaining how subjective *feel* is instantiated in the *brain.* And most people assume that there is a race to find a neurological explanation of the subjective properties of experience. But this common perception is actually impeding the search for a solution. For it is bad scientific method to try and jump over too many explanatory levels at once. And between phenomenal consciousness and neuroscience there are a number of distinct levels of scientific inquiry, including at least the *intentional* and the *computational* levels. It is rather as if the problem of *life* had come to be seen as the problem of explaining the distinctive properties of living things in terms of the indeterministic principles governing sub-atomic wave particles. Cast in those terms, the problem of life, too, would look well nigh insoluble! And in this case, of course, the correct approach—now more or less successful—is to seek an explanation in terms of biochemistry. Similarly, then, in the case of phenomenal consciousness: our best strategy is to go for an explanation in terms of some combination of causal role and intentional content, if we can.[2] And that means denying the real existence of qualia.

2. Reductive explanation and the 'explanatory gap'

What is it for something, in general, to be given a reductive natural explanation? A property or event is explained when we can show how suitable arrangements or sequences of lower-level properties or events (which do not themselves involve or presuppose the target phenomena) would constitute just such a property or event. So *life* is explained when we can see how the right sequences of biochemical events would give rise to such phenomena as reproduction, metabolism, and other distinctive properties of living things. Similarly for *speciation* when we provide an account in terms of natural selection. And so on. In ontological terms, reductive explanation requires at least metaphysical supervenience of the explained on the explaining. There must be no possible world where the lower-level facts together with all relevant laws of nature remain just as they are, but the explained facts are different or absent. Otherwise something would remain *unexplained*—namely, why in the actual circumstances the higher-level phenomena are *not* different or absent.

Chalmers (1996) argues that we can see in advance that phenomenal consciousness cannot be reductively explained—not even into intentional and/or functional terms. According to Chalmers, our concept of any given higher-level process, state, or event specifies the conditions which any reductive explanation of that phenomenon must meet. For example, our concept *life* contains such notions as *reproduction* and *energy production by metabolic processes*, which are amongst the functions which any living thing must be able to perform. And then a reductive explanation of life will demonstrate how appropriate biochemical changes and processes can constitute the performance of just those functions. The phenomenon of life is explained when we see just how those lower-level biochemical

---

[2] See Botterill and Carruthers, 1999, for defence of the scientific status of intentional psychology, and so also for vindication of the scientific reality of intentional content.

Peter Carruthers

events, suitably arranged and sequenced, will instantiate just those functions which form part of our concept *living thing*.[3]

According to Chalmers, our concepts of chemical, geological, biological, psychofunctional, intentional, etc. facts are broadly *functional* ones. Reductive explanations can then show how suitable arrangements of lower-level facts would constitute the execution of just those functions. But our concepts of phenomenally conscious states are not functional, but purely recognitional—we can just *recognize* the feel of pain, or of the experience of red when we have it. And the conceivability of zombie worlds and/or inverted feel worlds shows that phenomenal consciousness does *not* supervene metaphysically on lower level facts. If we can conceive of states which are functionally and intentionally identical to our conscious experiences while being phenomenally distinct, then we cannot be conceptualizing the felt aspect of those experiences in terms of functions and intentional contents. Rather our concepts, here, are presumably bare *recognitional* ones, consisting in our possession of immediate recognitional capacities for phenomenal states of various kinds. And if there can be worlds microphysically identical to this but in which phenomenal consciousness is absent or inverted, then phenomenal consciousness does not supervene on the lower-level phenomena in the way necessary for reductive explanation.

It is this which sets up the 'explanatory gap' between neurological or cognitive functions on the one hand, and phenomenal consciousness on the other. Chalmers claims, indeed, that we can see in advance that any proposed reductive explanation of phenomenal consciousness into neurological, or computational or intentional terms is doomed to failure. For what such 'explanations' provide are mechanisms for instantiating certain *functions*, which must fall short of the *feel* possessed by many types of conscious state. Since we do not conceptualize our conscious states in terms of function, but rather in terms of feel, no explanation of function can explain them. Hence the existence of the 'hard problem' of phenomenal consciousness, rendering the latter irredeemably mysterious.

Now, I agree that reductive explanations normally work by

[3] In fact it is science's track-record of success in providing such reductive explanations which warrants our belief that physics is closed in our world (that is, for thinking that physical processes cannot be altered or interfered with by higher-level processes—there is no top-down causation), and which provides the grounds for the claim that all natural phenomenon supervene (naturally and/or metaphysically) on microphysical facts.

66

specifying a lower-level mechanism for fulfilling some higher-level function. And I agree that we have available purely recognitional concepts of phenomenally conscious states. So no explanation of phenomenal consciousness can be *immediately cognitively satisfying*, in the sense of meshing with the way in which phenomenally conscious states are conceptualized. But explanation should be about properties, facts and events as *worldly* phenomena, *not* about the way in which we conceptualize those things.[4] While the 'explanatory gap' is of some *cognitive* significance, revealing something about the manner in which we conceptualize our experiences, it shows nothing about the nature of those experiences themselves. Or so, at any rate, I maintain.

Naturalists should have a 'thick' conception of facts, properties and events as worldly, concept-independent entities. From the perspective of naturalism we should believe both that there are real properties belonging to the natural world, and that *which* properties there are in the world is an open question, which cannot be read directly off the set of concepts which we happen to employ. And the question of which properties are immanent in the natural world is a question for science to answer. Moreover, we should hold that the *nature* of the properties picked out by our concepts is a matter for discovery (just as we discovered that our concept *water* picks out a property which is none other than H_2O); and that two or more concepts may turn out to pick out one and the same property.

If we are scientific realists then we think, not only that there is a mind-independent reality whose nature and causal operations science attempts to uncover, but also that science is gradually uncovering (or at least getting closer to) the truth about that reality (Kitcher, 1993). So it is to science that we should look to discover the set of naturally existing properties. If we idealize to the point at which we achieve a *completed* science, then we can say that the set of natural properties are the ones referred to by the predicate-terms in the various laws of that science. Or putting the point epistemically, we can say that whenever we have reason to believe in the truth or approximate truth of a scientific theory, then we also have reason to

---

[4] This isn't meant to deny that *explanation* is a partly epistemic notion, such that whether or not something is an explanation of a phenomena is relative to what we know already. My point is just that explanation is always *world-directed*. It is the wordly (that is concept-independent) events and properties themselves which we seek to explain (relative to our background knowledge), not the way in which those events and properties are conceptualized by us.

Peter Carruthers

believe in the existence of the properties picked out by the property-terms employed by that theory.[5]

We can then allow that we have purely recognitional concepts for some of our phenomenally conscious mental states. But it is not the existence of such concepts which particularly needs explaining (although this is *worth* explaining, and can be explained—see below). Rather, our target should be the properties which those concepts pick out. We may be able to specify the nature of those properties in such a way as to make it clear, not only how they can be available to immediate recognition, but also why they should involve the characteristic properties of subjectivity. A reductive explanation of those properties may still be possible, even though the concepts which we use to pick out those properties may not be functionally defined.

Consider, for comparison, some other domain in which people can come to possess purely recognitional concepts (at least concepts which are nearly so—see the paragraphs which follow). It is said, for example, that people can be trained to sex very young chicks entirely intuitively by handling them, without having any idea of what they are doing, or of the basis on which they effect their classifications. So suppose that Mary is someone who has been trained to classify chicks into As and Bs—where the As are in fact male and the Bs are in fact female—but without Mary knowing that this is what she is doing, and without her having any idea of what it is about the As which underpins recognition.

Then we ask Mary, 'Can you conceive of a world which is micro-physically identical with our own, except that the chicks which are As in our world are Bs in that, and vice versa? If *A* really does express a purely recognitional concept for Mary—if she really has no beliefs at all about the nature of *A-hood* beyond the fact that some chicks have it—then she should answer 'Yes'. For all she then has to imagine, is that she is confronted with a chick exactly like this A-chick in all micro-physical respects, but that it is one which evokes a recognitional application of the concept *B*. Plainly Mary should not—if she is sensible—conclude from this thought-experiment that *A-hood* is not a physical or functional property of the chicks. And if she did, she would reason fallaciously. For as we know, the property picked out by her recognitional concept is in fact the property of being male.

---

[5] This is the crucial premise needed for the defence of the reality of intentional properties, provided that intentional psychology has the status of a science. See Botterill and Carruthers, 1999, chs. 6 and 7.

Consciousness: Explaining the Phenomenon

It is unlikely of course that Mary will have no beliefs at all about the nature of *A-hood*. She will probably at least believe that *A-hood* is a perceptible property of the chicks. And if, like us, she believes that perception is a causal process, then she must believe that instances of *A-hood* can have some sort of causal impact upon her sense-organs. These beliefs may well lead her to believe that the property of *A-hood* is somehow or other constituted by physical facts about the chicks, and so to reject the possibility of a world where all micro-physical facts remain the same but *A-hood* and *B-hood* are reversed. But then the only differences here from recognitional concepts of feel are (first) that many of us may have *no* beliefs about the causal nature of introspective recognition. And (second) even if we do believe that introspection is causally mediated, we may lack any beliefs about the nature of the introspective process which imply physicality, in the way that we *do* believe that outer perception of the properties of physical objects requires those properties to have physical effects upon our sense-organs.

The morals of this example for phenomenal consciousness should be clear. Possessing purely recognitional concepts of *feel*, we can deploy those concepts in thought-experiments in ways which are unconstrained by the physical or functional facts. But nothing follows about the non-physical, non-functional, nature of the properties which those concepts pick out. So although we can conceive of worlds in which all the micro-physical facts remain as they are, but in which phenomenal consciousness is different or absent, it may be that there are really no such worlds. For it may be that phenomenal consciousness is constituted by some physical or functional fact, in which case there are no possible worlds where the facts of consciousness can be different while the constituting facts remain the same.

So much by way of ground-clearing: phenomenal consciousness consists in introspectively recognizable properties of subjective *feel* and *what-it-is-likeness*, which many are tempted to think are intrinsic and non-relational; but there is no reason of principle why such properties should not be reductively explained.[6] I turn, now, to provide just such an explanation. My thesis is that the properties involved in phenomenal consciousness are successfully reductively explained by dispositionalist higher-order thought (HOT) theory. I shall make no attempt to review alternatives, or to contrast my

---

[6] Of course *many* arguments for an explanatory gap have been offered, by a variety of thinkers; whereas I have only (briefly) considered one. For discussion and disarmament of others, see my 2000, chs. 2–4.

proposal with others on the market. In the space available to me here, I shall concentrate just on explaining my own positive proposal, and on displaying some of its virtues.[7]

3. Dispositionalist higher-order thought theory

According to dispositionalist HOT theory, phenomenally conscious states consist in *analog intentional contents* held in a special-purpose short-term memory store in such a way as to be available to a variety of down-stream conceptual systems (including various systems for belief-formation, and for practical reasoning), crucially including a 'mind-reading' or 'theory of mind' system *capable of HOTs about those very contents*. The architecture of the theory is represented in figure 1. The remainder of this section will be devoted to elucidating and commenting on this architecture, before we turn to consider the explanatory potential of the theory in the sections which follow.

On this account, perceptual contents are regularly passed to two or more short-term memory stores, C (conscious) and N (non-conscious), to be integrated with the subject's goals in the control of

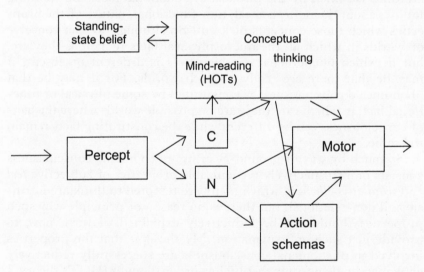

Figure 1. Dispositionalist HOT theory.

7 For detailed consideration of a range of alternatives to dispositionalist HOT theory—both first-order and higher-order—see my 2000 chs. 5-11.

70

action. C itself is defined, *inter alia*, by its relation to HOTs—any of the contents of C being *apt* to give rise to a HOT about itself, should circumstances (and what is going on elsewhere in the system) demand. This allows us to retain our beliefs in the richness of conscious experience (*contra* Dennett, 1991) without making outrageous demands on the mind-reading system which generates HOTs, since the account imposes no particular limit on the amount of information held in C at any one time. Certainly the contents held there can have a degree of richness and detail which far outstrips our powers of conceptualization and description, just as intuition suggests.

The model is consistent with, and partly motivated by, the evidence that our perceptual faculties sub-divide into a number of functionally distinct perceptual sub-systems, one of which provides a set of representations for conceptualization and decision-making, and the other of which feeds a different set of representations to guide our detailed movements (e.g. Milner and Goodale, 1993, 1995). So one set of percepts is available to be integrated with a variety of action schemas to guide movement, but is neither conscious nor available to conceptual thought; whereas the other set of percepts is available to a variety of belief forming and practical reasoning systems, and are conscious, but these are not the percepts which guide the details of our movements on-line. Just such a bifurcation of cognitive and sensorimotor perceptual systems is found in many other creatures besides ourselves. But according to dispositionalist HOT theory it had to wait on the evolution of a HOT-wielding, mind-reading, module—as one of the down-stream consumer systems for the contents of the conceptualizing system—in order for the contents of C to become phenomenally conscious.[8]

The contents of C, while perhaps being *imbued* with concepts (often or always), also involve representations more fine-grained than any concept. These representations are *analog* ones (or at least, they are analog in relation to the containing concepts—see below). To see the intended contrast here, think of the difference between a digital clock, on the one hand, and the traditional analog 'handed'

[8] Actually my belief in the modularity (and genetically chanelled nature) of the mind-reading system in ancillary to the main story being told here. The principle explanatory claims of dispositionalist HOT theory can go through just the same even if our mind-reading capacities are socially acquired, constructed through childhood theorising, or result from processes of mental simulation as some maintain. See Botterill and Carruthers, 1999 chs. 3 and 4, for discussion.

variety, on the other. On the face of the former, time is represented in discrete steps (one for each minute which elapses, say); on the face of the latter, the passing minutes are represented continuously, without discrete steps: the hands just move continuously around. Now strictly speaking, properties are only analog if—like *length* or *movement*—they admit of *continuous* variation: so that between any two such properties there is always a third. This might seem to present a problem for the account, since the process subserving perception are almost certainly *not* continuous but discrete—after all, any given brain-cell is either firing or at rest at any given moment. But we can in fact introduce a relativized variant of the same notion, saying that representations are analog relative to a certain conceptual repertoire if they admit of significantly *more* variations than there are concepts to classify them.

Some people insist that perceptual content is *non-conceptual* (e.g. Tye, 1995). In this connection Peacocke (1992) introduces the idea of what he calls 'scenario content', which is to consist of analog representations of the ways in which the space immediately surrounding the perceiver is filled, but without these filled spaces being categorized into objects or kinds. Now, I suspect that one aspect of this proposal, at least, is mistaken—namely, the claim that perception does not represent discrete objects. Data from infancy studies suggest that quite young infants have a firm grip on simple physical/mechanical causal principles, with expectations about what can move, and how (Sperber *et al.*, 1995). So I suspect that from the start these ways-of-filling-space are seen as dividing into objects which can move in relation to one another. But I am happy to allow that there may be a stage early in development (and perhaps also in evolution) when no concepts are yet applied to the represented fillings-of-space. Indeed, adults too, may sometimes have perceptions which are almost wholly non-conceptual in content. Think, for example, of someone from a hunter gatherer tribe who is introduced into some high-tech scientific laboratory, she may literally have no idea what she is seeing—just surfaces and filled shapes and potentially moveable objects.[9]

Normal adult perceptions are not like this, however. I do not *first* experience a distribution of filled spaces around me, and *then* come to *believe* that these are tables, chairs, people, and television sets. Rather, I *see* myself as surrounded by such familiar objects. Indeed,

---

[9] The hunter gatherer's perceptions will still not be wholly non-conceptual, since she will be able to apply colour concepts, like *red* as well as concepts like *rough*, *smooth*, and so on to what she sees.

a variety of considerations suggest that perceptual states are normally imbued with concepts. To mention just one; perceived similarity spaces can undergo a dramatic shift as a result of concept learning.[10] This has been demonstrated experimentally by psychologists (Lucy, 1992; Goldstone, 1994; Livingstone *et al.*, 1999). But the same point is also familiar to common sense. When I had my first job in the wilds of Scotland, there was little else to do but take up bird-watching on the estuary where we lived. At first I just saw crowds of little grey birds on the beach, but I later came to *see* the beach as populated by plovers, knots, dunlins, and red-shanks. As a result of concept-learning, the differences between the birds came to leap out at me in a phenomenologically salient way; I *saw* them as distinct. It soon became barely intelligible to me how I could ever have confused a plover with a dunlin, they looked so different.

So I say that the contents of C are analog, but normally imbued with concepts; whereas beliefs are wholly conceptual, or digitally 'chunked'. This way of drawing the percept/belief distinction seems to fit the phenomenology quite well. What I perceive is presented to me under concepts (I see *a car*, or *a person*, or *Mary*), but I am always aware of more subtle variations than I have concepts for. For example, imagine you are looking at a tree whose leaves are being shifted in the breeze. What you see comes to you imbued with the concepts *tree* and *leaf*; but the subtly shifting pattern of motion, and the precise shape which the tree outlines against the sky, are things for which you have *no* concepts. Nevertheless they are part of what is represented, and you can distinguish subtle variations in them.

Note that this already puts us in position to explain one of the puzzling features of phenomenal consciousness, namely its supposed *ineffability*. For any analog representation will be ineffable— in a sense—in relation to the concepts used to describe its content. For example, my visual system delivers representations of colour which are analog in the sense that they allow a seemingly-smooth spectrum of only-just-distinguishable shades of colour to be represented. My colour *concepts* are relatively few by comparison. Then any particular shade will be discriminable from its nearest neighbours; but the difference will be indescribable—it is a difference which will slip through the mesh of my conceptual net. The only way of describing the difference will be by means of an example, saying 'It is the shade of *that* object there as opposed to *this* object here'.

[10] For other arguments in its support, see my 2000, ch.5.

Peter Carruthers

What properties does the mind-reading system need to have, in order for the contents of C to be phenomenally conscious, on the present account? I maintain that it needs to be sophisticated enough to understand the appearance/reality or is/seems distinction; and it should contain some recognitional concepts of experience—e.g. *seems red, seems green, seems smooth* and so on.[11] If the conceptual systems already contain first-order recognitional concepts of *red, green, smooth*, and such like, then it would be a trivial matter to turn these into higher order recognitional concepts once the mind-reading system is armed with the is/seems distinction. This distinction is thought to emerge in children, together with an understanding of belief as a representational (and possibly false) state of the subject, somewhere between the ages of 3 and 4. (See Flavell *et al.*, 1987; Gopnik and Astington, 1988; Gopnik, 1993; Baron-Cohen, 1989; Clements and Perner, 1994—but see Fodor, 1992, and Leslie, 1994, for the claim that these capacities are available to children from the age of 2 or earlier.)

4. Explaining away qualia

Given the correctness of dispositionalist HOT theory, it is easy to explain why it so naturally *seems* to people that phenomenally conscious states possess intrinsic, non-relational properties (qualia). For phenomenally conscious states result from the availability of experience to *purely recognitional higher-order concepts*. These concepts have no relational components—they are not relationally *defined*. Someone deploying these concepts will then easily be able to *conceive* of worlds in which the corresponding feels are either absent or inverted while all relational facts remain the same. And then by eliding the distinction between concept and property, or by confusing conceptual with metaphysical possibility, it will be easy to think that the properties which our phenomenal concepts pick out are similarly intrinsic and non-relational.

Moreover, notice that our first-order perceptual states present many properties in the world *as* intrinsic. Our perception of a surface as *red*, for example, represents that surface as covered by a certain intrinsic—non-relationally individuated—property; namely, *redness*, of some or other shade. (It certainly does not present that

[11] This account applies most readily to outer perceptions of vision and touch, say, where the appearance/reality distinction has clear purchase, and less easily to bodily sensations like pain, where it does not. For a more rounded and slightly more complex account see my 2000 chs. 5 and 9.

Consciousness: Explaining the Phenomenon

surface as having the power to cause experiences of a certain sort in normal perceivers in normal circumstances, in the way that dispositionalist analyses of colour concepts maintain!). And then higher-order analog states—states of *seeming red*, *seeming green* and the rest—will be *seemings* of the presence of a certain *intrinsic* property. Small wonder, then, that we might naturally come to think of those states as *possessing* intrinsic properties (qualia).

But of course, as we noted in section 2 above, the *property* of phenomenal consciousness can consist in analog intentional content available to HOT—and so be relational and *non*-intrinsic—while our *concepts* of phenomenal consciousness are *non*-relational. So there is no special problem in explaining why people are so naturally tempted to believe in qualia.[12] The harder problem is to explain the defining feature of phenomenal consciousness—its *what-it-is-likeness* or *feel*.

5. Explaining subjective feel

How can dispositionalist HOT theory explain the subjective feel of experience? In particular, how can mere *dispositions* to deploy higher-order recognitional concepts confer on our experience the property of *feel* or *what-it-is-likeness*? Remember that what is to be explained is how a non-phenomenally-conscious perceptual state comes to acquire the properties of *subjectivity* and *what-it-is-likeness* distinctive of phenomenal consciousness. Yet it might seem puzzling how mere *availability* to HOT could confer these additional properties on a perceptual state. How can something which hasn't actually happened to a perceptual state (namely, being targeted by a HOT) confer on it—categorically—the dimension of subjectivity? For subjectivity surely *is* a categorical property of a phenomenally conscious experience. Worse still, indeed: when I *do* actually entertain a HOT about my experience—thinking, say, 'What a vivid experience!' —it is surely *because* the experience *already* has the distinctive subjective properties of phenomenal consciousness that I am able to think what I do about it (Robb, 1998). So, once again, how can we legitimately appeal to HOTs in the explanation of those very properties? The answer consists in a dose of 'consumer semantics'.[13]

[12] See my 2000, ch. 7 for more extensive development of the points made briefly in this section.
[13] For further development and elaboration of the explanation proposed in this section, see my 2000, ch. 9.

Peter Carruthers

Given the truth of some form of consumer semantics (e.g. teleosemantics, or functional or inferential role semantics), the contents of C will depend, in part, on what the down-stream consumer systems can do with those contents. And the attachment of a HOT consumer system to the outputs of an otherwise first-order conceptualizing perceptual system will transform the intentional contents of the events in C. Where before these were first-order analog representations of the environment (and body), following the attachment of a HOT system these events take on an enriched dual content—each experience of the world/body is at the same time a representation that just such an experience is taking place; each experience with the analog content *red*, say, is at the same time an event with the analog content *seems red* or *experience of red*. And the events in C have these contents categorically, by virtue of the *powers* of the HOT consumer system, in advance of any HOT actually being tokened.

My claim is that the very same perceptual states which represent the world to us (or the conditions of our own bodies) can at the same time represent the fact that those aspects of the world (or of our bodies) are being perceived. It is the fact that the faculties of thinking to which experiences are made available *can make use of them* in dual mode which turns those experiences into dual-mode representations. This is because, in general, the intentional content of a state will depend upon the nature and powers of the 'consumer systems' as Millikan (1984) would put it. The content possessed by a given state depends, in part, upon the uses which can be made of that state by the systems which can consume it or draw inferences from it. And similarly, then, in the case of perceptual representations: it is the fact that perceptual contents are present to a system which is capable of discriminating between, and making judgments about, those perceptual states *as such* which constitutes those states as second-order representations of experience, as well as first-order representations of the world (or of states of the body). If the content of a state depends partly on what the down-stream systems which *consume*, or make use of, that state can do with it, then the attachment of a mind-reading consumer system to first-order analog perceptual states may be expected to transform the intentional contents of the latter. In virtue of the availability of the analog content *red* to a consumer system with a recognitional concept of *seems red*, each perceptual state with the content *red* is already a state with a higher-order analog content *seems red* or *experience of red*. Each such state then has, as part of its content, a dimension of *seeming* or *subjectivity*.

76

There are a variety of different forms of consumer semantics: for example, teleosemantics, functional role semantics, and inferential role semantics; and each can be construed more or less holistically or locally. In fact I favour some form of inferential role semantics, where the *immediate* inferential connections of a state are particularly important determiners of content (see my 1996, ch.5 and Botterill and Carruthers, 1999, ch. 7). Thus for a state to have the content of *P&Q*, the subject must be disposed to infer *P* from it— but not necessarily to infer from it ~*(~Pv~Q)*. There are powerful reasons for preferring some form of consumer semantics to any kind of pure causal co-variance semantics (Botterill and Carruthers, 1999, ch. 7). And there is independent reason to think that changes in consumer semantics can transform perceptual contents, and with it phenomenal consciousness (Hurley, 1998). Consider the effects of spatially-inverting lenses, for example (Welch, 1978). Initially, subjects wearing such lenses see everything upside-down, and their attempts at action are halting and confused. But in time—provided that they are allowed to move around and act while wearing their spectacles—the visual field rights itself. Here, everything on the input side remains the same as it was when they first put on the spectacles; but the planning and action-controlling systems have learned to interpret those states inversely. And as a result, intentional perceptual contents become re-reversed.

If consumer semantics is assumed, then it is easy to see how mere dispositions can transform contents in the way dispositionalist HOT theory supposes. For notice that the consumer-system for a given state does not *actually* have to be making use of that state in order for the latter to carry the appropriate content—it just has to be *disposed* to make use of it should circumstances (and what is going on elsewhere in the cognitive system) demand. So someone normalized to inverting spectacles does not actually have to be acting on the environment in order to see things right-side-up. She can be sitting quietly and thinking about something else entirely. But still the spatial content of her perceptual state is fixed, in part by her dispositions to think and move in relation to the spatial environment.

Consider, here, the implications of some form of inferential role semantics, for the sake of concreteness. What is it that confers the content *P&Q* on some complex belief-state of the form 'P#Q'? (The sign '#' here is meant as a dummy connective, not yet interpreted.) In part, plainly, it is that one is disposed to infer 'P' from 'P#Q' and 'Q' from 'P#Q' (Peacocke, 1992). It is constitutive of a state with a conjunctive content that one should be disposed to deduce either one of the conjuncts from it. But of course this disposition can remain un-activated on some occasions on which a conjunctive thought is entertained. For example, suppose I hear a weather-forecaster say, 'It will be windy and it will be cold', and that I believe her. Then I have a belief with a conjunctive content even if I do nothing else with it. Whether I ever form the belief that it will be windy, in particular, will depend on my interests and background concerns, and on the other demands made on my cognitive resources at the time. But my belief still actually—and categorically—has a conjunctive content in virtue of my inferential dispositions.

So a dose of consumer semantics is just what dispositionalist HOT theory needs to solve the categoricity problem. Indeed, notice from the example above that in any particular instance where I *do* exercise my inferential dispositions, and arrive at a belief in one of the conjuncts, we can cite my prior conjunctive belief as its cause. So it is *because* I *already* believed that it will be windy and cold that I came to believe that it will be windy in particular. But for all that, my preparedness to engage in just such an inference is partly constitutive of the conjunctive content of my prior belief. So, too, then, in the case of phenomenal experience: if I think, 'What an interesting experience!' of some perceptual state of mine, it can be *because* that state is *already* phenomenally conscious that I come to entertain the higher-order thought; but it can also be by virtue of my disposition to entertain HOTs of just that sort that my perceptual state has the kind of content which is constitutive of phenomenal consciousness in the first place.

We can easily explain, too, how our higher-order recognitional concepts of experience can 'break free' or their first-order counterparts, in such a way as to permit thoughts about the possibility of experiential inversion and such like. Here is how the story would go. We begin—in both evolutionary terms and in normal child development—with a set of first-order analog contents available to a variety of down-stream consumer systems. These systems will include a number of dedicated belief-forming modules, as well as a practical reasoning faculty for figuring out what to do in the light of the perceived environment together with background beliefs and desires. One of these systems will be a developing mind-reading module. When the latter has reached the stage of understanding the subjective nature of experience and has grasped the is/seems distinction, it will easily—indeed, trivially—become capable of second-order recognitional judgments of experience, riding piggyback on the subject's first-order recognitional concepts. So if the subject had a recognitional concept *red*, it will now acquire the concept *seems red*, knowing that whenever a judgment 'red' is evoked by experience, a judgment of 'seems red' is also appropriate on the very same grounds.

This change in the down-stream mind-reading consumer system is sufficient to transform all of the contents of experience (and imagination), rendering them at the same time as higher-order ones. So our perceptual states will not only have the first-order analog contents *red, green, loud, smooth*, and so on, but also and at the same time the higher-order analog contents *seems red, seems loud, seems smooth*, and so on. The subject will then be in a position to form recognitional concepts targeted just on these higher-order contents, free of any conceptual ties with worldly redness, greenness, loudness, and smoothness. (This can either be done by *fiat*—dropping or cancelling any conceptual connection with redness from the recognitional concept *seems red*—or by introducing new concepts of the form *this experience*.)[14] And once possessed of such concepts, it is possible for the subject to wonder whether other people have experiences of *seems red* or of *this* sort when they look at a ripe tomato, and so on.

Notice that this account of the subjectivity of phenomenally conscious experience makes essential appeal to analog higher-order representations. So in one sense it is quite right of Browne (1999) to accuse me of being a closet higher-order experience (or 'inner sense') theorist. Like such theorists (e.g. Lycan, 1996) I believe that phenomenal consciousness constitutively involves higher-order analog (non-conceptual or partly conceptual) contents. But I get these for free from dispositionalist HOT theory by appeal to some or other form of consumer semantics, as outlined above. No 'inner scanners', nor any special faculty of 'inner sense', need to be postulated; nor are the states which realize the higher-order analog contents distinct from those which realize the corresponding first-order contents, in the way that higher-order experience theorists normally suppose. If this makes me a 'closet introspectionist' (Browne) then I am happy to concur; but it is introspectionism without costs.

[14] Of course Wittgenstein (1953) famously argued that the very idea of private concepts of experience of this sort is impossible or conceptually incoherent. In due deference to Wittgenstein, I spent a good many years of my life trying to find a viable version of the Private Language Argument, one manifestation of which was my Oxford D-Phil thesis (1979; see also my 1986, ch6.) I ultimately came to the conclusion that there is no good argument in this area which doesn't presuppose some form of verificationism about meaning or quasi-behaviourism about the mind. But I don't need to argue for this here.

Peter Carruthers

What we have here is, I claim, a good and sufficient explanation of the defining feature of phenomenal consciousness—its subjectivity, or what-it-is-likeness; and it is, moreover, an explanation which is fully acceptable from a naturalistic perspective. That feature gets explained in terms of the dual representational content possessed by all phenomenally conscious states (they have both 'objective' or world/body representing content and 'subjective', or experience-representing content), by virtue of their availability to both first-order and higher-order consumer systems.

6. Dormative virtues

Someone might object that the account provided here has all of the hallmarks of an explanation in terms of *dormative virtue*—that is to say, all the hallmarks of no explanation at all. For recall the line just taken: it is *because* my experience *already* has a given higher-order analog content that I think, 'What an interesting experience!'; but it can also be because that state is of a kind which is disposed to cause HOTs of just this sort that it possesses a higher-order content in the first place. The account then seems formally analogous to this: if I fall asleep after drinking a soporific cocktail, it can be *because* that drink is *already* a soporific that I come to lose consciousness; but it can also be by virtue of my disposition to lose consciousness in just this way that the cocktail is soporific in the first place.

The first point to make by way of reply is that explanations of the 'dormative virtue' sort are perfectly appropriate in their place. It can be both true and explanatory to say that I fell asleep because I drank a liquid containing a soporific. This is to explain one particular event (me falling asleep) in terms of another which is its cause, and to indicate that there is *some* property (not further specified) of the cause such that events of that kind are correlated with sleep in a law-like way. And it can be both true and explanatory to say of the liquid in question—opium, as it might be—that it is a soporific. This is to provide a partial functional specification of its properties. Where dormative virtues definitely become *non*-explanatory is if we appeal to them in trying to answer the question, 'Why does opium put people to sleep?' (Bad answer: 'Because it is a soporific'.) For this question is a request to *specify* the underlying mechanism, not just to be told that such a mechanism exists. (That is, we don't just want to be told, 'Because it has some property which tends to cause sleep'—we already knew that.)

In the same way, it can be both true and explanatory to say that

Consciousness: Explaining the Phenomenon

I came to have a belief with the content *that it will be windy* because I already had a belief with the content *that it will be windy and cold.* This is to explain one event in terms of another with which it is connected in a law-like manner. And it can be both true and explanatory to say that *and*-beliefs tend to cause beliefs in their individual conjuncts. This is to provide a partial functional specification of the nature of conjunctive content. Where explanation by content runs out, is when we ask the question, 'Why do people with conjunctive beliefs tend to believe the individual conjuncts?' For this, too, is a request to specify the underlying mechanism, needing to be answered by appeal to some sort of computational account, for example, and not by an appeal to content. Likewise, then, for the relations between higher-order analog contents and higher-order recognitional judgments: appeals to them are only non-explanatory if our question is *why* such contents give rise to such judgments at all.

Notice too, that in one respect saying that I came to believe *that P* because I already believed *that P&Q* is quite unlike saying that I fell asleep because I took a soporific. For to say the latter is *just* to say that I fell asleep because I drank something which tends to make people sleep, since a soporific is nothing other than a substance which causes sleep. Conjunctive beliefs, in contrast, aren't identical with beliefs which cause belief in the individual conjuncts, since introduction-rules are just as important as elimination-rules in specifying the contents of the logical connectives. The functional specification of conjunction by its elimination-rules is only a partial one. So to explain my belief that *P* in terms of my belief that *P&Q* is to give a good deal more information about the cause, of a functional sort, than merely to say that it has some property which tends to cause *P*-beliefs.

Likewise for higher-order analog contents; only more so. To say that someone is in a perceptual state with the analog higher-order content *seems red* is not just to say that they are in a state which tends to make them judge that they are experiencing red. This may be a partial characterization of the content of the state, but it is *only* partial. In addition we need to say that the state has an analog content, that it is also an analog representation of red, normally caused by exposure to red, and so on. So here, too, the explanation of my higher-order judgment is a good deal more informative than a mere 'dormative virtue' one. Indeed, it is particularly important to stress the analog nature of the higher-order contents in question. For this means that there is no end of possible higher-order judgments, each employing one of an unlimited range of potentially-available higher-order recognitional concepts, to which those

81

Peter Carruthers

contents could give rise. On the present account, it only requires the subject to have an understanding of the is/seems distinction in general, and to possess *some* higher-order recognitional concepts, for *all* of the subject's perceptual (and imagistic) states which are available to such concepts (i.e. which are contained in C) to acquire a dimension of *seeming*. This means that there is richness of content in higher-order experience which goes *far* beyond a mere disposition to make a few types of higher-order judgment.

In general then my answer to the 'dormative virtue' challenge is this: higher-order analog contents are just as real, and just as categorical in nature, as are any other species of intentional content; and causal explanations by appeal to them can be explanatory. But just as with other types of content, their nature is determined, in part, by their effects on the down-stream consumer systems—in this case subjects' capacities to make higher-order recognitional judgments about their experiences. So the one question which this account cannot (and is not designed to) answer, is *why* people tend to make such higher-order judgments at all. Here the answer, 'Because they undergo higher-order analog contents'—although it does have a good deal of additional information—is not really an explanatory one.[15]

Conclusion

The 'hard problem' of phenomenal consciousness (Chalmers, 1996) is not so *very* hard after all. Common-sense notions of cause and intentional content give us all that we need for a solution. Phenomenally conscious states are analog intentional states available to a faculty of higher-order recognition. In virtue of such availability, those states have a dual content—world/body representing, and also experience/seeming representing. So it is by virtue of such availability that phenomenally conscious states acquire a dimension of seeming or subjectivity. Put differently: phenomenally conscious states are analog intentional states with dual content (both

[15] Of course it *would* be informative to answer this question by saying, 'Because there are intrinsic properties of people's experiences of which they are aware', *if* such properties existed. But (a) there are no good reasons to believe in the existence of any intrinsic, non-intentional, properties of experience (qualia), and (b) it is easy for a higher-order theorist to explain why people are so naturally tempted to believe in such properties. See my 2000, chs. 2, 3, 4 and 7.

Consciousness: Explaining the Phenomenon

first and second order); where such contents result from availability to both first and second-order consumer systems.[16]

Bibliography

Aglioti, S., DeSouza, J. and Goodale M. 1995. 'Size contrast illusions deceive the eye but not the hand', *Current Biology*, **5**, 679–85.
Baars, B. 1988. *A Cognitive Theory of Consciousness* (Cambridge: Cambridge University Press).
Baars, B. 1997. *In the Theatre of Consciousness* (Oxford: Oxford University Press).
Baron-Cohen, S. 1989. 'Are autistic children behaviourists?' An examination of their mental-physical and appearance-reality distinctions', *Journal of Autism and Developmental Disorders*, **19**, 579–600.
Block, N. 1995. 'A confusion about a function of consciousness', *Behavioural and Brain Sciences*, **18**, 227–87.
Botterill, G. and Carruthers, P. 1999. *The Philosophy of Psychology* (Cambridge: Cambridge University Press).
Bridgeman, B. 1991. 'Complementary cognitive and motor image processing', in G. Obrecht and L. Stark (eds) (Plenum Press).
Bridgeman, B., Peery, S. and Anand, S. 1997. 'Interaction of cognitive and sensorimotor maps of visual space', *Perception and Psychophysics*, **59**, 456–69.
Browne, D. 1999. 'Carruthers on the deficits of animals', *Psyche*, **5**, <http://psyche.cs.monash.edu.au/v5/>
Carruthers, P. 1979. *The Place of the Private Language Argument in the Philosophy of Language* (Oxford D.Phil thesis. Unpublished).
Carruthers, P. 1986. *Introducing Persons*. (London: Routledge).
Carruthers, P. 1996. *Language, Thought and Consciousness* (Cambridge: Cambridge University Press).
Carruthers, P. 2000. *Phenomenal Consciousness, Naturally* (Cambridge: Cambridge University Press).
Castiello, U., Paulignan, Y. and Jeannerod, M. 1991. 'Temporal dissociation of motor-responses and subjective awareness study in normal subjects', *Brain*, **114**, 2639–55.
Chalmers, D. 1996. *The Conscious Mind* (Oxford: Oxford University Press).

[16] For the most part this chapter weaves together material from my 2000, chs. 2, 3, 5, 8 and 9; reproduced here with the permission of Cambridge University Press. Thanks to Colin Allen for the objection which gave rise to section 6, to Dudley Knowles and Tim Schnoeder for comments on an earlier draft, and to all those who participated in the discussion of my presentation of earlier versions of this chapter at the Universities of Bolton and Glasgow, and to the Royal Institute of Philosophy conference, 'Naturalism, Evolution and Mind', held in Edinburgh in July 1999.

Peter Carruthers

Clements, W. and Perner, J. 1994. 'Implicit understanding of belief', *Cognitive Developmen* **9**, 377–95.

Dennett, D. 1991. *Consciousness Explained* (London: Penguin Press).

Dretske, F. 1995. *Naturalising the Mind* (Cambridge, MA: MIT Press).

Flavell, J., Flavell, E. and Green, F. 1987. 'Young children's knowledge about the apparent-real and pretend-real distinctions', *Developmental Psychology*, **23**, 816–22.

Fodor, J. 1992. 'A theory of the child's theory of mind', *Cognition*, **44**, 283–95.

Goldstone, R. 1994. 'Influences of categorisation on perceptual discrimination', *Journal of Experimental Psychology: General*, **123**, 178–200.

Gopnik, A. 1993. 'How we know our own minds: The illusion of first-person knowledge of intentionality', *Behavioural and Brain Sciences*, **16**, 1–14.

Gopnik, A. and Astington, J. 1988. 'Children's understanding of representational change and its relation to the understanding of false belief and the appearance-reality distinction', *Child Development*, **59**, 26–37.

Hurley, S. 1998. *Consciousness in Action* (Cambridge, MA: Harvard University Press).

Kitcher, P. 1993. *The Advancement of Science* (Oxford: Oxford University Press).

Leslie, A. 1994. 'Pretending and believing', *Cognition*, **50**, 211–38.

Livingstone, K., Andrews, J. and Harnad, S. 1999. 'Categorical perception effects induced by category learning'. *Journal of Experimental Psychology*, General, **128**, 325–49.

Lucy, J. 1992. *Grammatical Categories and Cognition* (Cambridge: Cambridge University Press).

Lycan, W. 1996. *Consciousness and Experience* (Cambridge, MA: MIT Press).

Marcel, A. 1983. 'Conscious and unconscious perception: an approach to the relations between phenomenal experience and perceptual processes', *Cognitive Psychology*, **15**, 238–300.

Marcel, A. 1998. 'Blindsight and shape perception: deficit of visual consciousness or of visual function?', *Brain*, **121**, 1565–88.

McGinn, C. 1991. *The Problem of Consciousness* (London: Blackwell)

Millikan, R. 1983. *Language, Thought and other Biological Categories*. (Cambridge, MA: MIT Press).

Milner, D and Goodale, M. 1993. 'Visual pathways to perception and action', *Progress in Brain Research*, **95**, 317–37.

Milner, D and Goodale, M. 1995. *The Visual Brain in Action* (Oxford: Oxford University Press)

Nagel, T. 1974. 'What is it like to be a bat?', *Philosophical Review*, **81**, 2, 127–36.

Obrecht, G., and Stark, L. (eds) 1991. *Presbyopia Research* (Plenum Press).

Peacocke, C. 1992. *A Study of Concepts* (Cambridge, MA: MIT Press).

Robb, D. 1998. 'Recent work in the philosophy of mind', *Philosophical Quarterly*, **48**, 527–39.

Consciousness: Explaining the Phenomenon

Rosenthal, D. 1986. 'Two concepts of consciousness', *Philosophical Studies*, **49**, 329–59.
Sperber, D., Premack, D. and Premack A. (eds) 1995. *Causal Cognition* (Oxford: Oxford University Press).
Tye, M. 1995. *Ten Problems of Consciousness* (Cambridge, MA: MIT Press).
Weiskrantz, L. 1986. *Blindsight* (Oxford: Oxford University Press).
Weiskrantz, L. 1997. *Consciousness Lost and Found* (Oxford: Oxford University Press).
Welch, R. 1978. *Perceptual Modification* (Academic Press).
Wittgenstein, L. 1953. *Philosophical Investigations*. Translated by Elizabeth Anscombe (Oxford: Blackwell).

Norms, History and the Mental

FRED DRETSKE

Many people think the mind evolved. Some of them think it *had* to evolve. They think the mind not only has a history, but a history essential to its very existence.

Of those who think it had to evolve[1], some think it because they discern, or think they discern, a normative quality to mental affairs, a way mental states and activities (*qua* mental) are supposed to be, that can only be understood by conceiving of mentality as a product of an evolutionary process. Without a process like natural selection (or learning), processes capable of grounding a difference between how things are and how they are supposed to be, there is nothing to provide the requisite contrast with existing fact, the sort of contrast implied by speaking (as we do in cognitive affairs) of beliefs, perceptions, and inferences as correct or incorrect, mistaken or fallacious, right and wrong, veridical and illusory. If this normative quality is really essential to cognitive affairs, and history is the only source of normativity, then history is to minds what it is to fossils. Without the right history, there aren't any.

Since the arguments for this view are not entirely convincing—even to someone like me who accepts their conclusion—and the consequences of the view, I keep being told, are preposterous[2], I

[1] I am thinking of Millikan, 1984 & 1993b; Papineau, 1993; Dretske, 1986 & 1995 and, depending on which way they go on representation, probably also Lycan, 1996 (see p. 75 where he expresses sympathy with a teleological view of representation) and Tye, 1995 (see sections 5.4 and 7.4). Neander, 1995 sympathetically explores a teleological (thus, historical) view of representation without actually embracing it.

[2] A favoured way of dramatizing this is by invoking Swampman, a creature imagined by Donald Davidson, 1987 who materializes by chance when a bolt of lightning strikes a decaying log in a swamp. Miraculously, Swampman is, molecule for molecule, the same as Davidson. Since Swampman has no significant history—certainly none of the kind that would (according to historical accounts of the mind) give him thoughts and (maybe even) experiences—he lacks these mental states even though he is physically and (therefore) behaviourally indistinguishable from Davidson. Swampman is a zombie. For those who think the mind (particularly the phenomenal mind) supervenes on the current physical state of the body, this is preposterous.

Fred Dretske

take this occasion to re-examine the matter. If I am to continue believing not just that the mind is a product of historical development, but, like a fossil, can only exist in that way, I need better reasons than I've already got. I'm not sure I can produce them, but I hope the exercise of looking for them will prove philosophically useful. It was for me.

1. Normative Concepts

Philosophers of science used to worry a lot about theory-laden concepts. A theory-laden concept is one whose correct application to an object presupposes that a certain theory, or fragment of a theory, is true of that object. There cannot be objects of that sort, objects to which the concept applies, unless the theory, or theory-fragment, is true. Showing the theory false has the consequence that a concept loaded with it, (and, therefore, implying the truth of it), applies to nothing. There are no such objects.

Norwood Russell Hanson (1958) did much to sensitize philosophers to theory-laden concepts and the role they played in science. He used the ordinary concept of a wound to illustrate the idea. To be a wound it is not enough to be a cut or incision in a person's flesh, the sort of gash an assailant might make in wounding a person. To qualify as a wound, the cut must have a particular origin, a certain kind of history. Surgeons do not wound patients on whom they perform appendectomies (not, at least, if they are doing their job right) even though the cuts they make may be indistinguishable from genuine wounds. When made by a surgeon for an approved medical reason, the incision is not made with the right purpose to qualify as a wound. It has the wrong history. Having the right history is, if you will, the 'theory' the concept wound is loaded with.

Concepts come laden with norms[3] as well as theories and history. Think of the difference between murdering and killing. Murder is

[3] The following discussion of norm-loaded concepts is, I think, independent of what view one takes of the embedded norms. If one is a subjectivist about these things—thinking, perhaps, that to say that something is wrong (bad, not the way it ought to be, etc.) is merely to assert (or evince) personal feelings and attitudes toward it (e.g., that you don't like or approve of it), then norm-laden concepts are concepts that S cannot correctly apply to x unless S (not necessarily anyone else) has the right feelings or attitudes toward x. For a recent defence of an 'expressivist' analysis of norms see Gibbard (1990).

a norm-loaded concept because it requires the killing to be done is a morally or legally objectionable way. To murder X is to kill X wickedly, with malice aforethought, inhumanely, or barbarously.[4] That is why you can't murder, though you can kill, someone accidentally or while trying to save their life. When accidental or done with benevolent motives the killing isn't wicked, wrong, bad, or malicious[5]—hence, not murder

This is not to say that killings can't be wrong. Of course they can. It is just that killings are not—whereas murders are—necessarily wrong. Murders depend on norms for their very existence. Killings do not. Take away norms and, in one stroke, you extinguish murder just as wounds and fossils are eliminated by removing their history. Killings, cuts, and bones (?) remain, yes, but not wounds, murder, and fossils.

The norms expressed in describing an act as murder are moral or, perhaps, legal in nature. There are other kinds of norms. Broken or defective, for instance, are terms that imply something about how objects to which they apply are, in some non-moral and non-legal sense, supposed, or supposed not, to be. To say that a mechanism (or bodily organ) is defective is to say that it is not in the condition it is supposed to be in. If you or I deliberately make a thing the way it is in order to illustrate a point, as a prototype, or as a work of abstract art, or if it materializes randomly that way out of cosmic dust, it isn't defective no matter how much it looks and behaves like object that (with a different history) is defective. The standards implied in describing a mechanism (organ, etc.) as defective come from its history—often from the intentions and purposes of a designer or maker. For this reason, defective things have to have a history. If they don't, they aren't defective. This, incidentally, is why Swampman could not have a broken leg or defective vision even if his physical twin, Donald Davidson, did.

Injury, healthy, strained, stretched, diseased, flawed, ill, sick, damaged, spoiled, ruined, marred, contaminated, defiled, corrupted, infected, malformed—they are all like that. Nothing can be any of these things unless it, or the processes leading up to it,

[4] For legal nitpickers: there is a legal form of (first-degree) murder that does not require malice on the part of the killer. Felony murder—a death (even if accidental) brought about in the commission of a felony is (at least *was*) classified as murder in some jurisdictions.

[5] Though something else may be bad or wrong—e.g., the negligence (driving while drunk) that led to the accident. Thus, the result may still be labelled murder.

Fred Dretske

are subject to norms. If something is marred or damaged, for instance, it departs in some degree from a standard that defines how it should be. Many of these standards come from us, the designers and builders of devices. It is our purposes, the way we intend things to be, that makes them—when they fail to be that way—damaged, spoiled malformed, flawed, and so on. If a gadget is my creation, if I made it to do X, then it is broken or defective if it doesn't do X—exactly what I designed it to do. If I want my gadget—in every other respect exactly like a clock—to lose time, if that was my purpose in building it the way I did, it is defective, not working right, if it doesn't lose time.[6] I am the origin of this norm.

Things are subject to multiple standards. Sometimes, for example, we intend things to be in a condition they are not—relative to some other standard—supposed to be in. There is no inconsistency in saying that an object is supposed to be in a state that (relative to another standard) it is not supposed to be in.

2. Are Mental Concepts Normatively Loaded?

If mental concepts are norm loaded, then minds (or those parts of the mind we pick out with norm-laden concepts) cannot exist without norms. This creates a problem: where do these norms come from? They cannot come from us—from our intentions, purposes, and desires—the way norms governing our own creations (e.g., my slow-running gizmo) come from us since the norms we now seek are ones on which intentions, purposes, and desires themselves depend for their existence. So, if one is a realist about the mind, if one thinks of mentality as existing independently of the interpretive and explanatory stances of others, then the norms constituting these mental states have to come from somewhere else. Where could that be?

This is a problem if mental concepts are norm-laden. But are they? Some of them appear to be. Mistakes, the sort of thing cognitive agents are prone to make, are, after all, judgments (i.e., takings) that are wrong or improper in some way. One cannot believe, perceive, or infer without risking misrepresentation, illusion, and fallacy. That is part of the game. Maybe cognition

---

[6] If one thinks of clocks as functional devices—objects that are *supposed* to tell the (*right*) time—then the gadget I build, not having that function, is not a clock despite being physically indistinguishable from a (slow-running) clock.

can occur (in an omniscient being?) without error, but the possibility of mistake, the possibility of getting it wrong, of committing a fallacy, is part of what we mean when we speak of someone as judging, inferring, or concluding that so-and-so is true. If, then, the possibility of mistake (if not mistakes themselves) are part of what we mean in describing an act or practice as cognitive, then cognition is norm-laden in the sense that nothing merits this description unless, somewhere in the background, there are norms relative to which results can be deemed wrong, bad, or incorrect. If you can't make a mistake, if what you are doing isn't the sort of thing in which mistakes are possible, then what is happening might be described as digestive or immunological, but it isn't cognitive. It is not believing, judging, reasoning, perceiving, or inferring.

At one time this line of reasoning seemed right to me and I took it to show that there was a problem for naturalistic accounts of the mind. The problem—or what seemed to me a problem—was to determine the source of these cognitive norms. Where did they come from? How does one get a mental OUGHT, a SUPPOSED TO BE, from a biological IS? David Hume taught us that it is a fallacy to conclude that something ought (morally) to be so from premises describing only what (as a matter of fact) is so. Why isn't it also a fallacy to suppose (as naturalistic theories of the mind do) that normatively loaded mental states arise from, and are thus reducible to, the norm-free facts of physics and biology?

One response to this problem (championed by Ruth Millikan, 1984 & 1993) is that the facts of biology are not norm free. An organ or a trait's proper function—roughly speaking, what it is selected to do—is, Millikan insists, itself a normative concept.[7] If it is a thing's proper function to do F, then it is supposed to do F. Thus, norm-laden cognitive discourse (Millikan speaks of false beliefs as defective and 'true' and 'false' as normative terms (Millikan, 1993, p. 72)) can be grounded in biological norms. There is no fallacious derivation of a cognitive OUGHT from a biological IS; only a transformation of a biological into a cognitive OUGHT. She describes her purpose (Millikan, 1993, p. 10) as defending this biological solution to 'the normativity problem,' the problem of accounting for false beliefs, misperceptions, bad inferences, errors, and so on. This, I conjecture (but see footnote #8), is why she speaks in the title of her

---

[7] See also, K. Neander, 1995, p. 112, who says that biological norms underwrite semantic norms. Not everyone agrees, of course, that natural selection yields norms. Fodor, 1996, p. 252; Bedau, 1993; Matthen, 1997, and others are sceptics.

Fred Dretske

first book (Millikan, 1984) of language and thought as biological categories.[8]

The problem to which Millikan's biological solution is a solution no longer seems like a problem to me. Beliefs and judgments must be either true or false, yes, but there is nothing normative about truth and falsity. What makes a judgment false (true) is the fact that it fails (or succeeds) in corresponding to the facts and failing (or succeeding) in corresponding with the facts is, as far as I can see, a straightforward factual matter. Nothing normative about it. An arrow (on a sign, say) can point to Chicago or away from Chicago. There is a difference here, yes, but the difference is not normative. Aside from our purposes in putting the sign there or in using it as a guide (in which case our attitudes give rise to norms about where the sign is supposed to be pointing), there is nothing right or wrong, nothing that is supposed-to-be or supposed-not-to-be, about an arrow pointing to Chicago. There might be something normative (i.e., conventional or rule-governed) about what an arrow points at (i.e., whether an arrow points with the pointy or the feathery end), but, given the conventions governing this fact, there is nothing additionally normative about an arrow pointing at Chicago. The same is true of beliefs. There may be norms involved in something's meaning that Chicago is that way (more of this in a moment), but, if that is what it means, there is nothing additional normative about its being true or correct. Peacocke[9] claims that 'correct' and 'incorrect' are normative because whether X is correct or not depends on the way the world is. But whether X is pointing at Chicago also depends on the way the world is. It depends on where Chicago is. That doesn't make 'pointing at Chicago' normative.

For understandable reasons we dislike false beliefs and do our best to avoid them. This dislike and avoidance leads us to use normative language in describing false beliefs. We speak of them as mistakes or misrepresentations where the prefix 'mis' signifies that the judgment or belief is not only false, but is wrong, bad, or improper in some way. But the practice of describing false beliefs in this normative way

[8] Since first writing this I have been told, by no less an authority than Ruth Millikan, that this was *not*, in fact, her intention at all. When she speaks of the 'normativity' problem, she is using the word 'norm' and related expressions in a technical way, in quite a different way from the way I am using them in this paper. Despite her protests, I nonetheless leave this paragraph as I originally wrote it because, frankly, this is such a natural—I am tempted to say unavoidable—way to interpret her introduction to (1993). I am not—not by any means—the only one who interprets her this way. Still, on these matters, she is the boss. Hence, this footnote.

[9] C. Peacocke (1992), p. 126.

doesn't show that there is anything essentially normative about false beliefs anymore than it shows that there is something essentially normative about the weather (e.g., a blizzard) on the day of our picnic because we describe it as awful. The fact that cognition requires the possibility of error, and that errors are bad does not mean that cognition requires norms—not unless errors are necessarily bad. But why should we believe this? Bad, yes, at least most of the time, but not necessarily bad. The only fault with fallacious reasoning, the only thing wrong or bad about mistaken judgments, is that, generally speaking, we don't like them. We do our best to avoid them. They do not—most of the time at least—serve our purposes. This, though, leaves the normativity of false belief and fallacious reasoning in the same place as the normativity of blizzards on the day of a picnic and belching at the dinner table—in the attitudes, purposes, and desires of people who make judgments about the weather and table behaviour.

Some have argued that it isn't truth and falsity (correct and incorrect) that are norm-laden, but the concept of belief itself. Beliefs, by their very nature, and unlike wishes, hopes, desires, doubts, imaginings, and pretences, are mental states that aspire to, they aim at, truth and, therefore, fail or are defective in some way when they are not true. A belief can be false, yes, just as a (defective) heart can fail to pump blood, but a belief, even when false, is supposed to be true just as the defective heart is supposed to pump blood. A belief that it is raining, unlike a hope or fear that it is, aims at the truth about rain. That is the job, the purpose, the raison d'être of beliefs. Anything that lacks this purpose or goal is not a belief any more than a device that isn't supposed to pump blood is a heart. So if, in the natural world, there are no OUGHTS, nothing that confers on brain states the goal of truth, then neither are there, in the natural world, any beliefs.

This view is aggressively promoted these days[10], but I do not find

[10] I heard Paul Boghassian defend it at a conference in Palermo, Sicily, in August 1997, but I do not attribute specific arguments to him since, lacking a copy of the paper, I am forced to rely on my feeble memory of an oral presentation. Peacocke (in 1992, Chapter 5) argues that content (hence, belief) is normative and Kripke, 1982 that meaning (and presumably, therefore, also thought) is. I take up an argument by David Velleman, 1989, 1998 and Bernard Williams, 1973 below. Brandom, 1994 defends a Kantian (vs. a Cartesian) view according to which mental states like judgment and belief (involving concepts) are inherently normative. On the Kantian view of things, concepts have the form of *rules* that bring with them entitlements and commitments. Peacocke and Brandom distinguish different kinds of norms (Peacocke's 'normative liaisons' are similar to Brandom's 'consequential commitments'), but I think my arguments against the *essential* normativity of mental content apply to both.

Fred Dretske

it plausible. I agree that beliefs are necessarily true or false. If I didn't understand what it was to be true or false I could hardly understand what it was to be a belief. But I do not see that I need go farther than this. This seems like enough to distinguish beliefs from other mental states like wishes, desires, hopes, doubts, and pains (I return in a moment to whether it suffices to distinguish beliefs from suppositions, imaginings, assumptions, etc.). Why, in order to understand what a belief is, do I also have to think of a belief as something that aims at the truth? If I deliberately deceive you, is the resulting belief supposed to be true? Aren't people supposed to be deceived by a well executed trompe l'oeil, a magician's trick, or a clever disguise? My inclination is to say that such beliefs are supposed to be false. My reason for saying this is the same as my reasons for saying that anything one deliberately brings about (e.g., a slow running clock) is (given one's purposes) supposed to be the way one intends it to be. So if I design a device to be (or produce) F, if that is my purpose, the device, given my purpose, is supposed to be (or produce) F. If F happens to be a false belief in you (or even in me), then your (my) belief is supposed to be false in the same way my 'clock' is supposed to tell the wrong time.[11]

David Velleman (1998) following Bernard Williams (1973) argues that a belief's aiming at the truth would explain the difficulty of believing at will.[12] The explanation is that believing a proposition at will would entail believing it without regard to whether it was true, something which is impossible for an attitude that aims at the truth. This is a nice point, but before we take it as a reason to think that belief aims at the truth, we need an argument that it is the best explanation for not being able to believe at will. I don't think it is. Given that so many other mental states—including many of the propositional attitudes—are also not under the control of the will (you can't just decide to be afraid that P, to desire that P, to be sorry that P, to regret that P, to be hungry, depressed, etc.), and given that none of these aim at the truth, why suppose that belief, alone, does so? Why not suppose, instead, that what makes these attitudes

[11] Recalling our early remark (about multiple standards) it may be objected that although the belief, *given my intentions*, is supposed to be false, it is, *given (merely the fact) that it is a belief*, supposed to be true. That may well be so, but we are here examining arguments for thinking it *is* so, and we haven't yet found any of those.

[12] He also mentions the argument that it would explain (what has come to be known as) the normativity of content. Since it is the normativity of content that is now in dispute, this argument, in *this* context, doesn't carry any weight.

involuntary (when they are) is something about the way they are brought about? In perception, for example, we are typically caused to believe by events (experiences) over which we have no voluntary control. That is why we (typically, at least) cannot believe at will.

Velleman points out that we cannot distinguish beliefs from other propositional attitudes (e.g., imaginings) in terms of motivational force because other propositional attitudes also have a motivational role. In imagining that she is an elephant, a child might well be motivated to behave in an elephant-like way. So belief that you are an elephant cannot be distinguished from imagining that you are an elephant in terms of the role it plays (together with desire) in explaining elephant-like behaviour. Both have this role. And so they do. But the question is not whether beliefs are the only thing that (together with desires) have a motivational role, but whether the role beliefs (together with desire) have in explaining behaviour isn't unique. Isn't this role sufficiently different from the role that imaginings have to enable us to distinguish beliefs from imaginings (entertainings, suppositions, assumptions, etc.) in terms of their distinctive functional role? It seems to me that it surely is. If a little girl behaved, and was disposed to behave, in all the ways a person who believed he was an elephant behaved, I would say—and I don't see how one could help saying—that the little girl had, tragically, slipped over the edge from pretense into actual belief. It is functional role, not what it aims at, that distinguishes belief from other factive attitudes.

Debates about the normativity of meaning (of words) or content (of beliefs) are sometimes couched in terms of a concept's extension and the 'rules' (hence, norms) governing its application (see Kripke, 1982). Concepts have extensions: cows and only cows are in the extension of the concept cow. This concept can only be correctly applied to cows. If someone falsely applies it (on a dark night) to a horse (i.e., believes of the horse that it is a cow), this is an incorrect (i.e., false) application of the concept. So far so good. Aside from our desires and intentions to avoid what is false, though, why is the false application of a concept something that is wrong, bad, or improper? What rule or norm does it violate? A belief that 37 plus 84 is 111 is certainly false; it does not correctly pick out a trio of numbers in the extension of plus, but what rule is broken by applying plus to these three numbers?

It will be said that if we do not care whether we get the right (correct, true) answer—or if we deliberately try to get a wrong answer—then what we are doing is not adding 37 and 84. We are fooling around, doodling, or, perhaps, trying to make somebody

Fred Dretske

think we don't know how to add. But we are not adding. We can add 37 and 84 and get the wrong answer, yes, just as we can break the rules of chess (unintentionally or when cheating) and still be playing chess, but in order to be properly described as adding two numbers (just as playing chess) we have to view ourselves as falling within the purview of the rules (hence, norms) constituting the activity we are engaged in. We must feel constrained by the rules of arithmetic that determine what the right answer is just as, when playing chess, we are supposed to follow the rules of the game. That, after all, is what makes cheating, cheating. If we do not feel bound by these rules, if we take to be irrelevant the criticism (in the case of addition) that we forgot to carry the '1', then we are not really adding. Addition, we will be told, is a rule (norm) constituted activity— the same as playing chess or baseball. And what is true of addition is true of all concepts. Norms are built into—they constitute—the concepts we apply. If we do not respect these norms, do not feel the entitlements and commitments they give rise to, then we are not really applying concepts.[13]

This, it seems to me, is a confusion between two quite different things—the norm-free concepts (meanings) we intentionally apply, on the one hand, and the norm-generating intentions with which we apply them on the other. All intentional acts, in virtue of being intentional (or goal directed[14]), give rise to norms, those prescribing what you have to do to reach your goal. You cannot be hiding from a predator, driving to Chicago, or ironing your shirt[15] without

[13] I am grateful to Tim Schroeder for helpful discussion on this point. He convinced me that what I said (in an earlier draft) on this point was much too superficial to capture the position I was arguing against. Maybe it is still too superficial, but it is an improvement.

[14] What I say in the text is probably better said about goal-directed activities and the means one adopts to achieve these goals. Some intentional actions are not goal directed in the relevant sense. To use a familiar example, one intentionally destroys the children's hospital. One knows one is going to destroy it when one deliberately drops the bombs on the nearby munitions plant. That, though, isn't one's goal, one's purpose, in dropping the bombs. The goal is destruction of the munitions plant. I skip over these complications here. I am grateful to Michael Bratman for clarification here.

[15] Some verbs (like 'hide') have the relevant intentions already built in. Unlike driving to Chicago (which you can do without intending to get to Chicago) you can't be hiding from X without intending or trying to conceal yourself from X. I think adding is more like hiding; you can't do it unintentionally. My intuitions about these matters (admittedly shaky) tell me that if you unintentionally add two numbers (while trying to multiply

96

intending to do all the things you believe necessary to do these things. You are not really hiding from X (though you may be pretending to hide from X) if you do not care whether X can see you or if you deliberately make attention-grabbing noise. You are not driving to Chicago if you ignore or take to be irrelevant information to the effect that that isn't the way to Chicago. All intentional acts, in virtue of being intentional, bring the actor under the purview of norms in the sense that the actor is obliged (ought) to adopt the means she believes necessary (in the circumstances) to do what she intends to do. If you feel no constraint or obligation to do what you acknowledge to be necessary for doing A, then you are not—not really—intending to do A. The same is true in applying concepts. If the act of applying a concept is intentional (it needn't be), it will fall under the purview of norms, but not because concepts or their application is a norm-constituted activity, but because the act of applying concepts, when it is intentional, generates norms associated with the actor's intentions and desires. Doing A intentionally commits the actor to doing whatever she believes necessary to doing A and, thus, exposes her to the 'should's' and 'supposed-to's' that such commitment brings with it. If the application of a concept is not an intentional act—as it isn't, for example, in the case of many perceptual judgements (e.g., seeing that the glass is empty)—then, as far as I can see, norms are absent. All that is left is truth or falsity.

This, by the way, is why conceptual role semantics (generally speaking, meaning as use) is so much more plausible for language than thought. Saying (asserting, claiming) that P (unlike believing that P) is, generally speaking, a purposeful, goal-directed, action, and, thus, the language of entitlements, commitments, rules, and norms more easily finds a home here. But, even here, I submit, the norms emerge from the associated intentions, not the meanings applied in the intentional act.

I am not, let me emphasize, denying that beliefs aim at the truth. I am not denying that beliefs ought to be true or that their function is to get things right. I am only denying that this is essential to them, that if, for whatever reason, they don't aim at the truth, they cease to be beliefs. I am quite happy to admit, for instance, that perceptual systems have a job, a function, a purpose—that of providing information to (higher) cognitive centres for the guidance

---

them, say) you were not (at the time you added them) adding them. You were multiplying them. I shall here assume that the actions I describe (e.g., driving to Chicago, ironing your shirt) are intentional in the relevant sense—directed at a goal (of, e.g., getting to Chicago, ironing your shirt).

Fred Dretske

of action. Since this is their job, they are not doing what they are supposed to be doing, not doing their job, if they do not deliver this information. It follows, therefore, that the output of perceptual processes—perceptual experiences and beliefs—are supposed to be veridical. They are supposed to correspond in some reliable way to the world about which they carry information. If they do not, the systems producing them are not doing their job, not doing what they are supposed to be doing. The normativity of perceptual beliefs and experiences thus derives from the teleofunctions of the mechanisms producing them, and these teleofunctions emerge from the historical (selectional) process that shaped those mechanisms.

All this I agree with. Given the fact that perceptual systems have an evolutionary history of the right sort, it is in fact their job (= biological function) to provide the brain with information about the environment in and on which actions are to be performed. But this isn't the point. This, by itself, isn't enough to show that perceptual concepts are norm-laden. It isn't enough to show that perceptual beliefs and experiences cannot exist without norms. For we don't yet have an argument that the teleofunctions that give rise to those norms are essential to perceptual experiences and belief. Why can't we simply agree that perceptual systems (just like the kidneys, heart, and lungs) have biological functions that they obtain from a process of natural selection and, given these functions, are supposed to do various things—whatever it is their function to do. Why can't we say all this and still deny that such a historical development is necessary to the beliefs and experiences, *qua* beliefs and experiences, that these systems produce? Why are such historically derived norms essential? If Swampman's eyes and ears supply information to Swampman's brain in the standard way (as they certainly will if Swampman is molecularly indistinguishable from Davidson), and if this information is actually used (as it clearly will be) to negotiate Swampman's way through his environment, why should we deny that this is perception simply because the information is being provided by organs that (lacking an evolutionary history) lack the biological function of supplying it? Lacking the relevant functions, they are not supposed to supply it, yes, but why is that critical to the mentality of the process and its products? That is exactly what the arguments we have so far been examining (those appealing to the norm-laden character of cognition) were supposed to supply, and, given their failure, what we still lack convincing arguments for.

3. Intentionality

We have so far concluded that although we may need history to explain norms, we do not need history to explain mentality because mentality, though subject to norms (isn't everything?), is not constituted by them. We can have mentality without norms and, thus, without the kind of history that might—arguably, at least—be required to ground norms.

There is, however, another possibility, the possibility that history, although not required for the normativity of cognition, is required for some other aspect of our mental life.[16] This is a possibility I mean to raise in the remainder of this paper. The upshot of this brief look will be that although we do not need history to explain the normativity of mental affairs, we may need it to explain another aspect of our cognitive affairs—the aboutness or intentionality of cognitive states.[17]

Thought and experience are intentional in the philosopher's sense of this word; i.e., they are about things and the things they are about need not exist in order for one to think about or experience them. If one need not stand in any actual relation to orange blobs in

[16] The fact that history may be needed to explain the intentionality, not the normativity, of the mental is not always clearly distinguished. Neander (1995, p. 110), for example, speaks of grounding intentionality in biological facts (functions), but then (p. 112) says that functions are needed to underwrite the normative notion of mental (semantic) content. Millikan moves back and forth between intentionality and normativity as the feature of mental affairs that proper functions are supposed to ground. Given her technical use of the word 'normative,' though (see footnote 8), this may not, in fact, be a movement but simply a re-phrasing. MacDonald (1989, especially p. 189) has a clear discussion of these matters.

In (Dretske 1986 & 1986) I described misrepresentation as a problem for a naturalistic approach to the mind, but I did not clearly specify whether I thought this problem was a normative problem or just a problem about intentionality. I don't think I was clear about it then. History, I would now say, is necessary for misrepresentation, but not because misrepresentation (and, therefore, representation) is essentially normative, but because it is essentially intentional.

[17] I do not assume (though I argue for it elsewhere—Dretske, 1995) that intentionality is the 'mark of the mental.' Arguably, at least, itches, tickles, and pains (mental states in good standing) do not possess it. Nonetheless, I do assume (without here arguing) that intentionality is an essential characteristic of *cognitive* states. Such mental states and processes as perception, memory, judgment, and inference, involve representation, and representation, I assume, is intentional.

Fred Dretske

order to think about them, what makes one's thoughts about them? What makes a thought that pumpkins are orange a thought that they are orange rather than yellow or blue? What makes perceptions (dreams, hallucinations) of orange things subjectively so different from perceptions (dreams, hallucinations) of blue things? If we begin by assuming, as I do, that experiences and thoughts are brain states, what makes some conditions of this grey matter about orange while others are about blue and still others about nothing at all?

One tempting answer to this question is that although intentional properties (being about orange pumpkins) are not real relations (real relations require the existence of their relata), they can be analysed into real relations if (and only if?) intentional properties are grounded in relationships that existed in the past. What makes this bit of stuff, A, about that bit of stuff, B, what establishes the semantic connection between them, is not that A and B stand in some relation to one another (that can't be right since B need not even exist for A to be about it), but, instead, that A (or appropriate ancestors—earlier tokens—of type A) and B (or earlier tokens of B) stood in appropriate (causal?) relations to each other. If no presently existing condition of the brain—neither its intrinsic properties nor its current extrinsic relations—makes it about orange pumpkins, it must be the brain's past relations to orange pumpkins (or orange things and pumpkins[18]) that gives it this intentional property.

The thought here (I'm putting it crudely, but I'm trying to capture an intuition, not construct air-tight arguments) is that if a brain can get itself connected to things that do not now exist (perhaps never existed), and if such connections are not secured by presently existing relations to the sort of thing it is now connected with, then actual relations must have done their work in the past. Being 'connected' to orange pumpkins—thinking about or experiencing them—requires an appropriate history because that is the only way existing connections with non-existing objects—i.e., intentional relations—can be grounded in real (i.e., non-intentional)

---

[18] I skip over complications relating to primitive vs. complex concepts. Obviously one can think about unicorns (orange pumpkins) without ever having been related to a unicorn (an orange pumpkin) in the past. But the idea (an old idea) is that one's capacity to think about unicorns (orange pumpkins, etc.) depends on one's past relations to (perceptions of?) instances of the conceptual constituents of the complex concept involved in the thought. Even if one needn't have been related to unicorns (orange pumpkins, etc.) to think about them, one needs (in order to have the idea of a unicorn, an orange pumpkin, etc.) to have been related to horses and horns (orange things and pumpkins, etc.) in order to have these thoughts.

relations to actual objects. If some bit of grey matter is about the colour orange (in the way an experience is of the colour orange) and there does not exist, at the time of the experience, anything that is orange, then, just possibly, what makes this grey matter about orange (rather than red or blue) is its past relations to orange (rather than red or blue) things.

This, I admit, is a creaky argument. Those who do not share my reductionistic proclivities will not be attracted by it.[19] It depends on a philosophically questionable assumption that intentional properties must be grounded in real relations to existing objects. It depends, that is, on the assumption that if S, a conscious being, is intentionally related to f, this connection must be the result of relations S (or, perhaps, ancestors of S) bears (or bore) to objects having f. This is not an assumption that will go unchallenged. It is a variant of the methodological idea (reductionism) that Jerry Fodor expressed by saying that if intentionality is real, it is really something else. I like this idea. But then I would. I'm a reductionist.

The manner in which concepts like thought and experience are, according to this approach, history-laden is, I admit, different from the way that concepts like murder and impaired are norm-laden. Certain conceptual connections lie on the surface, others do not. Almost anyone, after a few minutes reflection, will agree that if something is broken or impaired, it is not in a condition, or not behaving the way, it should be. Everyone, not just philosophers, will agree that murder has, while killing lacks, a normative character. That, it seems, is part of what we all mean—and would, furthermore, readily admit to meaning—in contrasting killing and murder. Not everything, though, lies so close to the conceptual surface. Some connections are more deeply buried. The relations between intentional concepts and history are like that. They are more deeply buried. They are, nonetheless, recoverable. They are recoverable in the same way the (for me) less obvious historical implications of concepts like wound, broken, and impaired are recoverable. Or if causal theorists are right—as I believe they are—the way that the relation between seeing (X) and causation (of perceptual experience

[19] Nor will those, like Jerry Fodor, 1990, who think that semantic connections can be established by real relations between universal properties (assuming that counterfactual supporting dependency relations count as real relations). I don't have the space to say why I think this doesn't work. Suffice it to say that I agree with Adams and Aizawa that Fodor's (Asymmetric Dependence) Theory of mental content does not avoid the relevance of history to mental content. It merely hides it. For all the details see Adams and Aizawa, 1994a (pp. 225 & 233), 1994b, and 1997 (p. 280).

Fred Dretske

by X) is recoverable. If it is, indeed, true that you cannot see (hallu-
cinate and dream of, yes, but not see) the Eiffel Tower unless the
Eiffel Tower is actually (part of) the cause of your experience, and if
it is also true (as it appears to be) that this fact is not evident on casual—not even (for many) prolonged—reflection, then I see no reason
why the historical nature of intentional concepts must be evident.
The fact that it is not evident should be no more an objection to the
historical character of intentional (representational, semantic)
concepts than it is to the causal character of perceptual concepts.

Where does that leave us? It leaves us with a conclusion—that
intentional concepts are history-laden—the plausibility of which
depends, critically, on the questionable premise that semantic connections must be grounded in genuine (presumably causal) relationships.[20] There are other questionable premises, but this one, I think,
is the most contentious. I think it is true, but others will surely dis-
agree. I do not know how to convince them I'm right. All I can do
is ask what else, besides the past, could make something in your
head about the colour orange. If nothing else could, then intentional
concepts are history-laden. Swampman is a zombie. If something
else could, what is it?[21]

[20] A logical point. In the first part of this paper I argued that although
history explains norms we don't need history to explain mentality because
mentality is not *essentially* normative. Now, however, I am arguing that since
mentality is essentially intentional, and the only way to explain intentionality
is historically, mentality is necessarily historical. Doesn't all this imply that
mentality is (also) necessarily normative since it can only be explained by
something—viz., history—that makes the product, mentality, normative?

Yes it does *if* one agrees (not everyone does) that history (e.g., natural
selection) gives rise to norms. But even if we put this point aside, the logical structure of my argument is not that mentality can exist without
norms but that one cannot *argue* for the necessity of history to mentality
by invoking history as the only way to explain normativity. One can't do
this because the only thing essentially normative about mentality is the
normativity that come from its history, and if there is no reason to think
history essential, there is no reason to think that norms are constitutive of
mentality. So one cannot argue for the necessity of history *from* norms.
That would be circular. We have to argue for history from some
independent basis and that, I am suggesting, is intentionality.

[21] My thanks to the participants of the Notre Dame Conference on
Varieties of Dualism (March 1998) for useful feedback and criticism on an
early draft of this paper. I want especially to thank John O'Leary-
Hawthorne, Fritz Warfield, Al Plantinga, and Marian David for helpful
comments. I would also like to thank philosophers in the audience at the
University of Delaware—especially Fred Adams, Chris Boorse, Steve
Kimbrough, and Mike Rea—for very helpful questions and discussion.

Bibliography

Adams, F. & Aizawa, K. 1994a. 'Fodorian Semantics', in S. Stich and T. Warfield (eds) (Oxford: Basil Blackwell), pp. 223–42.

Adams, F. & Aizawa, K. 1994b. '"X" means X: Fodor/Warfield Semantics', *Minds and Machine,* **4**, 215–31.

Adams, F. & Aizawa, K. 1997: 'Rock beats scissors: historicalism fights back', *Analysis,* **57**, 273–81.

Bedau, M. 1993. 'Naturalism and Teleology', in S. J. Wagner and R. Warner (eds) (Notre Dame, IN: University of Notre Dame Press), pp. 23–51.

Bogdan, R. (ed.) 1986. *Belief: Form, Content, and Function* (Oxford: Oxford University Press).

Brandom, R. 1994 *Making it Explicit* (Cambridge, MA: Harvard University Press)

Davidson. D. 1987. 'Knowing one's own mind', *Proceedings and Addresses of the American Philosophical Association,* **60**, 441–58.

Dretske, F. 1986. 'Misrepresentation', in R. Bogdan (1986), pp. 17–36.

Dretske, F. 1995. *Naturalizing the Mind* (Cambridge, MA: MIT Press).

Fodor, J. 1990. *A Theory of Content and Other Essays* (Cambridge, MA: MIT Press).

Fodor, J. 1996. 'Deconstructing Dennett's Darwin', *Mind and Language,* **11.3**, 246–62.

Gibbard, A. 1990. *Wise Choices, Apt Feelings* (Cambridge, MA: Harvard University Press).

Hanson, N. R. 1958. *Patterns of Discovery* (Cambridge, UK: Cambridge University Press).

Kripke, S. 1982. *Wittgenstein on Rules and Private Language* (Oxford: Blackwell).

Lycan, W. 1996. *Consciousness and Experience* (Cambridge, MA: MIT Press).

MacDonald, G. 1989. 'Biology and representation', *Mind and Language,* **4.3**, 186–99.

Matthen, M. 1997. 'Teleology and the product analogy', *Australasian Journal of Philosophy,* **75.1**, 21–37.

Millikan, R. 1984. *Language, Thought, and Other Biological Categories* (Cambridge, MA: MIT Press).

Millikan, R. 1993a. *White Queen Psychology and Other Essays for Alice* (Cambridge, MA: MIT Press).

Millikan, R. 1993b. 'Introduction', to Millikan (1993a) (Cambridge, MA: MIT Press), pp. 3–12.

Neander, K. 1995. 'Misrepresenting and malfunctioning', *Philosophical Studies,* **79**, 109–41.

Papineau, D. 1993. *Philosophical Naturalism* (Oxford: Basil Blackwell).

Peacocke, C. 1992. *A Study of Concepts* (Cambridge, MA: MIT Press).

Stich, S. and Warfield, T. (eds) 1994, *Mental Representations* (Oxford: Basil Blackwell).

Fred Dretske

Tye, M. 1995. *Ten Problems of Consciousness* (Cambridge, MA: MIT Press).

Velleman, J. D. 1989. *Practical Reflection* (Princeton: Princeton University Press).

Velleman, J. D. 1998. 'How Belief Aims at the Truth', paper read at the 1998 *Chapel Hill Philosophy Colloquium*.

Wagner, S. J. and Warner, R. (eds) 1993. *Naturalism: A Critical Appraisal* (Notre Dame, Indiana: University of Notre Dame Press).

Williams, B. 1973. Deciding to Believe: in *Problems of the Self* (Cambridge, UK: Cambridge University Press), pp. 136–51.

What has Natural Information to do with Intentional Representation?[1]

RUTH GARRETT MILLIKAN

'According to informational semantics, if it's necessary that a creature can't distinguish Xs from Ys, it follows that the creature can't have a concept that applies to Xs but not Ys.' (Fodor, 1994, p. 32)

There is, indeed, a form of informational semantics that has this verificationist implication. The original definition of information given in Dretske's *Knowledge and the Flow of Information* (1981, hereafter KFI), when employed as a base for a theory of intentional representation or 'content,' has this implication. I will argue that, in fact, most of what an animal needs to know about its environment is not available as natural information of this kind. It is true, I believe, that there is one fundamental kind of perception that depends on this kind of natural information, but more sophisticated forms of inner representation do not. It is unclear, however, exactly what 'natural information' is supposed to mean, certainly in Fodor's, and even in Dretske's writing. In many places, Dretske seems to employ a softer notion than the one he originally defines. I will propose a softer view of natural information that is, I believe, at least hinted at by Dretske, and show that it does not have verificationist consequences. According to this soft informational semantics, a creature can perfectly well have a representation of Xs without being able to discriminate Xs from Ys.

I believe there is some ambivalence in Dretske's writing about natural information, especially noticeable when comparing KFI to *Explaining Behavior* (1991, hereafter EB), but if we ignore some of Dretske's examples, the explicit statement of the theory in KFI is univocal. This theory is also strongly suggested in Fodor's work on mental content (Fodor, 1990; 1994; 1998) and seems to be consonant with J. J. Gibson's use of 'information' as well.

According to Dretske,

A signal *r* carries the information that *s* is F = The conditional probability of *s*'s being F, given *r* (and *k*), is 1 (but, given *k* alone, less than 1). (KFI, p. 65)

[1] This paper also appears as 'Appendix B' in Millikan, 2000.

Ruth Garrett Millikan

Dretske's '*k*' stands for knowledge already had about *s*. Knowledge that p is belief that is caused by information that p. It follows that a signal carries the information that *s* is F when either it alone, or it taken together with some other signal that has also been transmitted to the receiver, returns a probability of 1 that *s* is F. Thus, I suggest, we can drop the parenthetical 'and *k*' in the formulation and just say that a signal carries the information that *s* is F if it is an operative part of some more complete signal, where the conditional probability that *s* is F, given the complete signal, is 1 but would not be 1 without the part. Thus we eliminate reference to knowledge.

What is meant by saying, in this context, that the occurrence of one thing, 'the signal,' yields a probability of 1 that another thing, '*s* being F,' is the case? In a footnote, Dretske explains:

> In saying that the conditional probability (given *r*) of *s*'s being F is 1, I mean to be saying that there is a nomic (lawful) regularity between these event types, a regularity which *nomically precludes* *r*'s occurrence when *s* is not F. There are interpretations of probability (the frequency interpretation) in which an event can fail to occur when it has a probability of 1 ... but this is *not* the way I mean to be using probability in this definition. A conditional probability of 1 between *r* and *s* is a way of describing a lawful (exceptionless) dependence between events of this sort... (KFI, p. 245)

and in the text he tells us:

> Even if the properties F and G are perfectly correlated ... this does not mean that there is information in *s*'s being F about s'*s* being G ... For the correlation ... may be the sheerest coincidence, a correlation whose persistence is not assured by any law of nature or principle of logic. ... All Fs can be Gs without the probability of *s*'s being G, given that it is F, being 1. (KFI, pp. 73–4)

The probability that *s* is F given *r* must follow, it appears here, *given merely logic and natural law*. That is, the necessity must be strict natural necessity.[2]

The next question concerns the reference classes intended when referring to 'the probability that *s* is F, given *r*.' *r* was said to be a signal and *s* being F would seem to be a state of affairs, but if there are causal laws necessitating the one given the other, these laws must be general. There must be certain general aspects under which we are considering *r*, and the fact that *s* is F, by which they are

---

[2] The necessity may go in either temporal direction. For example, an effect might carry information about another effect of the same cause.

connected in a lawful way. They cannot be connected in a lawful way merely as an individual occurrence and an individual fact. It must be a certain type of signal that determines, with a probability of 1, a certain type of fact. And this will yield two reference classes for the probability, the class of signals of a certain type and the class of facts of a certain type, such that the probability that a signal of that type is connected with a fact of that type is 1. What reference classes are intended, then, when it is said that a certain *r* carries the information that a certain *s* is F? When Dretske says that the pointer on my gas gauge being at the $^{1}/_{2}$ mark carries the information that my gas tank is half full, in which two reference classes are these two conditions being considered, so as to make that so?

Clearly the reference classes cannot be (1) all pointers on gas gauges that point to the one half mark and (2) all gas tanks that are in the same cars as those gauges. For some gas gauges are broken or disconnected or badly calibrated, and even if none were, it would not be a matter of natural law that they couldn't be broken or disconnected or badly calibrated. Rather, as Dretske emphasizes in KFI, a reference must be made here to the presence of certain 'channel conditions.' In this case, channel conditions consist in a fairly intricate collection of surrounding conditions including various connecting parts the presence of which is needed before natural laws will guarantee that the gas gauge will read half full only if the gas tank is half full. One kind of thing carries information about another in accordance with strict natural necessity only given specified channel conditions. The two reference classes concerned contain only members connected by these channel conditions.

We can contrast this to the notion of a *ceteris paribus* law. According to the classical view, a *ceteris paribus* law is one that is true in accordance with natural necessity given certain surrounding conditions, where exactly what these conditions are is not specified, indeed, may or may not be known. Usually the idea is, however, that whatever these conditions, they are for the most part realized in the contexts in which the law is used. The *ceteris paribus law*, then, makes reference to both kinds of probability that Dretske mentioned above. First, given the surrounding conditions to which it implicitly refers, it holds true with a probability of 1 in accordance with strict natural necessity. Second, the surrounding conditions to which it implicitly refers are themselves assumed to hold true with high statistical frequency.

But on the above reading of Dretske's definition of information, the second sort of probability is not involved. The frequency with which the channel conditions hold, relative to which a certain kind of signal bears information about a certain kind of fact, is not part of the definition of information. Suppose, for example, that many gas gauges are badly calibrated (indeed, they are) so that the gas tanks connected to them are half full when the pointer is on the one quarter mark, others when the pointer is on the three quarters mark, and so forth. In each case, when the gas tank is half full, no matter what it reads, the pointer carries the information that it is half full, relative to its own particular channel conditions. How often each of these various kinds of channel conditions holds is quite irrelevant. To be sure, Dretske often talks as if the relevant reference class in which *this* reading on *this* gas gauge should be put is restricted to those times when this very same gas gauge does or, counterfactually, would have given this same reading. Still, the assumption has to be that we are talking only about times when this very same gas gauge is found surrounded by the very same relevant channel conditions. Or suppose the reference class consists only of this particular reading on this particular occasion, the idea being just that if the tank had not been half full the pointer would not have pointed to this number. This way of thinking of the matter is in every way equivalent. The point is that the counterfactuals have to be run on the assumption that the relevant channel conditions still hold, and nothing has been said about how often conditions of this sort do hold in the world.

This is the only way I can see to interpret Dretske's definition and remarks on information quoted above. On the other hand, this way of interpreting Dretske's definition of information does seem to be inconsistent with certain things he says about 'natural meaning,' 'natural signs,' and 'indication' in EB, despite the fact that he explicitly associates all three of these with signals that bear 'information' in the sense of KFI (EB, p. 58). Dretske tells us, for example, that although otherwise such tracks would indicate quail, '[i]f pheasants, also in the woods, leave the very same kind of tracks, then the tracks, though made by a quail, do not indicate that it was a quail that made them.' (EB, p. 56). Here, not natural law but statistical frequencies at the source end of the information channel appear to be determining whether the tracks carry natural information. And Dretske tells us that '[t]he red spots all over Tommy's face.mean [natural meaning] that he has the measles, not simply because he *has* the measles, but because people without the measles don't have spots of that kind.' (EB, p. 56). Contrast Fodor, who seems to use the term 'information' more in the way we interpreted it above following the explicit definition in KFI. He says, 'If the tokens of a symbol have two kinds of etiologies, it follows that there are two kinds of information that tokens of that symbol carry. (If some 'cow' tokens are caused by cows and some 'cow' tokens aren't, then it follows that some 'cow' tokens carry information about cows and some 'cow' tokens don't).' (Fodor, 1990, p. 90). Fodor also often speaks of 'covariation' between represented and representation, which is plausible only if one imagines a reference to some one definite though unspecified channel of influence, making the signal depend nomically on whether s is F and vice versa. Fodor's usage fits not only Dretske's original definition but also a cautious physician's offering: 'Those spots may mean Tommy has the measles, but they could also mean scarlet fever. I think we had better take a culture.' Dretske's modified claim, that if some people with spots like that don't have the measles then those spots don't mean measles, apparently refers instead to statistical frequencies at the source.

Alternatively, perhaps it refers to the frequency of certain channel conditions. It might well be, for example, that given certain channel conditions, only measles virus would cause spots like that, but that given other channel conditions, only strep bacteria would. Just as, given certain channel conditions, only a half full tank of gas would cause that reading, but given other channel conditions, only a quarter full tank would. Then by Dretske's original definition, Johnny's spots might mean measles even if on another child they would mean scarlet fever. But if Dretske's modification here involves assigning certain channel conditions themselves a probability of one, such a probability would also seem to be merely a statistical frequency.

Indeed, both Dretske's KFI and his EB waver at points between the two kinds of probability in discussing information. Dretske tells us, both in KFI and in EB, that if his doorbell rings, that carries the information that someone is at the door. But in EB we are told,

> It is partly the fact, presumably not itself a physical law, that animals do not regularly depress doorbells ... that makes a ringing doorbell *mean* that some *person* is at the door ... as things *now* stand, we can say that the bell would not be ringing if someone were not at the door. It therefore indicates or means that someone is at the door. But this subjunctively expressed dependency, though not a coincidence, is not grounded in natural law either ... Normally, though, these things don't happen ... And this is no lucky coincidence, no freaky piece of good fortune ... There must actually be some condition, lawful or otherwise, that explains the persistence of the correlation ... [for the doorbell to indicate a person]. (EB, p. 57).

Ruth Garrett Millikan

But, of course, if the condition that explains the correlation is not lawful but 'otherwise,' then it is grounded in mere facts about the state conditions characterizing the world at certain times and places—either conditions at the source or existent channel conditions. It has the status merely of a local statistical frequency—based lawfully, perhaps, hence explainably, upon prior local statistical frequencies, but that does not change it's essential nature as merely a statistical frequency.

The vacillation here seems to be twofold. First, it concerns whether or not mere statistical frequencies at the source, rather than strict natural law, should be allowed to determine signals as bearing 'natural information.' Second, it concerns whether we should count a signal that is not univocal except as harnessed to a particular information channel. But, of course, most of the interesting examples of signals carrying 'information,' defined Dretske's original way, are of a sort that either do not always carry the same kind of information (because channel conditions vary) or if they do, that is a matter of convenient empirical fact, not natural necessity. The fact that a signal carries 'information,' defined Dretske's original way, has no bearing whatever upon whether, by the mere fact that the signal has arrived, one can tell anything about *what* information, if any, it carries.[3]

I propose to stay for a while with Dretske's original definition of natural information. To my knowledge, no other well defined notion of natural information is currently available. Allowing merely statistical considerations on board poses an intractable problem concerning the reference classes within which the frequency of 1 should be required to hold. Do spots like that mean measles if small pox, though now extinct, used to, and may in the future, cause spots like that? If the Skinner-trained pigeons in your neighbourhood start pressing doorbells, how close may my neighbourhood be to yours for my ringing doorbell still to carry the information that a person is at my door? More important, mixing frequencies with natural necessities muddies the issues involved in trying to understand phenomena connected with intentional representation. These issues can be seen much more clearly if we separate issues of natural law from issues that concern mere frequencies. For clarity, I will call natural information purified of all mere frequencies, natural information as originally defined by Dretske, 'informationL' (for 'law").

[3] Dretske worries about something close to this in KFI pp. 111–23, but he does so in the confusing context of worrying about what 'knowledge' is, and thus he never confronts the basic problem—or so I would argue, but my main project here is not Dretske exegesis.

InformationL is an entirely objective commodity and it is ubiquitous. Often its channels are complex, and such as seldom if ever to be duplicated. Channels that are often duplicated tend to be fairly simple channels, such as reflections in calm water. Channels carrying reflections in choppy water, though not much more complex, are seldom repeated. The more numerous and irregular the intervening media between source and signal are, the less likely repetition becomes.

InformationL is everywhere, but the problem, of course, is to interpret it. For no signal that makes up only part of the world can carry the informationL that its own channel conditions hold. And that means that it cannot carry the information that it carries informationL, nor what code this information is in. This opens the question why an organism could possibly care whether or not it ever encounters any of this ubiquitous but uncommunicative informationL. What good will it do an animal to have informationL?

The problem is twofold. First, a signal carrying informationL is, as it were, in code. It is of no use to an organism unless the organism can 'read' the code. Second, the informationL that reaches an organism is not all in the same code.

Consider first the easy problem, that of reading the code. Suppose that the information all arrives in the same code. Then for a signal to be of use to a creature—to be 'read' by it—it would only be necessary that the creature should be guided by the signal in a way that diverts it from activities less likely to benefit it to ones more likely of benefit it, this likelihood being contingent on the fact conveyed by the signal. For example, if the fact conveyed is the relative location of water, given that the creature is thirsty, all that is needed is that the signal should cause the creature to turn toward the location indicated. The beneficial activity need not, of course, be overt. It might be an inner state change. The basic idea here is well known, I believe, and has been given numerous expressions, for example, by Dretske and myself.

The 'same code' problem is the harder one, and is itself two-sided. First, we have not yet offered a reason to suppose that informationL about the same thing always or ever reaches an organism in the same code or packaging. Second, we have offered no reason to suppose that the same packaging always or ever carries the same informationL, indeed, any informationL. Why suppose, for any signal that the organism receives, that all signals of that kind reaching the organism, carry the same informationL. But for the organism to be able to use the informationL it receives, the same kind of informational content needs to affect the organism in the same kind of way, and different kinds of informational content need to affect it in different ways. Information about the same must, as it were, look the same to the organism, and information about different things must look different to the organism. (This may put us in mind of Fodor's 'formality constraint' (1980).)

A central tenet of contemporary ecological psychology of the sort introduced by J. J. Gibson is that there is far more consistency in the natural information received by an organism than was formerly supposed. The claim is, first, that if you look for the right aspect of the signals that arrive by way of the ambient energy surrounding an organism, you find that a surprising number of superficially or apparently different channels of informationL can be described as really being the same channel once you have located the right high order invariances in the signals. And it is these invariances, these univocal codes,[4] that the evolving animal has become sensitive to, so as to 'pick up' the relevant information and use it.

Second, the Gibsonian claim is that the very same relevant channel conditions are present under environmental conditions that the animal frequently or nearly always finds itself in, or that it knows how to manoeuvre itself into. In the animal's normal environment, the relevant channel conditions are always the same, or always possible for the animal actively to intercept, so that relevant features of the source lawfully produce informationL about themselves in the same code. There are 'ecological laws' such that the signals covary with the relevant environmental features.

Third, the Gibsonian claim is that informationL of this sort that is relevant to the animal's needs is much more complete than had previously been supposed. Information about exactly those environmental conditions to which the animal needs to adjust is frequently presented in an unequivocal way. 'The stimulus is not impoverished.'

These three claims are not generally separated in the tradition of Gibsonian psychology, but they are independent. Gibsonian 'information' is not only informationL, but also lawfully carries complete information needed for guidance with respect to important aspects of the environment, and is frequently present in the environment, coming in always through the very same information channels, that is, exemplifying the very same *ceteris paribus* laws, arriving in a

[4] Gibsonians protest that the natural information used by organisms is not in the form of a 'code.' Their point, however, is merely that it is constituted by changing energy structures that do not require translation into some other medium in order to be used by the organism.

single code. All the animal has to do is to tap into these rich sources of information (for example, by developing eyes with lenses) and funnel them directly into guidance of appropriate behaviour.

Mechanisms by which various perceptual constancies are achieved, such as recognition of same colour, same shape, same size, same voice, and so forth, through a wide spectrum of mediating conditions, in so far as these constancies are sometimes detected over wide ranges of input in accordance with univocal principles, illustrate the use of Gibsonian information. Then it is a very complex signal indeed, one in which the significant invariances are (from the physicist's point of view) highly derived, that yields informationL through a complicated but still univocal channel in a single code. The job of tapping into such informationL channels and using the information to guide useful action is, as a biological engineering feat, extremely challenging. Yet natural selection has managed to solve many of these problems.

Surely there does exist in our world at least a certain amount of Gibsonian information, or at least very close to that, which serves as the bedrock foundation making sentient life possible at all. This foundation guides the most basic immediate responses to the environment of all animals, and also supports all information gathering activities and faculties that make use of less tractable, less user-friendly, forms of information which are also naturally found in the environment. But there is also much useful informationL in the environment that is not fully Gibsonian.

InformationL becomes less Gibsonian, for example, as it becomes less ubiquitous. Darkness and dense fog, for example, impede transmission of normal visual information. InformationL becomes less Gibsonian as it arrives in more alternative packagings, in alternative codes. For example, we use a number of alternative visual cues for depth. More interesting are cases in which the same signal form varies in the information it carries. Consider light and sound when reflected off smooth surfaces. Like a gas gauge that carries informationL but reads '$^1/_4$' when it is half full, reflections carry perfectly good informationL but informationL that needs to be read differently than usual. A puddle in the woods is not a hole in the ground with upside down trees hanging inside. Animals, after brief exposure, generally treat reflections simply as irrelevant noise in the data, holes in the normal flow of information. But a kitten's first experience with a mirror can be very amusing to watch, a dog will bark at its own echo, sometimes for hours, and a Canada goose once spent a whole afternoon doing a mating dance to his reflection in the basement window of our building on the Connecticut

Ruth Garrett Millikan

campus. We humans, on the other hand, are able to tap into many such sources of informationL and to read them correctly. We can comb our hair in the mirror, we understand that Clinton is not inside the TV set nor our friends inside the telephone. We build gadgets to collect thousands of different kinds of informationL— various indicators, metres, gauges, scopes, audios, videos, and so forth—and we learn to read them correctly.

When a variety of channels of informationL about the same are intermittently available to an organism, the animal must understand when each is open, distinguishing informationL both from mere noise and from informationL arriving in similar vehicles but differently coded. Nor should we take for granted that an animal can integrate the sources of informationL that it uses. There is a story circulating (though probably apocryphal[5]) that certain venomous snakes strike mice by sight, trace the path of the dying mouse by smell, and find it's head (so as to swallow it first) by feel, and that none of these jobs can be done using any other sensory modality. The lesson is, anyway, logically sound. InformationL about the same that comes in a variety of codes requires 'translation' if it is to be used in a versatile way.

Suppose then that informationL about the same things arriving through a variety of media is translated by mechanisms in the organism into a common code.[6] Insofar as this result is achieved, whatever appears in that code is correlated always in the same way with the same source or kind of source of information in the environment, even when the channels that control this effect are variable. In this way, a great deal of informationL that is not fully Gibsonian as it originally reaches the organism may be translated into the practical equivalent of Gibsonian informationL inside the organism. As I will now argue, however, relatively few things that an animal needs to know can be communicated in this direct way.

InformationL depends on a channel between the information source and the signal producing a correspondence between the two in accordance with natural necessity. But unfortunately, relatively few things that an animal needs to know about can figure as sources for this kind of information. The mouse, for example, needs to know when there is a hawk overhead, but there are no natural laws that apply to hawks overhead and hawks only. The existence of

[5] The original source seems to be the zoologist Sverre Solander, who gives no references and, despite requests, has offered no data yet to my knowledge.
[6] By 'translated into a common code' I mean only that sameness or overlapping in content is marked. See (Millikan, 1997 & 2000 Chapter 10).

hawks is not a matter of law, nor, for any given channel, is the nonexistence of things other than hawks that might cause the same effects as a hawk on the output of that channel, a matter of natural necessity. Similarly, if there are channel conditions under which cows cause mental 'cow' tokens as a matter of natural law, surely there can be none under which mental 'cow' tokens are caused by cows. They might instead be caused by something that looked like a cow, or sounded like a cow, or smelled like a cow, or all three, but that wasn't a cow. It is the *properties* of objects like hawks and cows that enter into natural laws, not the hawks and cows themselves, and it is never a matter of natural law that only hawks or cows have these properties.

There is, of course, an old-fashioned way out of this difficulty. You can argue that it is a matter of nominal definition that cows and only cows have certain properties, and then argue that information concerning the copresence in one and the same object of all these defining properties could indeed be transmitted through an information channel. Then there might be natural informationL about the presence of a cow. As a preliminary, however, first notice that you can't take this route for information concerning individuals. Even quite primitive animals are often able to recognize and keep track of various of their conspecifics individually, to learn things about them, and so forth. But there are no laws that concern any individuals as such. No signal can carry the informationL that it is *Johnny* who has the measles. Second, although a classical position that some still occupy gives natural kinds such as gold and water definitions in terms of necessary and sufficient characteristics, it is no longer plausible that biological kinds, such as cow, can be defined that way. A large proportion of the kinds that we name in everyday speech are 'historical kinds,' kinds that are not defined by their possession of certain properties at all, but instead through 'historical' connections—connections in the spatial/temporal/causal order—that their members have to one another (Millikan, 1999 & 2000, Chapter 2). Exactly as with individuals, these kinds cannot be subjects of informationL. They fall under no laws, not even *ceteris paribus* laws, and they support no counterfactuals.

Thus we are returned to the problem addressed earlier when Dretske observed that it is not a matter of natural necessity that your ringing doorbell 'indicates' there is some person at the door. In what sense of 'natural information' then, exactly, does the doorbell carry natural information? Is there a way to define a softer notion of 'natural information' to do the work required here?

To answer this we must have firmly in mind what work it is that

Ruth Garrett Millikan

is required. What do we need a theory of natural information for? In this context, we require it to support a theory of 'intentional' representation, in the sense introduced by Brentano. This is the kind of representation that displays Brentano's mark of the mental. Intentional representations can represent nonexistent things, for example, nonexistent facts. They can be misrepresentations. All agree, of course, that natural information is not itself intentional, that it cannot misrepresent or be false. 'Informational semantics,' as Fodor calls it, is an attempt to show how, despite this difference, intentional representation still rests at base on natural information.

How to move from a theory of natural information to a theory of intentional representation is, however, a problem. That is what Fodor's theory of 'asymmetrical dependency' is designed to do (Fodor, 1990 Chapter 4). And that is what Dretske's addition of teleology is designed to do—his claim that it is only a function, not always realized, of intentional representations to carry natural information (Dretske, 1981 & 1991). Fodor's asymmetrical dependency theory seems, quite explicitly, to rest on informationL, but I won't argue that case here. Rather, I will try to show how teleology can be combined with a theory of soft natural information to produce the variety in forms of intentional representation that animals require. But there has been some confusion about the relation of teleological accounts of intentionality to informational semantics. So let me first remark on that relation.

Naturalized teleological theories of the content of representations are attempts to explain Brentano's mark of intentionality: How can representations be false or represent nonexistent things? But teleological theories are only overlays, minor additions, veneers superimposed, on prior underlying theories of representation, and there can be considerable variety among these underlying theories. When looking at any teleological theory, the first thing to ask is on what kind of more basic theory of representation it rests.

Suppose, for example, that you think of mental representations as items defined in a classical functionalist way, in accordance with patterns of causal/inferential dispositions. And suppose that you have a theory that tells what dispositional relations one of these representations must have to others, and the collection as a whole to the world, for it to be a representation, say, of its raining. Then the teleological theorist, call her Tilly, will come along and point out that surely some of the causal roles of actual representations in actual people's heads correspond to bad inferences. What you must say, says Tilly, is that what the representation represents is determined by what it's causal role *would* be if the head *were* operating correctly, that is, in the way it was designed, by evolution or learning, to operate. Similarly, suppose that you think of mental representations as items that 'stand in for' the things they represent, running isomorphic to them, with differences in the representations producing differences in the behaviours guided by them, thus making the behaviours appropriate to the presence of the things represented. Then Tilly will come along and point out that some representations are false, that is, not isomorphic to things in the world as required to guide behaviour appropriately. What you must say, says Tilly, is that the representations represent what would need to be in the world, running isomorphic to them, if the cognitive systems were operating correctly. That is, what a teleological theory of content does is to take some more basic theory of content, point out that the application of that theory to actual creatures requires idealizing them in certain ways, and then offer the teleological principle to explain which idealization is the right one to use in interpreting intentional contents, namely, the one that fits how the cognitive systems were designed or selected for operating. You give your naturalistic analysis of what a true or correct representation is like, and Tilly merely adds that systems designed to produce true representations don't always work as designed, claiming that correctness in perception and cognition is defined by reference to design rather than actual disposition.

Accordingly, the teleologist who is an information semanticist begins with the idea that representations are signals carrying 'natural information' and then adds teleology to account for error. My claim is that adding teleology to informationL will not yield the rich variety of intentional representation that either we or the animals employ, but that there is a softer kind of natural information that does underlie all intentional representation. This softer kind, however, offers no help whatever to the verificationist.

Let us return, for a few moments, to the animal whose perceptual/cognitive systems are capable of translating informationL about the same things arriving through a variety of media into a common code. Whatever appears in that code is correlated always in the same way with the same source or kind of source of informationL in the environment. But, Tilly reminds us, it is not plausible that errors will never occur. If this arrangement has been built by natural selection, however, it will at least be a *function* of these mechanisms, which tap into and converge these channels of informationL, to produce signals that carry informationL in a univocal code. Their function is to transmit signals that are controlled by certain external sources of information so that these sources then control the behavior of the organism in ways that are adaptive. Surely this is the sort of thing that Dretske had in mind in saying that the function of a representation is to indicate (Dretske, 1986 & 1991). Or, being very careful, what has really been described here is not the function of the representations themselves, but the function of certain mechanisms that produce representations. The first job of such a mechanism is to complete a specific type of channel of information flow, or to bring to focus in a single code a number of such channels, so as to produce an informationL-bearing signal in a specific code. This is the way to add teleology to the idea that intentional representation is, at root, natural informationL. False intentional representations result when such a mechanism fails to perform this job properly.

I say that I think this is what Dretske has in mind. Dretske has sometimes wavered, however, on whether it can be a function of information gathering systems to gather information about affairs that are distal to the organism. I will explain.

The job of bringing information arriving through different channels, perhaps through complex media, in different codes, to a focus is obviously difficult and very risky. Tilly is surely right that systems responsible for accomplishing this feat inevitably will sometimes fail. Recall the Canada goose in love with itself, and the dog trying to communicate with its echo. When this sort of thing happens, however, it is not usually because there is anything wrong with the organism. Without doubt, perhaps definitionally, almost none of the mistakes in informationL gathering that are made by healthy animals are due to malfunction of the animals' informationL-focusing systems. Mistakes are due to an uncooperative environment, which fails to supply those informationL channels that the animal has been designed or tuned to recognize and employ. Gibson to one side, concerning some informationL that an animal needs to gather, the environment may be rife with decoy channels, nor is there anything the animal can do about that, perhaps, without evolving completely different perceptual systems. Both Dretske (1986) and Neander (1995) have concluded from this, however, that the information gathering systems of animals may not actually have the function of gathering information about *distal* affairs at all. The argument is that when representations of distal affairs are apparently mistaken, since typically this is not because the animal's information systems are failing to function properly, it must be that that these systems do not have as their function to gather this kind of information. Neander then seriously claims that all representation must be only of proximal stimuli. The effect, of course, will be a very strong form of verificationism indeed. The organism can only represent what it can verify conclusively, granted it's not sick or damaged.

But the idea that nothing can have a purpose or function that it requires help from anything else to achieve is mistaken. Consider the can opener on the wall in my kitchen. It is not now opening cans. It is not now performing its function. It would need my help in order to do that. Certainly it doesn't follow that it is malfunctioning, or that opening cans is not its function.[7] In the case of information gathering systems, exactly as with can openers or, say, with the famous walking mechanisms in cockroaches, a cooperative environment plays a lead role in helping them serve their functions. (Nor, of course, does it follow that it is the environment's function to help cockroaches walk or to help us focus information.)

Let us now look more closely at the result of adding teleology to natural informationL to produce intentional representation. The first job of a system that uses informationL to produce representations is to complete a specific type of natural-informationL channel so as to project that informationL into some standard code. But systems of this kind also have jobs beyond. The codes into which they translate informationL must be ones that the behavioural systems of the animal are able to use. The problem, posed first during evolutionary development, then to the developing individual animal, is to coordinate these two kinds of systems. Suppose, however, that the representation-producing systems and the behavioural systems fail to cooperate on some task. Suppose that a signal carrying informationL about one state of affairs is used by the behavioural systems in a way appropriate instead to some contrary state of affairs. For example, the informationL that the height to be stepped up is, say, eight inches, is coded in a representation that guides the legs to step up only seven inches. Which has erred, the perceptual side of the system or the motor side of the system? Is the representation wrong, or is its use wrong? Has the message been written wrong, or has it been read wrong? What does the *intentional* representation say: eight inches or seven inches?

Notice that the signal, as carrying informationL, definitely says eight inches. Compare the informationL carried by a miscalibrated

---

[7] If, however, you do insist, as Neander does, that in the *ordinary* sense of 'function' things really can't have distal functions, then I refer you to the definition of 'proper function' stipulated in Millikan (1984), in accordance with which most of the many proper functions that most biological items have are distal, and I suggest that the notion of function we need to use to gain insight here is 'proper function' as there defined.

Ruth Garrett Millikan

gas gauge. The miscalibrated gauge carries informationL telling the *actual* level of the gas in the tank. If we interpret it wrongly, that does not make it carry the informationL we wrongly take it to carry. What it itself naturally means just is whatever it *actually* carries informationL about, even though in a difficult or uninterpretable code. In the same way, the coded informationL about the height of the step cannot be wrong. The attributes *right* and *wrong*, *true* and *false*, don't apply to the code considered as a natural sign.

Recall that a signal carries informationL, not as considered within the reference class of all items in the world having the same physical form, but only as a member of the class of signals linked to sources through the same kind of information channel, that is, in accordance with the same natural necessities implemented through the same mediating conditions. As an *intentional* representation, however, the representation of the height of the step is a member of a different reference class altogether. It is a member of the class of all representations like it in form,[8] produced by the same representation-producing systems, for use by the same representation-using systems. In this class there may also be representations identical to it but that carry natural informationL in a different code, and representations that carry no natural informationL at all. In which code, then, is its *intentional* content expressed?

Exactly here is the place to apply teleology, as I see it, to the analysis. We suppose that the system that codes and uses the information about the step is a system where the coding and using parts of the system have coevolved, either phylogenetically and/or ontogenetically. During evolution of the species and/or during learning or tuning, they have been selected or adjusted for their capacities to cooperate with one another. The operative features of both halves of the system have been selected for and/or tuned as they have because these features and settings have sometimes succeeded in guiding behaviour appropriate to the informationL encoded. If this is so, inevitably it is true that these coordinations were achieved by settling on some single and quite definite code. Only if there was constancy or stability in the code employed by the representation maker and user could coordinations have been achieved systematically. It is this code then that the representation producer was designed to write in, and it is this code that the representation user was designed to read. And it is this code that determines the *intentional* content of the message about the height of the step. In any particular case of

---

[8] More accurately, the class of all representations that the systems designed to use it are designed to identify as having the same content. See (Millikan, 1997 & 2000 Chapter 10).

error, whether it is the representation producers or the representation users that have erred depends on whether or not the natural informationL appears in this code.

My proposal is now that we should *generalize* this result. Intentional representations and their producers are defined, are made to be such, by the fact that it is their job to supply messages that correspond to the world *by a given code*. That is the essence. But notice that *that* formulation makes no reference to informationL. If that is the essence of the matter, then the *mechanisms* by which the producers manage to produce messages that correspond by the given code drops out as irrelevant to their nature as intentional representation producers. If there exist systems with the function of supplying messages that correspond to the world by a given code but that manage to achieve this result, when successful, *without tapping into any channels of natural informationL*, they too will be producers of intentional representations. They will be producers of intentional representations that are not defined with reference to natural informationL. I will now argue that such systems do exist, indeed, that the bulk of our mental representations necessarily are of this type. Rather than informationL, they tap into channels of softer natural information. How should we define this 'softer' form of natural information?

Dretske wishes to eliminate *de facto* perfect correlations that are 'lucky coincidences' or 'freaky piece[s] of good fortune' as possible supports for any notion of natural information. But does anything stand in the middle between, on the one hand, statistical frequencies resulting from lucky coincidence and, on the other, the necessity of natural law? The answer Dretske gave to this question, though inadequate, I believe, is still a very interesting one. He said, '[t]here must actually be some condition, lawful or otherwise, that explains the *persistence* of the correlation' [emphasis mine]. About this I remarked earlier that the fact that a local statistic is based lawfully upon prior local statistics, hence that a correlation is explainable, does not alter its nature as a mere statistical frequency. If the frequency of black balls in the urn today is 1, and if nothing disturbs the urn, then by natural necessity it follows that the frequency of balls in the urn tomorrow is 1. That does not change the probability of being black if a ball in the urn into a probability of some kind other than mere statistical frequency. It does not help being-a-ball-in-the-urn to carry the informationL being-black.

But it does do something else. It explains how, by sampling the urn today and adjusting my expectations of colour accordingly, this adjustment in expectation can turn out to be adequate to my experience tomorrow, *not by accident but for good reason*. Many statistical frequencies *persist* over time in accordance with natural necessity, and many produce correlate statistical frequencies among causally related things, in accordance with natural necessity. If measles are producing spots like that in this community today, then measles will probably be producing spots like that in this community tomorrow. Measles, after all, are contagious. And if a nose like that is correlated with the presence of Johnny today it will probably be correlated with the presence of Johnny tomorrow. Johnny's nose, after all, tends to sustain both its shape and it's attachment to Johnny. There are no laws that concern individuals as such, but there are many kinds of local correlations that do. Notice, however, that whether the persistence of a correlation may be explained in this sort of way does not depend on its being a perfect correlation. Conditional probabilities of 1 have nothing to do with the matter.

This yields a way that an organism may come to possess systems that produce representations that correspond to the world by a given code *often enough* to have been selected for doing that job, but that do this job without tapping into any natural informationL. Systems of this sort run on bare statistical frequencies of association—on correlations—but on correlations that persist not by accident but for good reason. Probably these correlations typically obtain between properties of the not-too-distant environment that *do* supply informationL to the organism, and more distal properties, kinds, situations, individuals, and so forth, of interest to the organism but that *don't* supply it with informationL. The intentional contents of representations of this sort are determined not by any natural informationL that it is their function to carry, but merely by the codes in which their producers were selected to write, so as to cooperate with the systems designed to read them.

It follows that a representation producer, basing its activities on past local statistical frequencies, may indeed be representing Xs, and yet be unable perfectly to distinguish Xs from Ys. There may be no dispositions under which it has a disposition infallibly to distinguish Xs from Ys. *To perform properly*, its representations of Xs—its code tokens of a certain type—must correspond to Xs, but this does not entail that there exist any information channels at all, actual or possible, through which it could infallibly discriminate Xs from Ys. That having grown up with grey squirrels around, I am thinking of grey squirrels has nothing to do with whether I can discriminate grey squirrels from Australian tree possums, even if someone introduces tree possums into my neighbourhood. Similarly, the determinacy of content of my representation of cows is not threatened by the possibility of a new species arising that I couldn't distinguish from cows, or by the possibility of Martians arriving with herds of facsimile cows. The alternative that I should sometimes actually be at the other end of an informationL channel from cows is not even coherent.

Consider, in this light, Pietroski's tale about the kimus and the snorfs (1992). The kimus are attracted by the red morning glow over their local mountain so that they climb up it each day. Thus they conveniently avoid their chief predators, the snorfs, who don't take to mountain terrain. Pietroski claims that since no current kimu would recognize a snorf if it ran into it head on, it is implausible that the perception of red means snorf-free terrain to the kimus. A mere correlation between the direction of the red glow and the direction of the snorfs is not enough to support intentional representation. Now first, we should note that the injection of phenomenology here is perversely distracting. The question is not whether a red qualia, should there exist such things, could mean *no snorfs this direction* rather than *red*. Bats perceive shapes by ear and, goodness knows, maybe squares sound to them like diminished seventh chords do to us. Pietroski's question should be whether *any* inner representation that merely directs the kimu towards the sunlight could represent for it the snorf free direction. Nor should the idea be that the kimu reads or interprets the inner representation as meaning 'the snorf- free direction' the way you or I would interpret a sign of snorfs. To interpret a sign of snorfs, you or I must have a prior way of thinking of snorfs, and that, by hypothesis, the kimus do not have. The question, put fairly, is whether something *caused* by red light could *constitute* an inner representation of the snorf-free direction for the kimus. Also, we should be clear that the kimus' sensitivity to and attraction by the red light is not supposed to be accidental, but is a result of natural selection operating in the usual way. Kimu ancestors that were not attracted to red light were eaten by the snorfs.

Put this way, the situation is parallel to that of certain tortoises, who are attracted to green things, because green correlates with edible vegetation. They will move on the dessert toward any green seen on their horizon. Nor do the nutritious properties of the vegetation produce the green light. These properties are merely correlated with green light. Can the green mean 'chow over there' to the tortoise? Obviously not in so many words. But your percept of an apple doesn't mean 'there's an apple over there' in so many words either. If the green doesn't mean chow over there to the tortoise, then what on earth *could* mean chow over there to anyone? Is it really

Ruth Garrett Millikan

plausible that there could be a genuine informationL channel open to any of us, for you or for me, that would communicate the informationL that there was chow on the table? Does human chow, as such, figure in any causal laws? If not, then in what sense are we 'able to discriminate' when it is chow time? Unless, that is, we rely on mere statistical correlations.

Besides natural informationL, then, we should recognize another equally important kind of support for intentional representation, resting on what may also be called 'natural signs' carrying—to keep the terminology parallel—'informationC' (for 'correlation'). Natural signs bearing informationC are, as such, instances of types that are correlated with what they sign, there being a reason, grounded in natural necessity, why this correlation extends through a period of time or from one part of a locale to another. One thing carries information about another if it is possible to learn from the one something about the other not as a matter of accident but for a good reason. But no vehicle of information is transparent, of course. How to read the information through its vehicle has to be discovered, and it has to be possible to learn this in an explainable way, a way that works for a reason. The vehicle carries genuine information only if there is an ontological *ground* supporting induction that leads from prior experience to a grasp of the information carried in new instances. There must be a connection between the various instances exhibiting the correlation, a reason for the continuation of the correlation. Correlations that yield true belief only by accident do not carry genuine information.

Natural signs carrying informationC are correlated with what they represent because each sign instance is connected with what it represents in a way that recurs for a reason. Typically, however, the correlations are not perfect, and informationC, like informationL, cannot be false by definition. A token indistinguishable from a natural sign but that is not connected in the usual way with its usual represented is not a natural sign. The correlations that support informationC may be weak or strong. For example, a particular instance of a small shadow moving across the ground is a natural sign carrying informationC that a flying predator is overhead if it is actually caused by a flying predator, but the correlation that supports this natural signing, though it persists for good reason, may not be particularly strong.

If we allow ourselves to use the term 'natural information' to cover informationC as well as informationL, then, we must keep firmly in mind that this sort of natural information has nothing to do with probabilities of one. Nor does the presence of this kind of information directly require the truth of any counterfactuals. If a shadow is a natural sign of a predator it does not follow that if a predator weren't there a shadow wouldn't be there, hence that such shadows can be used to discriminate predators from non-predators. Nor does it follow that if a shadow weren't there a predator wouldn't be there—not on a cloudy day. Thus it is that a creature can perfectly well have a representation of Xs without being able to discriminate Xs from Ys

Bibliography

Bogdan, R (ed.) 1986. *Belief: Form, Content, and Function* (New York: Oxford).

Dretske, F. 1981. *Knowledge and the Flow of Information* (Cambridge, MA: MIT Press).

Dretske, F. 1986. 'Misrepresentation', in Radu Bogdan (ed.) (New York: Oxford), pp. 17–36.

Dretske, F. 1991. *Explaining Behavior* (Cambridge, MA: MIT Press).

Fodor, J. A. 1980. 'Methodological Solipsism as a Research Strategy in Cognitive Psychology,' *Behavioural and Brain Sciences*, **3**, 63–73.

Fodor, J. A. 1990. *A Theory of Content* (Cambridge, MA: MIT Press).

Fodor, J. A. 1994. *The Elm and the Expert* (Cambridge, MA: MIT Press).

Fodor, J. A. 1998. *Concepts: Where Cognitive Science Went Wrong* (Oxford: Oxford University Press).

Millikan, R. G. 1984. *Language, Thought, and Other Biological Categories* (Cambridge, MA: MIT Press).

Millikan, R. G. 1997. 'Images of Identity', *Mind*, **106**, 499–519.

Millikan, R. G. 1999. 'Historical kinds and the special sciences', *Philosophical Studies*, **95**, 45–65.

Millikan, R. G. 2000. *On Clear and Confused Ideas; an Essay about Substance Concepts* (New York: Cambridge University Press).

Neander, K. 1995. 'Misrepresenting and malfunctioning', *Philosophical Studies*, **79**, 109–41.

Pietroski, P. M. 1992. 'Intentionality and teleological error', *The Pacific Philosophical Quarterly*, **73**, 267–82.

Locke-ing onto Content

FRANK JACKSON

Our reading is a passage from John Locke, *An Essay Concerning Human Understanding*, Book III, Chapter II, § 2.

> When a man speaks to another, it is that he may be understood; and the end of speech is that those sounds, as marks, may make known his *ideas* to the hearer. ... Words being voluntary signs, they cannot be voluntary signs imposed by him on things he knows not. That would be to make them signs of nothing, sounds without signification.

What is Locke telling us in this passage?

Suppose that you and I are involved in some kind of conspiracy, and we have agreed that I will put a pot plant on the balcony of my flat if the 'coast is clear'. What I will do is put the plant on the balcony when I *believe* that that the coast is clear; I won't put a pot plant on the balcony when the coast is clear independently of my opinion on the subject. To enter an agreement to do such and such when things are thus and so is to do such and such when you believe that things are thus and so. The point here is not one about what counts as success in following an agreement. When you agree to stop when the light turns red, you succeed in following that agreement to the extent that you stop when the light turns red, whether you believe that it has or not. The point is one about what it is to enter into the agreement or to seek to follow it. Just as to seek the Golden Mountain is to go where you believe it is, so to seek to follow an agreement is to do what you believe is in accord with it. Locke's point is that language—or anyway language in its assertoric use—rests on voluntary, if largely implicit, agreements to use words and sentences to stand for how we take things to be. Moreover, the very great utility of language tells us that speakers who share a language know, by and large, what other speakers are claiming about how they take things to be when they use their shared language. Or, to put the point in the now familiar jargon, we use language to tell about the contents of our beliefs, and the manifest success of this activity shows that very often we succeed.

I will be concerned with the implications of this Lockean point for teleological theories of content, and for a dispute over the sense in which properties determine reference.

127

Frank Jackson

I start by saying something about what I mean by content. In section two, the longest section, I discuss the problem the Lockean point raises for certain versions of teleological theories of content. In section three, I argue that what we learn from Locke favours causal descriptivism over causal theories of reference proper.

1. Content and representation

The word 'content' is a term of art which has become especially prominent in recent discussions in the philosophy of mind and language. It means different things to different people. What I mean by it—and, I confess, what I think everyone should mean by it, but I am biased—is best approached by reflecting on the fact that thought and language represent. What I believe, for example, represents how I take things to be; what I desire represents how I want things to be; and what I say or write is how I am, in language, representing things as being (via, as Locke says, agreements to convey to one another how we take things to be).

Now, there is a crucial distinction between how some thought or sentence is representing things as being, and what makes it the case that the thought or sentence is so representing things as being. This distinction is crucial whenever we discuss structures that represent. For example, one question is how a petrol gauge is representing things as being—as it might be, that the tank is half-empty; but a quite separate question is what makes it the case that the gauge is representing that the tank is half-empty. It is in addressing the second question that we need to talk about such facts as that the gauge's pointer is half-way between E and F, that typically the position of the pointer and the level of petrol in the tank co-vary, and, on some views, what the gauge was designed to do (see e.g., Dretske, 1995). The same point applies to language. We need to keep apart the question of how a sentence represents things as being, from what makes it the case that it is so representing things as being. Discussions of the second question involve questions of word usages—in the sense of conventions as David Lewis (1969) puts it, intentions to communicate as H. P. Grice (1957) puts it, or voluntary agreements as Locke puts it—entered into by users of the sentence and of the various words that make it up, the beliefs (ideas) in the minds' of those users, and the inferential profile of the sentence in some given language.

However, discussions of the first question do not involve these questions. What I am saying about how things are when I say to you

'There is a tiger right behind you' is not something about my mind, or about word or sentence usage, or about inference patterns. What I am saying is something distinctly disturbing about how things are in the region of space just behind you.

By 'content', I mean how things are being represented as being—the first question. This means that, for us, content is, somehow or other, construable in terms of a division among possibilities. For to represent how things are is to divide what accords with how things are being represented as being from what does not accord with how things are being represented as being. In slogan form: no division, no representation. To bring the point out, reflect on how you would feel if someone offered to tell you where the best beer in Edinburgh was to be found, but nowhere in their offer could you detect which places they were giving ticks to and which they were giving crosses to. But to give ticks and crosses is to make a division.

The best-known account of content (in our sense, and from now on I'll suppress this qualification) is the possible worlds one made famous by Lewis (1986) and Robert Stalnaker (1984): roughly—that is, leaving aside niceties to do with egocentric content and self-ascription—the content of a thought or sentence is the set of possible worlds where it is true. And the most famous objection to this account is, of course, that it makes the content of logically equivalent sentences identical; it makes, for famous example, the content of the sentence 'A is an equilateral triangle' the same as that of 'A is an equiangular triangle'—and the same goes for the corresponding beliefs. Fortunately, we need take no stance on this issue. For all I argue here, the possibilities could be much more fine-grained than possible worlds—or (same point expressed in different words) the possible worlds could be thought of in a more-fine grained sense than is usual. For instance, the possibilities at which 'A is an equilateral triangle' are true and those at which 'A is an equiangular triangle' are true might be construed in a way that makes them differ: perhaps the first involves sides in a way in which the second involves angles. Indeed, this is one way of thinking of accounts of content that appeal to structured entities involving concepts: the structure for 'A is an equilateral triangle' differs from the structure for 'A is an equiangular triangle' in that one has the concept *side* where the other has the concept *angle*. In consequence, the first involves sides where the second involves angles.

Speaking for myself, I am happy to count the content of the sentence 'A is an equilateral triangle' and the sentence 'A is an equiangular triangle' identical, and likewise for the corresponding beliefs. We need to keep the contents of sentences and of beliefs sharply distinct from the sentences and beliefs themselves; we need, that is, to keep contents distinct from the vehicles of content, and I cannot see how to secure this with the various, more fine-grained accounts of possibilities. When I look at the details of these more fine-grained accounts of possibilities—ones that make the set of possibilities at which it is true that A is an equiangular triangle a different set from that at which it is true that A is an equilateral triangle, it seems to me that facts about content are being run together with facts about vehicles of content. But that is another story.

In what follows, we are going to think of content in terms of divisions among possibilities—the content of a thought or linguistic item is given by the possibilities at which it is true or obtains or is satisfied or ...—without enquiring closely into the nature of these possibilities. With this in mind, we can now turn to the lesson from Locke for the content of thought and, in particular, for teleological accounts of the content of thought.

2. The teleological theory of content

The teleological theory of content takes many forms, depending, *inter alia*, on whether it is selectional history that delivers the relevant *telos*, and on whether it is the *telos* of the state whose content is in question or the *telos* of some underlying structure that generated the state which is crucial. We will frame our discussion in terms of one well-known version of the teleological theory. I think that much of what I say would apply to other well-known versions of the theory but I won't pursue the point here. According to the version we will be concerned with, the contents of mental states are given by the selectional histories of certain brain states which are these mental states—perhaps in the sense of being identical with them or perhaps in the sense of constituting them. David Papineau expresses his version of this style of teleological theory by saying that, roughly, the belief that P is the state selected to co-vary with P, and the desire that P is the state selected to bring about P. (Papineau, 1993, p. 94). The division effected among possibilities is between those that the state is selected to co-vary with in the case of belief, and those it is selected to bring about in the case of desire, and the rest.

The important point for us is that content is given by an aspect of causal history, rather than by current causal and functional roles. It is, of course, this point that is prominent in the famous swampman debate. Swampman's states play the same current functional roles as our states; the reason that teleological theories have to deny intentionality to swampman—or, at least, have to deny that swampman's states have anything like the same intentional contents as our states—is that his states lack the kind of history teleological theories see as crucial for content.

Now, causal histories are not as epistemically transparent as current functional roles. I can see here and now what this lump of metal is doing—holding the door open, or stopping the papers from flying off my desk, or being the example I have chosen to make a philosophical point, or .... I cannot see here and now what this lump of metal was *designed* to do. Again, typically, whom Fred parties with is easy to ascertain; whom his great grandparents partied with is much harder to ascertain. Likewise, although I cannot see inside the skins of my fellow human beings, their interactions with the environment can make obvious the kind of functional roles their internal states are playing. By contrast, the selectional histories of those internal states are often far from obvious and only become known after hard work by evolutionary biologists.

The problem raised by Locke's point will now be obvious. Locke's point tells us that the way we acquired language and its evident utility depend on the contents of very many of our beliefs and desires being pretty much common knowledge; but if content is given by selectional history, these contents will be very far from common knowledge.

There are, it seems to me, basically two ways for teleologists to go in response to this point. One is to multiply contents; the other is to multiply ways of latching onto contents.

Teleologists might insist that our intentional states have both informational content and selectional content, meaning that they are in general different contents, not that they are the same content under different names. We have different divisions among possibilities, rather than the same division differently labelled. Informational contents are the contents we share around when we talk and write to each other. They are the ones Locke's point applies to. They are the ones we know via the way our fellows interact with their environments. They are the ones that are pretty much common knowledge in lots of cases. They are the ones people who have never heard of the theory of evolution know about. Selectional contents, on the other hand, are the states of affairs that play the selectional roles teleologists talk about. Thus, on Papineau's version, the selectional content of a belief would be, roughly, the state of affairs that it is selected to co-vary with, and the selectional content of a desire would be the state of affairs it is selected to bring about.

Frank Jackson

There are three problems (at least) for teleologists in multiplying contents. The first is that it makes the teleological theory less interesting. It started life as a bold claim about *the* content of intentional states. It is now a claim that we can use selectional history to identify *one* of the contents of intentional states. Teleologists might restore boldness by insisting that selectional content is the really important content. Although our beliefs, for example, have in general two contents, it is their selectional contents that are important. But now one has to wonder what the word 'important' means here. Informational content is the one that matters for finding our way around the world, for passing on information about it, and the only one many of us know about.

The second problem for multiplying contents is one of internal consistency. The arguments used by teleologists are not of the 'let a thousand flowers bloom' kind. They are explicitly designed to show that the alternative accounts of content fail.

The third problem is that it makes what we believe and desire indeterminate to a substantial extent, for the contents of our beliefs and desires are *what* we believe and desire. We can live with the idea that there is some imprecision in what we believe and desire, and with the idea that, in the case of creatures whose powers of detection and rational action fall a long way short of ours—frogs, would be an example—there is *substantial* indeterminacy in what they believe and desire. However, it is a brave person who thinks we are in the same kind of position as the frogs.

In view of these problems, I think that teleologists should go the second way in response to the Lockean challenge. They should multiply ways of latching onto contents, rather than the contents themselves. Here is one way the second way might be fleshed out. There is just one content for each intentional state—where this, of course, needs to be read in a way that does not rule out cases where the content is to some degree imprecise—and it is given by selectional history. If Papineau's version of teleonomy is right, *the* content of my belief is the state of affairs it is selected to co-vary with. However, in the case of behaviourally sophisticated, complex organisms like us, the contents that selectional considerations identify are, except in highly unusual circumstances (of which swampman's is the most extreme and famous illustration), one and the same as those identified in the way we all grasp, the way that draws on a state's more or less current functional roles. In the case of less behaviourally sophisticated creatures—the frogs I mentioned a moment ago might be an example, with their notorious inability to distinguish flies from lead shot—this is not true, but it is, runs the second way, true for us.

This explains how content gets to be common knowledge; it does so by virtue of the fact that we can identify it through 'folk' functional roles, as we might call them. Here, the term 'folk functional roles' is simply a tag for the roles which interactions with the environment tell us about and which we draw on to assign content. We do not assign content by looking at tea leaves or reading the stars; nor do we assign content by magic, or by telepathy, or by wild guessing—or if we do use one of these methods, we do a very bad job. Somehow or other, we assign content by drawing on what people do, in the sense of how they move through their worlds. How we do it, the extent to which we implicitly infer facts about internal processing as well as more obvious 'external' facts, the sense in which it is correct to use the term 'inference' to characterize what is going on, and the extent to which we draw on our own cases, perhaps carrying out some kind of simulation, are among the issues that excite much controversy, but we can set these issues to one side here.[1]

The second way remains a version of teleonomy because it insists that, although for us the states of affairs that play the selectional roles are typically one and the same as those that play the folk functional roles, when they differ, the first 'win'; when they differ, the contents of the intentional states in question are given by the states of affairs that play the selectional roles, not those that play the folk roles.

Here I will press two objections to this second way.[2] The first objection is that this second way is inconsistent with one of the main arguments given for teleological theories of content. This main argument is that, out of the at-all-plausible approaches to content, only selectional histories identify contents with sufficient precision. Many teleologists' argue, to take one well-known example, that they alone can handle the 'embarrassment of riches' problem for functionalist treatments of content—the problem that one and the same state has many different, possible and actual, causes and effects. Here is Papineau's critical discussion of the idea that some version of 'arms length' or common-sense functionalism might explain how our intentional states might be about happenings in the world around us.

... why not [in the account of functionalism] simply extend our causal net to allow more distal causes of perception, on the input

[1] For discussion of these issues, see Jackson 1999.
[2] For an earlier version of the first point and for more on the various ways that the teleological theory might be understood, see Jackson and Braddon-Mitchell 1997.

Frank Jackson

side, and more distal effects of behaviour, on the output side? This would allow us to analyse the truth conditions of beliefs as those distal circumstances which cause them, and the satisfaction conditions of desires as those distal states of affairs they give rise to ... (Papineau, 1993, p. 58).

This move, however, is fatally afflicted by the disease known as 'disjunctivitis'. The belief that there is an ice-cream in front of you can be caused not only by a real ice-cream, but also by a plastic ice-cream, or a hologram of an ice-cream, or and so on. So, on the current suggestion, the belief in question ought to represent either-a-real-ice-cream-*or*-a-plastic-one-*or*-any-of-the-other-things-that-might-fool-you. Which of course it doesn't.

Similarly with desires. The results which follow any given desire include not only the real object of the desire, but also various unintended consequences. So the current suggestion would imply that the object of any desire is the disjunction of its real object with all those unintended consequences. Which of course it isn't. So even if we widen functionalism's causal roles to include distal causes and effects, we still need somehow to winnow out, from the various causes that give rise to beliefs, and the various results that eventuate from desires, those which the beliefs are about, and which the desires are for.

This is where an appeal to teleological considerations seems to yield a natural and satisfying answer. We can pick out a desire's real satisfaction condition as that effect which it is the desire's biological purpose to produce. And, similarly, we can pick out the real truth conditions of a belief as that which it is the biological purpose of the belief to be co-present with. (Papineau, 1993, p. 58).

This argument cannot be pressed by an advocate of the second way. The second way's plausibility depends precisely on the claim that folk functional roles, which are of course the kinds of roles that figure in arm's length and common-sense functionalism, do serve to identify content. The leading idea is precisely that the folk roles pick out the very same contents as the selectional roles.

My second objection to the second way turns on the point that Shakespeare's opinions about what his friends were thinking were often justified. I said that the second way holds that, for behaviourally sophisticated creatures like us, the folk roles typically pick out the contents of intentional states. But, in fact, it needs to hold, in addition, that this fact is a known one. To meet Locke's point, teleologists must hold that it is common knowledge that the folk roles pick out the contents of intentional states. Symptoms of measles do not tell us about measles unless we know that they are symptoms of measles.

We have learned to ask certain causal questions of proffered theories of intentional states and their contents; we ask, for example, whether some proffered theory can make good sense of how content properties are causally relevant to behaviour. I think we should also ask an epistemic question. We should expect from any proffered theory of intentional states and their contents, a good answer to why the folk roles deliver, and are known to deliver, so much reliable information about intentional states and their contents.

How might teleologists who favour the second way answer this question; how might they explain why we are justified in holding that the folk roles often tell us what someone believes and desires? They cannot say that it is a matter of meaning that they do—that would be to turn their view into a version of common-sense or analytical or arm's length functionalism. Nor can they say that we have established, as an empirical matter of fact, that the contents picked out by folk roles and the contents picked out by selectional roles are, in cases of creatures like us, very often the same, and that this fact justifies us in using the more readily available folk roles to determine what people believe and desire. This would mean that only those who have done the needed research would be justified in using folk roles to determine the contents of subjects' beliefs and desires, whereas in fact nearly all humans are justified in using the folk roles to determine content.

As far as I can see, the only explanation available for the teleologist is one in terms of reference-fixing by folk roles on biological kinds. (And this is, in fact, Papineau's view, as I understand it.) Here is an analogy to make the key idea clear. Why were people in 1600 justified in believing that the sea contained water although they would not have been justified in believing that it contained H_2O? Because they were justified in believing that the sea contained stuff of a kind that satisfied the reference-fixers (or folk markers, as they are sometimes called) for 'water'. They were justified, that is, in believing that there was an underlying natural kind common to most of the samples of potable, clear etc. liquids they were acquainted with—the kind that famously turned out to be H_2O— and that the sea contained it. In similar fashion, it might be argued that the folk roles for intentional content reference-fix on the states of affairs that play the important roles for creatures of our kind, and that the relevant important roles for creatures of our kind turn out to be selectional ones. For example, for creatures like us, the view would be, if we take Papineau's version of teleonomy, that the folk

135

roles associated with believing that P reference-fix on the role of being selected to co-vary with P. It is then necessary a posteriori that what a person believes is given by the state of affairs the belief state is selected to co-vary with.

Here is how the suggestion looks in display form:

S believes that P iff S is in the relevant important state for creatures of our kind that plays the folk role for belief that P. (Claim about reference fixing)

The relevant important state for creatures of our kind that plays the folk role for belief that P = the state with such and such a selectional relationship to P. (Empirical fact)

Therefore, S believes that P iff S is in such and such a selectional relationship to P. (Necessary *a posteriori* truth)

In Papineau's version, such and such a selectional relationship to P will come roughly to being selected to co-vary with P, but other varieties of teleonomy will favour some other articulation of the key, empirical second premise.

The problem with this reference-fixing account is that it makes it obscure why selectional roles count as the 'real' determiners of content, rather than the folk roles. For it is crucial to this account that premise one—the premise which identifies content in terms of folk roles—is true.

What about the suggestion I earlier put in the mouth of advocates of the second way—'although for [creatures like] us the states of affairs that play the selectional roles are typically one and the same as those that play the folk functional roles, when they differ, the first "win"; when they differ, the contents of the intentional states in question are given by the states of affairs that play the selectional roles...'? There are, however, two equally good ways of stating, for creatures where the states differ, the conditions under which they believe that P. We might say that these creatures count as believing that P because they are in a state which plays the selectional role for belief that P—roughly, if we follow Papineau, being selected to co-vary with P. Or we might say that they count as believing that P because they are in a state that plays the biologically important role of the state which in us plays the folk role for belief that P. The same point can be made about what makes water on Twin Earth water. You might say it is water because it is H_2O; or you might say it is water because it is the same natural kind as the potable, colourless etc stuff of our acquaintance on Earth. Either answer is as good as the other. So it remains obscure why we should call the resulting theory a teleological one rather than a folk one.

The point is especially pressing in the light of two problems—the first very familiar; the second less so—for thinking of the selectional roles as the really important ones. What we believe matters to us, and that points to current roles, not history, as being what is important. What I want, and I am sure that I am not alone in this, are states that reliably co-vary here and now with nice and with nasty things in my environment. That way I have the best chance of getting the nice things and of avoiding the nasty ones. A history of co-variation and of its playing a selectional role, is not, in itself, nearly as important for getting the nice things and avoiding the nasty ones.[3]

Secondly, a big part of what makes it true that a state's function is selected for is what happens to creatures that lack the state in question. A familiar concern for the teleological theory is the fact that when a structure which has a distinctive survival-enhancing role first arises, say through a random mutation, it has no content because there has been no time for selectional pressures to bite. The role it plays needs time to become a role that is selected for. Do we say that it has no content, though it will 'grow' to have content as time passes? Or do we say that it gets content in some derived sense by the very fact that it will grow to have content in some non-derived sense? The worry I wish to press, though, arises from considering the process whereby it becomes selected for. A big part of the process crucially concerns the nasty things that happen to creatures that missed out on the mutation. Do we really want to say that what someone believes or desires depends a lot on what happens to unfortunate others, perhaps largely causally isolated others?

Here is another way of putting the case that the reference-fixing account makes it obscure why selectional roles count as the 'real' determiners of content, rather than the folk roles. Consider the possible world where the underlying, important kinds for the creatures that have states playing the folk roles are 'creationist' ones. This world would be a kind of Twin Earth with 'creationism' for XYZ. It is the world in which the telos comes from God and not evolution. In this world, the right version of the displayed argument above is:

S believes that *P* iff *S* is in the relevant important state for creatures of our kind that plays the folk role for belief that *P*. (Claim about reference fixing)

[3] For more on this objection, see Jackson and Braddon-Mitchell (1997).

Frank Jackson

The relevant important state for creatures of our kind that plays the folk role for belief that P = the state with such and such a relationship to God. (Empirical fact)

Therefore, S believes that P iff S is in such and such a relationship to God.
(Necessary *a posteriori* truth)

In this world, the word 'belief' does not mean what our word 'belief' means any more than 'twater' means the same as 'water'. But what sense can the teleonomist who goes down the reference-fixing path give to its meaning being "worse" than ours, being any the less a word for an intentional state properly speaking?

3. Choosing between causal descriptivism and causal theories of reference

I now turn to the significance of our Lockean reading for theories of reference.

John Bigelow (1988) says that truth supervenes on being; by extension, reference supervenes on nature. Of course, there is a trivial sense in which reference supervenes on nature: if 't' refers to a and not to b, a differs from b in being that to which 't' refers. But I take it that the supervenience doctrine is highly plausible in a non-trivial sense also. If 't' refers to a and not to b, there must be something about a's nature as opposed to b's, in some wide but not trivial sense of 'nature', which makes this true.

Another way of putting essentially the same point is to say that there is no such thing as *bare* reference. A familiar issue in the philosophy of counterfactuals is whether a counterfactual can be barely true. Suppose that it is true that had such and such happened, then so and so would have happened. Can this be barely true, or must it be the case that, in some non-trivial sense, there must be something in virtue of which it is the case that had such and such happened, then so and so would have happened? My inclination is to deny that counterfactuals can be barely true, but I am much more confident in denying that reference can barely obtain. If 't' refers to a and not to b, there must be something about a that makes it so.

But if reference supervenes on nature, this means that a thing's properties determine that a term refers to it. For a thing's nature is simply a matter of its properties, in the easy-going sense of 'property' on which there is a property for every way things might be, including highly disjunctive ones. The sixty-four dollar

138

question, now, is whether these properties which determine reference are, or are not, properties in the minds of those who use the terms. Aristotle has properties that make it the case that 'Aristotle' refers to it, but is it or is it not the case that these properties are the properties associated with the word in the minds of those who use the word?

This question is central to the dispute between causal theorists of reference and causal descriptivism. Both views agree that 'Aristotle' does not refer to the thing which has the properties that first come to mind when Aristotle is mentioned. We learnt this from Saul Kripke (1980), though not in the sense that it was a brand new piece of knowledge. Kripke convinced us by appealing to our intuitions about how to describe possible cases where Aristotle failed to do the various things for which he is famous. In each case, we agreed with him that we should say that it was Aristotle who failed to do the things for which he is famous. This means that there is a sense in which we knew all along that the reference of 'Aristotle' does not go by the properties for which he is famous. Kripke make explicit to us something which we knew implicitly.

Causal theorists of reference and causal descriptivists also agree that the reference of 'Aristotle' is to the thing which has, inter alia, certain causal properties, including perhaps being a certain kind of causal origin of our usage of the word 'Aristotle'. The dispute between them is over what makes this true. Causal descriptivists hold, and causal theorists deny, that what makes this true is an association in the minds of users of the word with certain properties, including this causal property.

Locke's point favours causal descriptivism—and, as far as I know, the only place this is noted is in a footnote by Lewis (1997, p. 339, n. 22). Things could have had different names from those they actually have, and would have had different names had we entered appropriately-different arrangements for communicating how we take things to be. But, as Locke says, arrangements concerning we-know-not-what make no sense and could not be of any use to us. When Sydney got the name 'Sydney' instead of the name 'Melbourne'—as it would have, had a different naming tradition been followed back then—the namers knew what they were agreeing to name 'Sydney', and knew this independently of knowing that it is named 'Sydney'. But this requires associating properties with Sydney, including the ones the namers were attaching to the name 'Sydney' instead of to the name 'Melbourne'. There is no way of knowing which thing Sydney is independently of knowing its properties.

Frank Jackson

The point here does not turn on assuming the metaphysical doctrine that a thing is nothing more than its properties, whatever exactly that doctrine comes to. It turns on the epistemological doctrine that we cannot know that we are talking about a rather than b unless we know properties that discriminate between them.

4. Is content that transparent?

When I follow Locke and urge that we very often know what people believe and that this fact underlies our ability to acquire, and the utility of, language, I am not, of course, suggesting that we are infallible, or that we know in full detail what people are thinking or mean by their words. The claim is simply that we very often know, near enough, what people are thinking and mean by their words.

It is sometimes suggested that what we learned from Kripke (1980) and from Hilary Putnam (1975) has the consequence that what people are thinking, the contents of their thoughts, are much more opaque than I am allowing. In particular, I have come across the following line of argument. (I have, though, no reason to think that Kripke or Putnam would endorse it.) 'It took the discovery that water is H_2O to show that the content of "There is water hereabouts" is the same as the content of "There is H_2O hereabouts"; and the same goes for the thought that there is water hereabouts, and the thought that there is H_2O hereabouts. Further, this example is one among many. It follows that the contents of our thoughts and words are highly dependent on empirical facts in ways that imply that error and gross ignorance about what we are thinking and saying is endemic.'

However, as we are using the term 'content', it is not true that the content of 'There is water hereabouts' is the same as the content of 'There is H_2O hereabouts'. When English speakers use the sentence 'There is water hereabouts', the claim they are making about how things are is not the same as the claim they make when they use the sentence 'There is H_2O hereabouts'. If it were, the discovery that water is H_2O would not have been a discovery. The issue the example of water and H_2O raises, and the same goes for the many similar examples, is not whether serious error about content is endemic but how to formulate 'the division among possibilities' approach to content (in the sense of how things are represented as being) in the face of examples like this one. We had better not count the content of 'There is water hereabouts' and 'There is H_2O hereabouts' as one and the same on the ground that the sentences are true in the very same possible worlds.

140

One possible response, accordingly, is that although to represent is to make a division among entities, these entities should not be thought of as possible worlds as in the Lewis-Stalnaker scheme. Speaking for myself, though, I prefer a different response to the issue.

This response argues that the set of possible worlds that gives the content (in the sense of how things are being represented as being) of 'There is water hereabouts' is a different set from that which gives the content of 'There is H_2O hereabouts', despite the fact that they are true in just the same worlds. And it does this for an independently powerful reason. When we use the sentence 'There is water' to make a claim about how things are, we are making a claim about how things actually are. To give putative information about how things are is to give putative information about how they actually are (which is not to say that we can't and don't sometimes give information about how things would have been had ...). This means that if we wish to capture the content of 'There is water' in terms of possible worlds, in the sense which connects most closely to the information about how things are that we use the sentence to transmit, the possible worlds that are in accord with the sentence in the required sense are those which satisfy the condition: if this is how things actually are, the sentence is true. In other words, the partition the sentence effects qua vehicle of representation is not between the worlds where it is true and those where it is false, but between the worlds such that if they are actual, the sentence is true, and those such that if they are actual, the sentence is false. So, when we think about how to capture the content of 'There is water', we need to think about the worlds such that if they are actual, then 'There is water' is true. But if (*if*) Twin Earth is the actual world, if the way things actually are is that it is XYZ which is the clear, potable liquid that fills the ocean, acquaintance with which led us to coin the word 'water' (and the corresponding words in other languages) and there is no H_2O present at all, that sentence is true. True, if, as we well know, the actual world has H_2O playing the 'water' role, then the sentence 'There is water' is false at Twin Earth; it is irrelevant that XYZ exists in Twin Earth and plays the 'water' role there. But if we make the supposition that the way things actually are has XYZ playing the 'water' role, that is to suppose, in effect, that it 'turned out' that water is XYZ; which is why the sentence is true at Twin Earth under the supposition that Twin Earth is the actual world.

In sum, the content of 'There is water' is that there is stuff playing the 'water' role. Or, to put the matter in the terms of Kripke

Frank Jackson

(1980), the content of 'There is water' is given by the reference-fixers for 'water'. Or, in still other words, the content (in the sense of how things are being represented as being) of 'There is water' is the A intension of the sentence, (Jackson, 1998) or is the diagonal proposition (Stalnaker, 1978), or is the primary intension (Chalmers, 1996).

Thus, the possible worlds approach to representational meaning allows the content of 'There is water' to be different from the content of 'There is H_2O'. However, whatever you think of the way just sketched of how a possible worlds approach might capture the content of 'There is water hereabouts' and distinguish it from that of 'There is H_2O hereabouts', it is clear that the sentences do differ in how they serve to represent things as being—and the same goes for the thoughts we English speakers convey by using the sentences. So, any objection that starts from the claim that they are alike in content starts from somewhere false. At most, we have here a problem for possible-worlds treatments of content, not for the view that we know a lot about what people think and about what they mean in the sense of how they are representing the world to be with the words and sentences they produce.

Bibliography

Bigelow, J. 1988. *The Reality of Numbers* (Oxford: Clarendon Press).
Chalmers, D. 1996. *The Conscious Mind* (Oxford: Oxford University Press).
Cole, P. (ed.) 1978. *Syntax and Semantics: Pragmatics, vol. 9* (New York: Academic Press).
Dretske, F. 1995. *Naturalizing the Mind* (Cambridge, MA: MIT Press).
Grice, H. P. 1957. 'Meaning', *Philosophical Review*, **66**, 377–88.
Jackson, F. and Braddon-Mitchell, D. 1997. 'The Teleological Theory of Content', *Australasian Journal of Philosophy* **75**, **4**, 474–89.
Jackson, F. 1998. *From Metaphysics to Ethics* (Oxford: Clarendon Press).
Jackson, F. 1999. 'All That Can Be at Issue in the Theory-theory Simulation Debate,' *Philosophical Papers*. **XXVIII**, **2**, 77–95.
Kripke, S. 1980. *Naming and Necessity.* (Oxford: Basil Blackwell).
Lewis, D. 1969. *Convention.* (Cambridge, MA: Harvard University Press).
Lewis, D. 1986. *On the Plurality of Worlds.* (Oxford: Basil Blackwell).
Lewis, D. 1997. 'Naming the Colours', *Australasian Journal of Philosophy*, **75**, **3**, 323–42.
Locke, J. 1975. *An Essay Concerning Human Understanding.* (ed.) P. H. Nidditch (New York: Oxford University Press).
Papineau, D. 1993. *Philosophical Naturalism* (Oxford: Basil Blackwell).

Putnam, H. 1975. 'The meaning of "Meaning",' in *Language, Mind and Reality: Philosophical Papers, Volume 2* (Cambridge: Cambridge University Press), pp. 215–71.

Stalnaker, R. 1978. 'Assertion.' in P. Cole, (ed.) *Syntax and Semantics: Pragmatics, vol. 9* (New York: Academic Press), pp. 314–32.

Stalnaker, R. 1984. *Inquiry* (Cambridge MA: MIT Press).

The Evolution of Means-End Reasoning

DAVID PAPINEAU

1. Introduction

When I woke up a few days ago, the following thoughts ran through my mind. 'I need a haircut. If I don't get it first thing this morning, I won't have another chance for two weeks. But if I go to the barber down the road, he'll want to talk to me about philosophy. So I'd better go to the one in Camden Town. The tube will be very crowded, though. Still, it's a nice day. Why don't I just walk there? It will only take twenty minutes. So I'd better put on these shoes now, have breakfast straight away, and then set out for Camden.'

This is a paradigm case of what I shall call 'means-end reasoning'. In such reasoning, we consider the consequences of various courses of action, and choose the course best suited to our overall purposes. I take it to be uncontroversial that all human beings are capable of such means-end reasoning, and that this kind of reasoning guides many of our actions. Indeed I take it that this power of means-end reasoning is one of the most important differences—if not *the* most important difference—between humans and other animals.

Yet for some reason this topic has become unfashionable. Means-end reasoning seems to have disappeared from the theoretical agenda of many of those you would expect to be most interested, namely those who work on human cognition in a comparative or evolutionary context. There are now large industries devoted to theory of mind, to language, and to other 'modules' putatively characteristic of human cognition. But means-end reasoning itself gets brushed under the carpet, as somehow not quite the thing to talk about in modish theoretical society.

In this paper I want to make a plea for this somewhat old-fashioned topic. While language, and theory of mind, and no doubt other modules, have clearly played a crucial role in human evolution, I think that as good a case can be made for the significance of means-end reasoning. It is of course a tricky matter to chart the exact evolutionary dependencies between the different cognitive abilities peculiar to humans, and the remarks I make on this specific topic towards the end of this paper will be abstract and

David Papineau

speculative at best. But by that stage I hope at least to have persuaded you that means-end reasoning is a evolutionarily important topic in its own right.

My first task will be to be more specific about what I mean by 'means-end reasoning'. Care on this point is obviously needed, if I am to persuade you that 'means-end reasoning' is important for human evolution. For, if we set the standards too low, 'means-end reasoning' will be widespread throughout the animal kingdom, and not a peculiarly human adaptation. After all, nearly all animals have *some* ways of selecting behaviours which are appropriate to current needs and circumstances. Nor, in the other direction, will it do to set the standards too high, as requiring literacy or calculation, say. For then there will be no reason to suppose that 'means-end reasoning' has anything to do with human *biology*, however important it might be for the development of higher civilization.

Accordingly, in the next two sections I shall aim to specify an understanding of 'means-end reasoning' which is consonant with my claims about its importance for human evolution. After that I shall attempt to defend these claims

Before proceeding, however, it will perhaps be worth commenting on one specific influence that has diverted current theoretical fashion away from means-end reasoning. In many contemporary minds, I suspect, 'means-end reasoning' is thought of as antithetical to 'modularity'. This is because means-end-reasoning tends to be associated with the kind of general-purpose learner-and-problem-solver that traditional psychology took to be the seat of all animal intelligence. Enthusiastic advocates of modularity, however, reject this domain-general conception of animal intelligence, and argue that all real advances in cognitive power, and in particular the distinctive features of human psychology, consist of purpose-built 'modules' selected for specific intellectual tasks (cf. Cosmides and Tooby, 1992, p. 39 *et passim*). And so enthusiastic modularists tend to be impatient with talk of means-end reasoning, because they see it as a return to the bad old days of general-purpose learning and problem-solving.

However, I do not think of 'means-end reasoning' as opposed to modularity in this way. Insofar as there is a well-formed antithesis between general-purpose traditional mechanisms and modules, I would be inclined to place means-end reasoning on the side of the modules. Means-end reasoning may be domain-general in its *content*, in the sense that there is no limit to the kinds of information that it can operate with. But the same could be said of our linguistic abilities, yet these are widely taken to be the paradigm of 'modular' powers.

146

Moreover, means-end reasoning, as I think of it, is not to be thought of as providing a general interface between perceptual inputs and behavioural outputs, along the lines of the non-modular 'central system' that Jerry Fodor interposed between perception and action in his original *The Modularity of Mind* (1983). Rather, I take means-end reasoning to be an add-on that arrived late in evolution, in service of specific needs, and which itself interfaces with whichever pre-existing mechanisms co-ordinate perception and action.

Sceptics often respond to the modularist metaphor of the mind as a 'Swiss Army knife' by asking what decides which blades to use in which circumstances. This is a reasonable enough question, and some of my remarks later will indicate possible answers. But means-end reasoning itself does not play this role. Rather, means-end reasoning is a specialized mechanism, which gets activated when appropriate by whichever processes do co-ordinate the different aspects of cognition. From this perspective, means-end reasoning is simply another fancy tool in the Swiss Army knife, not some meta-device that co-ordinates the whole show.

2. Before Means-End Rationality

These last remarks are intended only as a pointer to my overall story. Details of the plot will be filled in as we proceed. The first step is to explain in more detail what I mean by 'means-end reasoning'. In this section I shall attack this question from the bottom up, so to speak. I shall consider how behaviour might be adapted to circumstances in animals who clearly lack means-end reasoning in any sense. By this means I hope to identify a sense of means-end reasoning in which there are interesting questions about its evolutionary emergence. The strategy, in effect, will be to isolate an important sense of means-end reasoning by considering what is lacking in those animals who manage without it.

I shall proceed abstractly, and in stages. I shall only consider very general features of cognitive design. And I shall start with the simplest possible such designs, and then proceed to more sophisticated ones.

Level 0—'Monotomata'—*Do R*

At the very simplest level, level zero, so to speak, would be the kind of animal that always does the same thing, **R**. For example, it might

David Papineau

move around at random, blindly opening and closing its mouth parts, thereby ingesting anything that happens to get in its way.

Level 1—'Opportunists'—If C, do R

A step up from this would be animals who suit their behaviour to immediate conditions **C**, saving their energy for situations where their behaviour **R** will bear fruit. For example, they move their mouth parts only when they detect the presence of food. (In such cases we can expect also that the behaviour **R** will itself be 'shaped' by sensitivity to conditions. The frog's fabled fly-catching behaviour fits this bill. Not only do the frogs shoot their tongues out at specific *times*, namely when the environment offers some promise of food; they also shoot their tongues out in specific *directions*, towards the point where the food is promised.)

Level 2—'Needers'—If C and D, do R

At the next level will be animals whose behaviour is sensitive, not just to current opportunities, but also to current needs. For example, we can imagine insect-eaters who don't shoot their tongues out at passing targets *unless* they also register some nutritional lack. Apparently frogs are not like this, and so are prone to overfeed. Even after their nutritional needs are satisfied, they still shoot their tongues out at passing flies. Still, even if frogs manage without a need-sensitive cognitive design, it can manifestly be advantageous to evolve one, and many animals have clearly done so.

Before proceeding to the next level of complexity, it will be well to enter a word of caution. It is natural, and indeed often very helpful, to characterize simple cognitive designs in representational terms, and I shall do so throughout this paper. But there are dangers of putting more into the representational description than the specified design warrants, and mistaking overblown representational description for serious explanation. In principle we should always demonstrate carefully that attributions of representational content are fully warranted. It would make this paper far too long to do this properly at every stage, but I shall try as far as I can to ensure that my representational descriptions are grounded in explicit specifications of cognitive design.

By way of illustrating the danger, consider the distinction I have just introduced between **C**s, which signify sensitivity to environmental '*conditions*', and **D**s, which register current *needs* (and so might thus be thought of as akin to 'desires' or, more cautiously, as '*drives*').

148

It might seem entirely natural to distinguish informational **C**s from motivational **D**s in this way. However, nothing I have yet said justifies any such contrast. After all, **C** and **D** appear quite symmetrically in the schematic disposition which heads this sub-section—**If C and D, do R**. So far we have been given no basis for treating these states as playing distinct roles in the regulation of behaviour.

Now I have raised this point, let me pursue it for a moment. To focus the issue, let me stipulate that both the **C**s and the **D**s are henceforth to be understood as *internal* states which trigger resulting behaviour **R**. (There must be some such internal states, if distal conditions and needs are to affect behaviour.) At first sight there may seem to be an obvious basis for distinguishing motivational **D**s from informational **C**s. If some **D** is triggered by low blood sugar level, say, then won't it play a distinctively motivational role, by contrast with an informational **C** that, say, registers passing insects? Isn't the **D** required to *activate* the animal, by contrast with the **C**, which just provides factual information, and so gives no motivational 'push'? But this is an illusory contrast. The **C** is equally required to activate the animal—however low its blood sugar, the animal won't stick its tongue out until there is something to catch. So far everything remains symmetrical, and both **C** and **D** should be counted as simultaneously motivational and informational—as 'pushmi-pullyu' states, in Ruth Millikan's terminology (Millikan, 1996). They can both be thought of imperatively, as saying 'Do **R** (if the other state is also on)', and also indicatively, as saying 'Here is an occasion for doing **R** (if the other state is also on)'.

A substantial division between motivational and informational states only arises when there is some extra structure behind the **C**s and **D**s. Without going into too much detail, let me give the rough idea. A state **C** will become informational rather than motivational when it ceases to be tied to any particular behaviour, and instead provides information that is used by many different behavioural dispositions. We can expect behaviourally complex animals to develop sensory states which respond reliably to external objects and properties and which are available to trigger an open-ended range of activities. This will be especially advantageous when animals are capable of learning (see level 4 below). When an internal state **C** ceases in this way to be devoted to any specific behavioural routines, it will cease to have any imperative content, and can be viewed as purely informational. (Cf. Millikan, forthcoming.)

Motivational states can become specialized in a converse way. Here again the states will cease to be tied to particular behaviours.

David Papineau

But in the motivational case this won't be because the states come to provide generally useful information, but rather because they acquire the distinctive role of signalling that certain *results* are needed. The reason this detaches motivational states from specific behaviours is that different behaviours will be effective for those results in different circumstances. Such motivational **D**s can still perhaps be thought of as having some informational content—blood sugar is low, maybe—but they will be different from purely informational **C**s, given that they will have the special responsibility of mobilizing whichever behaviours will produce some requisite result, whereas informational **C**s will have no such result to call their own.

Level 3—'Choosers'—If Ci and Di, do Ri, WHEN Di is the dominant need

Once animals have states whose role is to register needs, then there is potential for another level of complexity. It would be advantageous to have a mechanism to decide priorities when some **Ci** and **Di** prompt behaviour **Ri**, and another **Cj** and **Dj** prompt incompatible behaviour **Rj**. The obvious system is somehow to compare **Di** with **Dj**, and select between **R**s depending on which need is more important. It is not hard to imagine mechanisms which would so rank needs in either a qualitative or quantitative way.

Level 4—'Learners'—AFTER experience shows that Ci, Di and Ri lead to reward, then (as before): If Ci and Di, do Ri, when Di is the dominant need

So far I have implicitly been supposing that the prompting **C**s and **D**s are 'hard-wired' to the responsive behavioural **R**s—that is, that the relevant **C**, **D**→**R** links have been established by inter-generational genetic evolution and will develop in any animal which matures normally. *Learning* adds a further level of animal sophistication. By 'learning' here I simply mean that the **C**, **D**→**R** links can be influenced by the animals' specific experience of which behaviours produce which results in which circumstances. The obvious way to allow this is via mechanisms which will reinforce **C**, **D**→**R** links just in case **R** in **D** and **C** leads to some specific result.

In the schema above I have characterized the relevant reinforcing result simply as 'reward'. This raises a number of issues. One is whether the removal, or reduction, of the need-registering **D** is always implicated in the 'reward' which reinforces the likelihood of **R** given **C** and **D** in future. A mechanism along these lines is suggested by the fact that many drives, like hunger, or thirst, have functions (ingestion of food, or water) whose fulfilments are standardly necessary and sufficient for the reduction of the drives themselves. So learning mechanisms in which these drive reductions led to reinforcement would thereby select behaviour which was suited to fulfilling the functions of the drives (that is, getting food, or water).

Still, it is not obvious that all drives are designed to produce results which will then, as a matter of course, assuage those drives. For example, when there are signs of danger, an animal will need to identify anything unusual in its environment. Suppose there is some drive **D**—alertness, vigilance—which registers the need to identify anything unusual, and whose function is to get the animal to make such identifications. It wouldn't seem a good idea for this drive to be assuaged whenever it succeeds in fulfilling its function. If you find something unusual, you should become more vigilant, not less (and, conversely, your vigilance should be quieted if you fail to find anything unusual). More generally, there seems no reason to rule out drives which will continue through their own fulfilments, or even be enhanced by them. However, if there are such drives, then any associated learning mechanisms will not be able to use the drive's disappearance as a source of reinforcement, since this disappearance won't provide a good proxy for the drive's fulfilling its function. Rather, the learning mechanism will have to work with some other sign of a behaviour's being an effective means to the drive's fulfilment (such as actually finding something unusual).

I am not sure whether nature has in fact bequeathed any such leaning mechanisms to the animal kingdom, or whether all actual animal learning mechanisms work with drive reductions as reinforcers. A further issue, which arises whatever the answer to this question, is whether all animal learning derives from a single mechanism, which reduces all the drive-specific reinforcers (sating of hunger, quenching of thirst, perception of something unusual) to a common currency (the release of opiates, say), or whether there are a number of distinct learning mechanisms, one for each drive, each of which attaches behaviours to its own drive, depending on which behaviours have proved effective in past experience in fulfilling that drive's specific function. The latter option would allow the more sophisticated control of behaviour, but again it is an empirical question how far nature has availed itself of this opportunity.

At this stage I propose to stop my initial classification of cognitive structures. We have enough Levels to be getting on with. They will provide a basis, in the next section, for an initial characterization of 'means-end reasoning'.

But before proceeding it will be worth pausing briefly to remark

David Papineau

on the way that even these initial levels have shown the category of *drive* to be surprisingly many-sided. In a sense *drive* is a primitive version of *desire*, and I shall say a bit more in section 4(v) below about the extra elements in desire. But even before we get to the more sophisticated level of desires, drives themselves turn out to have a confusing number of facets. At the primitive Level 1, when need-registering drives are not really distinguishable from states which register environmental conditions, 'drives' simply signal the current appropriateness of some specific behaviour. Once drives do become so distinguishable, at Level 2, as registers of need rather than conditions, they will function to prompt whichever behaviours will satisfy those needs in current circumstances. A further role, which characterizes level 3, is to compete with other drives, when those other drives prompt incompatible behaviours. Note that the Level 2 role does not guarantee the Level 3 role: we can imagine an animal, like Buridan's ass, who functions well when only one need is active, but freezes in the face of more; more realistically, we can imagine animals who resolve competition between drives in some arbitrary non-functional way. And at Level 4 we find drives which play a yet further role, by reinforcing behaviours which lead to the reduction of drive (though this will only work, as I observed, for drives whose fulfilment leads naturally to their extinction). Again, this Level 4 role is not guaranteed by the roles at lower Levels, since the lower roles can be present in animals who do no learning at all.

At first, the notion of 'drive' can seem simple enough. But it turns out to pack in a number of dissociable features, which won't always be found together in real animals.[1]

[1] This complexity generates a corresponding uncertainty about the precise representational contents of drives. Even if we can distinguish drives as a kind from purely informational states, along the lines indicated when discussing Level 2, this does not yet decide which specific objects drives aim at. Perhaps we should deem them to be directed at any specific behaviours they may prompt (feeding behaviour, say); or perhaps their content is the specific results they are designed to achieve (ingesting of food); or perhaps, again, they represent the possibly different effects which will reinforce associated behaviours (such as raising blood sugar). I myself would argue in favour of the second answer, the specific result the drive is designed to achieve, given that this is the most basic function of any state which properly qualifies as a drive. But the rationale for assigning specific contents is a messy business, not only for motivational states like drives, but also for informational ones, and in what follows I shall not aim explicitly to justify any such specific attributions. For those readers who feel queasy about loose representational talk, I can only say again that I shall always aim to ground my attributions of representation in explicit specifications of cognitive design.

The Evolution of Means-Ends Reasoning

3. General Knowledge

Let me now draw attention to one striking feature of animals at Levels 0 to 4 (I shall call these '*simple* animals' from now on). They nowhere explicitly represent any general information of the form 'All As or Bs', or generic causal information to the effect that 'As cause Bs', or even conditional information about present circumstances like 'If A were to occur, then so will B'. In line with this, let me now specify, as a first approximation, that by means-end reasoning we should understand the use of this kind of explicit general[2] information to guide action. This initial definition of means-end reasoning will soon need to be significantly refined and qualified, but it will do to get us started.

Note that I have defined means-end reasoning in terms of using *general* information to guide actions, rather than in terms of using *any* information. This is because even simple animals clearly use particular information about their circumstances to guide behaviour. From Level 1 upwards they have states whose function is to represent particular features of their environment. Even so, no simple organisms explicitly represent any *general* facts. It is one thing to be able to represent the whereabouts of a particular pond, or apple, or lion. It is another to represent that the ponds contain water, or that apples are a source of food, or that lions are bad for your health.

This last point means that we cannot equate my question of which animals have means-end reasoning with the perhaps more familiar question of which animals should be counted as having *beliefs*. For the issue is not whether the animals have *any* powers of explicitly representing information, but whether they have the power of explicitly representing *general* information. I have no objection to saying that simple animals, certainly from Level 2 upwards, have particular beliefs about particular circumstances. But this won't qualify them as means-end reasoners, on my definition, given that they will still lack beliefs on general matters.

There is also a rather more general reason for not wanting to pose my issue of means-end reasoning in terms of the possession of beliefs. This is because many philosophers, most importantly Daniel Dennett (1978, 1987), take an 'interpretational' approach to the ascription of beliefs. Dennett holds that the attribution of beliefs answers to the 'intentional stance', as opposed to the 'design

---

[2] There are philosophical contexts in which it is important to distinguish between generalizations, generic causal claims, and particular conditional claims. For present purposes, however, nothing will be lost if we lump these together under the heading of 'general information'.

David Papineau

stance', and thus that such attributions are justified as soon as they help to make sense of behaviour, even if there is nothing corresponding to the attributed belief in the organisms' causal workings. On this view, even very simple animals might be held to have general beliefs (ponds contain water, say) on the grounds that their behaviour can usefully be rationalized by this belief, even if there is nothing in them which explicitly represents this information.

Fortunately, we can by-pass this largely terminological issue about the meaning of 'belief'. Suppose I concede to Dennett, for the sake of the argument, that even simple animals can have general 'beliefs' in his sense. It doesn't at all follow that they do means-end reasoning in my sense. For I did not define means-end reasoning in terms of general *'beliefs'*, but in design-level terms, as a matter of using general representations to guide behaviour. Whatever you think about the meaning of 'belief', there remains a substantial issue, namely, about which animals actually do use general representations in this way. In what follows I shall try to keep the waters clear by continuing to avoid the terminology of 'belief'.

Some readers may be wondering at this point why I am so sure, by my own lights, that simple animals *don't* use general representations to guide their behaviour. Isn't there a sense in which just such general representations are embodied in these animals' dispositions to behaviour? Take an animal who is disposed to drink from ponds when it is thirsty, precisely because in its individual or ancestral past this has proved an effective route to water. In this kind of case, it seems eminently natural to say that this disposition, which certainly guides the animal's behaviour, represents the fact that drinking from ponds will yield water. After all, it is precisely because this behaviour has produced this result in the past that the animal now has the disposition, and correspondingly it is precisely insofar as drinking will yield water in this case that the disposition will fulfil its biological function. Shouldn't we thus think of the disposition itself as the present embodiment of the general information that drinking from ponds will yield water?

I do not especially want to contest such attributions of content. I am happy to allow that this kind of disposition embodies information about the general response-to-outcome connection (**C&D**, **R→O**) which was responsible for instilling the disposition in the first place.

So, given this concession, I need to tighten up the definition of means-end reasoning, if this is to define a kind of thinking unavailable to simple animals. In my initial definition of means-end reasoning, I referred to '*explicit*' representations of general information. Maybe I can make something of this phrase, and argue that general information is only *implicitly* represented by dispositions to action, not explicitly. If means-end reasoning specifically requires explicit representations of general information, and mere dispositions to behaviour fail on this requirement, then there it will no longer follow that simple animals automatically qualify as means-end reasoners.

One way of developing this thought would be to hold that genuine explicit representation requires some kind of sentence-like vehicle, some articulated physical state to which we can ascribe a content. Simple organisms' representations of particular facts, involving definite modifications of sensory processors, would be so explicit. But their putative representation by mere behavioural dispositions would fail on this score, so this thought would go, because such dispositions do not have the kind of physical tangibility required for fully explicit representation.

However, I don't think that there is much substance to this line of thought. After all, dispositions to behaviour must have some kind of physical embodiment. An animal who is disposed to drink from ponds must differ in some substantial causal way from an animal who hasn't yet learned to do this. So why not let this real difference, whatever it is, serve as the vehicle of the content 'pond drinking yields water'? Moreover this vehicle, whatever it is, will interact appropriately with representations of needs and conditions in generating behaviour. The animal will only drink from the pond when this vehicle (which we are taking to represent 'pond drinking yields water') engages appropriately with the state which represents the need for water and the state which represents the presence of the pond, along the lines of the classical practical syllogism. So, on all these counts, there seems no reason not to count the disposition as a perfectly explicit representer: it must have some physical embodiment; and moreover that embodiment will interact with other uncontroversial representers in a way appropriate to its putative content.

Still, perhaps there is another way in which such putative dispositional representers of general information fail to be sufficiently explicit. In more familiar cases, general representations can be combined, one with another, to deliver new general representations. We can take 'valleys contain ponds' and 'ponds contain water', to generate 'valleys contain water'. But there is nothing in simple animals to allow anything like this. Their behaviour dispositions may embody general information, but they have no system which processes these items of general information to yield new such

David Papineau

general information. At most, as outlined in the last paragraph, these dispositional representers will interact with items of particular information ('here's a pond') and drives ('water needed') to generate particular behaviours, as in the standard practical syllogism.

To make the point graphic, imagine a simple animal who has information along the lines of *shaking those trees will yield fruit* implicit in one behavioural disposition, and information like *throwing missiles will repel bears* implicit in another. If it is a simple animal, it will have no way of putting these together so as to figure out that it would be a good idea to shake a tree when a bear is prowling nearby and no missiles are yet to hand. Of course, this information may itself come to be embodied implicitly in some disposition, if natural selection or learning instills a specific disposition to shake trees and throw the resulting fruit when bears are nearby. But the general point will still apply. While the organism will have various bits of general information implicit in its various behavioural dispositions, it will have no system for combining them and using them to infer the worth of behaviour that is not already directed by its cognitive architecture.

This represents an extremely significant limitation. It means that simple animals will never be led to perform behaviours except those which they, or their ancestors, have performed successfully in the past. This is because the only items of information that can enter into their practical syllogisms, so to speak, are of the form 'In **C&D**, **R** leads to **O**', where **R** is some behaviour previously performed when **C** and **D**, and **O** the outcome whose past achievement has led to their present disposition to do **R** given **C** and **D**. There is no possibility of their inferring that some **R** will lead to some **O** in some **C** and **D** from other items of general information, and then acting accordingly. They are limited to acting on **C&D**, **R→O** connections that they or their ancestors have directly experienced.

So let me now specify that means-end reasoning requires 'explicit' representation of general information in the specific sense that *such information can be processed to deliver new items of general information.* Whether or not behavioural dispositions in simple animals carry 'explicit' general content in other senses, they do not satisfy this requirement, since simple animals cannot combine their behavioural dispositions to generate new dispositions. Because of this, simple animals cannot perform novel actions. In effect, then, I have now defined means-end reasoning as the ability to perform novel actions. (The notion of 'novelty' required here merits further discussion. I shall return to this in section 4(i) below.)

Given this definition, we are now finally in a position to consider the importance of means-end reasoning for the evolution of higher cognition. To focus this issue, let me propose the strong hypothesis that means-end reasoning in the sense now specified is a biological adaptation peculiar to human beings. This paper certainly won't provide a knockdown defence of this hypothesis, and indeed as we proceed various modifications will prove to be necessary. Still, it will provide a useful peg on which to hang the discussion.

In the rest of this paper, I shall consider two lines of objection to the claim means-end reasoning is a biological adaptation peculiar to humans.

First, there are those who think that means-end reasoning is *too easy*, and therefore widespread throughout the animal kingdom. Against this I shall argue, in the next section, that non-human animals are sophisticated in many different ways, but that there is no compelling reason to think them capable of means-end reasoning in particular.

Second, there are those who think that means-end reasoning is *too hard*, and therefore no essential part of our evolutionary heritage. On this view, means-end reasoning is simply a non-biological 'spandrel' which has spun off from other distinctive abilities that evolution has bequeathed to humans. Against this I shall argue, in the final section, that standard explanations of this form do not work, and that in any case there are general reasons why no spandrel could fill the role played by human means-end reasoning.

4. Non-Human Sophistication

I suspect that many readers who have lived through the cognitive revolution in psychology will have started to feel increasingly impatient during the analysis of the last two sections. Don't we now know that most animals are far too sophisticated to be understood in terms of simple links between stimulating **C**s, driving **D**s and responsive **R**s? That was how the original behaviourists and their various neo-behaviourist successors tried to understand animals. But surely, so the thought would go, we now realize that animals are much more elaborate than that. Animals are blessed with any number of refined cognitive devices which enable them to deal with their environments by figuring out sophisticated responses to their circumstances in real time. As a result, animals have any number of behaviours in their repertoire which are manifestly inexplicable on behaviourist grounds, and clearly display levels of behavioural control unavailable to the simple creatures discussed in the last section.

157

David Papineau

The first point to make here is that there is nothing in my analysis so far to commit me to behaviourism about simple animals. I may have schematized matters in terms of **C**s, **D**s and **R**s, but this in itself scarcely convicts me of thinking in behaviourist terms. Indeed a moment's thought will make it clear that there are a number of ways in which my simple animals transcend behaviourist limitations.

Behaviourism holds that all dispositions to actions (all **C, D→R** links) are instilled in animals by general learning mechanisms operating on spaces of sensory inputs and behavioural outputs. Nothing in my analysis of simple animals commits me to any such blanket view about the sources of input-output links. True, I have allowed, at Level 4, for the possibility of learning by instrumental conditioning. But this does not mean that simple animals cannot also have structured 'hard-wired' links between inputs and outputs which do not derive from learning. After all, input-output links must be so 'hard-wired' in animals below Level 4; and even at Level 4 there can be 'hard-wired' links alongside the learned ones. Moreover, nothing I have said about simple animals implies that, when there is instrumental learning, at Level 4, it must derive from 'content-free' mechanisms which are equally ready to link any perceptual inputs with any behavioural outputs. Instrumental learning may be highly constrained, with only a limited range of input-output paths being available for shaping by individual experience.

Similar points apply to the inputs and the outputs themselves. Behaviourism assumes minimally structured spaces of sensory qualities as inputs and behavioural atoms as outputs. But nothing commits me to this strongly empiricist picture. I have, it is true, assumed *some* distinction between perceptual inputs and behavioural outputs in section 2 above (and I shall comment on this distinction further in section 4(i) below). But beyond this I have said nothing to imply that inputs and outputs must be simple or unstructured. So I have left it open that simple animals may have highly structured hard-wired input devices (perceptual 'modules', if you like), and highly structured hard-wired output devices (behavioural 'modules').[3]

---

[3] When I talk of 'modules' in what follows, I shall use the term merely as a stylistic variant for 'mechanism' or 'system'. In my view, the technical notion of a 'module' is a theoretical mess. Fodor, 1983 originally specified a number of necessary criteria for modularity, but omitted to tell us what to call the many interesting types of cognitive mechanism that satisfy some of these criteria but not others. Moreover, some of these criteria themselves turn out to involve a number of distinct and dissociable requirements: 'hard-wired', 'domain-specific' and 'informationally encapsulated' have proved particularly troublesome in this respect.

The Evolution of Means-Ends Reasoning

So, to repeat, nothing in my analysis commits me to behaviourism about simple animals. This clarification, however, is now likely to prompt a contrary reaction from committed cognitivists: 'All right, I see that when you say non-human animals are "simple", you are not saying that they are behaviourist dummies. You allow that their input and output modules, and the links between them, may be highly structured. But, if you allow this, why stop there? Why not credit animals with means-end reasoning as well? If you allow they have the mental wherewithal for sophisticated analysis of sensory stimuli, and for sophisticated control of behaviour, then why doubt that they can also figure out the best means to their ends? After all, it is clear that many specialized perceptual and behavioural systems in animals, like vision and navigation, involve complex computational processing of representations. Since this is clearly just the kind of processing required for means-end reasoning, wouldn't it be very surprising, to say the least, if evolution had never pressed such processing into the service of animal means-end reasoning? Means-end reasoning is manifestly a very powerful adaptive tool, once you have it. Given that the materials for such a means-end reasoner were readily to hand, so to speak, we should surely expect that evolution would have made use of them for just this purpose.'

Maybe recent connectionist ideas will make this line of thought seem less persuasive than it would have been a decade ago. The introduction of connectionist thinking into cognitive science has cast doubt on the presupposition that all perceptual or behavioural sophistication must rest on computational processing of explicit representations. From the connectionist perspective, the raw materials with which evolution builds brains are neural nets, not compositional computers. So perhaps means-end reasoners are not so easy to make, evolutionarily speaking, after all. For neural nets do not seem as immediately well-suited to the building of means-end reasoners as classical computations.[4]

Still, I shall not press this point. Questions of how means-end reasoners might or might not be built will be touched on again at the end of this paper. Let me at this stage mount a rather different challenge to the claim that non-human animals can perform means-and reasoning, simply by querying whether there are in fact any facets of non-human behaviour that cannot be explained by abilities at Levels 1–4.

Note in this connection that simple animals, I am thinking of

[4] Not that we should suppose it would be that easy to build a means-end reasoner, even if we could make use of classical computations. The 'frame problem' presents a substantial barrier to any such construction.

159

David Papineau

them, will certainly be able to display a wide range of sophisticated behaviours, despite their lack of means-end reasoning. Nothing stops such creatures from being sensitive to the most intricate features of their environment and performing extremely complex routines under the guidance of this information. Their cognitive mechanisms can be highly structured, both within their input and output modules, and in the links between them. All they lack is a system whose purpose is to put together items of general information in order to draw out further general conclusions.

It is perhaps worth emphasizing that input and output systems, as I am thinking of them, can be very complex indeed. One point I have not yet made explicit is that learning can take place within peripheral systems, as well as between them. Thus there could be perceptual systems which have acquired the ability, during individual development, to recognize animals or plants, or cars or aeroplanes, or individual faces or gaits, or musical compositions, or lack of pawn cohesion in the centre. Again, there could be behavioural systems which have acquired the ability to execute a forehand, or multiply by ten, or make a sandwich, or drive to work, or be apologetic.

Other complexities are possible. Thus, on the input side, some perceptual systems could receive information from others; while others could lay down their findings in memory stores (allowing information about particular circumstances to guide actions over a temporal distance, as it were). And, on the output side, the execution of behavioural routines could be guided by real-time informational resources deriving from special informational channels; moreover, there could also be nesting of behavioural routines, with more complicated modules being built up from simpler ones.[5]

At this stage a new suspicion about my line of argument is likely to arise. If I am packing all this into 'simple animals', isn't there a danger that simple animals are already performing means-end reasoning in the sense I have defined it? They may not have a definite 'theorem-prover' in their heads, a specific device that takes in sentence-like premises and derives conclusions via some mechanical realization of the predicate calculus. But, given the amount of cognitive structure I am allowing them, won't they satisfy my

[5] Note how the possibility of all these sophistications in simple animals undercuts the thought that there must have been strong selection pressure for means-end reasoning from an early stage in evolutionary history. If simple animals could already deal intelligently with every circumstance their environments threw at them, then why should they have undergone the selectional disadvantage of building an expensive theorem-prover?

requirements for means-end reasoning in any case, even without such a device?

In the rest of this section I shall consider five different ways in which this challenge might be developed. I should admit at this stage that some of these will lead to significant modifications to my strong hypothesis of non-human simplicity. However, even if the position I am left with is not exactly my strong hypothesis as originally advertised, it will still amount to a substantial claim about the distinctive abilities that humans use to select actions.

(i) Modular Combinations

The first thought I want to consider is that the combined operation of different elements in simple cognitive systems can itself amount to means-end reasoning as I have defined it. In particular, this arguably happens when input systems (or output systems) combine with input-output links to generate behaviour.

Recall how in section 3 above I allowed that dispositions to behaviour can properly be viewed as embodying general information. If an animal is disposed to drink from ponds when thirsty, because in its individual or ancestral past so drinking led to water, then I agreed that this disposition can properly be viewed as representing the general claim that drinking from ponds will yield water.

However, note now how a similar point could be made about perceptual dispositions. For example, if an animal is disposed to judge that a pond is present when it receives retinal stimulation X, because in its individual or ancestral past it formed this judgement when so stimulated, then shouldn't I equally allow that this perceptual disposition represents the general claim that stimulation X indicates ponds?

I am indeed happy to allow this. However, it now seems to follow that an animal will be performing means-end reasoning, in my sense, whenever two such dispositions combine to constitute a third, derived, disposition—to drink when thirsty on receipt of stimulation X. For at the representational level this derivation amounts to combining the general claims that 'stimulation X indicates ponds' and 'drinking from ponds will yield water' to generate the further general claim that 'drinking after stimulation X will yield water'.

Note in particular that an animal could well have this derived disposition even if stimulation X plus drinking had never been followed by water in its individual or ancestral past. Provided stimulation X had previously been followed by pond-judgments, and (different) pond-judgements plus drinking had previously been

161

David Papineau

followed by water, past experience would give the animal the premises, so to speak—which it could then put together to derive the experientially novel conclusion, that stimulation X plus drinking will be followed by water.

A similar point arises in connection with behavioural dispositions. For example, such a disposition could be held to embody the information 'in circumstances Y specific movements Z will constitute drinking from a pond', which together with 'drinking from ponds will yield water' will generate the possibly experientially novel conclusion 'in circumstances Y specific movements Z will yield water'.

My response to this line of thought is that while these derived dispositions are experientially 'novel' in one sense, there remains another important kind of 'novelty' which is possible for humans, but not simple animals. For note that the examples just given do not involve behaviour which is novel *from the perspective of the animal's perceptual and behavioural classifications*. After all, we are assuming an animal whose perceptual system classifies different stimuli together as *'ponds'* when sending information to other cognitive systems. So at this level, the level of the animal's perceptual classifications, there is nothing new in the fact that another pond yields water, given previous experience of ponds yielding water. Similarly, on the output side, an action needn't count as 'novel' just because it involves some uniquely discriminable sequence of movements, if these are simply one instance of a behavioural type which has previously been triggered as such by behavioural control mechanisms.

So let me now specify that the kind of novelty required for genuine means-end reasoning is novelty relative to the structure of the animal's perceptual and behavioural systems. Genuine novelty requires some new pairing within the animal's own perceptual and behavioural typology.

Some readers may feel that this is resting a lot on the animal's typology. This raises large issues, but in the present context let me simply observe that we have been committed to the reality of such typologies from an early stage. As soon as we reached Level 2 animals, with specialized informational systems, we were supposing a repertoire of perceptual judgements ('here's a pond', say) which maintain their identity across interactions with different drives and behaviours. And by Level 4 learners, if not before, we were supposing a repertoire of responses ('approach', 'retreat', 'drink', 'eat', say) which maintain their identity across prompting by different drives and perceptions. Given that these classifications were introduced earlier, and moreover that I then sketched their motivations,

162

there is nothing particularly ad hoc in now using them in characterizing behavioural 'novelty'.

(ii) Getting into Position

Ruth Millikan (forthcoming), following Randy Gallistel (1980), has pointed out how responses to conditions may be adaptive, not because they lead directly to advantageous outcomes, but because they are likely to put the animal in the way of some further condition which will then prompt a response which will lead to the advantageous outcome (or some further condition which will then prompt a response which is likely to put the animal in the way of some further condition ... which will then prompt a response which will lead to the advantageous outcome). So a bird, once it feels hungry, will be prompted to fly, and then, if it sees a fruit tree, will be prompted to approach it, and then, if it sees a fruit, will be prompted to peck it.

At first sight this might look like means-end reasoning as I have characterized it. When the bird takes flight, the virtue of this action lies in the fact that it is a means to seeing and approaching a fruit tree, which is a means to finding and eating a fruit, which is a means to food.

However, this is not a real instance of means-end reasoning in my sense. This is because such general facts as that flight is a means to finding fruit trees need not be represented anywhere in this bird, even in the generous sense in which I have allowed that such information can be represented in behavioural dispositions.

To see this, note that, for all that has been said so far, the *outcome* which has instilled the disposition to fly when hungry may be nothing other than that so flying has led to *food* in the past.[6] If this is so, then the disposition shouldn't be counted as representing anything except that flying when hungry leads to food. In particular, it won't represent that flying leads to tree-finding which in turn leads to fruit-finding. True, it is only in virtue of these further facts about these means that flying does lead to food. But if the aim of flying, as fixed by phylogenetic or ontogenetic history, has been food, rather than these intermediary means, then there will be no

---

[6] It would be different if the bird were able to *acquire* desires for some of the relevant means, such as finding fruit trees, since then a proximal behaviour like flying could be reinforced by achieving this desire, and not only by leading to food. I shall not be able to deal with the acquisition of desires fully in this paper, though I shall make some remarks on the subject in section 4(v) below.

David Papineau

rationale for taking the disposition to represent anything about these means. (That would be like taking my belief that aspirin cures headaches to represent facts about brain chemistry about which I am quite ignorant.)

It might seem arbitrary to think of the flying as aiming directly at food, rather than at the intermediary means. But note that animals get hungry when food is needed, and that the specific function of this drive is correspondingly to prompt behaviour which will lead to food. Given this, the phylogenetic or ontogenetic selection of flying when hungry will hinge crucially on whether flying leads to food, and not on whether it leads to other outcomes. (After all, if flying led to fruit trees, but not food, it wouldn't be selected; but if it led to food, but not via fruit trees, it would be selected.)

There may seem to be a problem in supposing that a behaviour (like flying) can be selected by a pay-off (food) from which it is removed by a long series of intermediate means. But note how such behaviours can evolve by accretion. Once hungry birds are disposed to eat when they see fruit, this will create selection pressure for hungry birds to approach when they see fruit trees. And once they are disposed to do this, then this will create selection pressure to fly when they are hungry. Perhaps this kind of process will work better in intergenerational genetic selection than in ontogenetic learning. For an ontogenetic learning mechanism will need somehow to connect the behaviour with the distal pay-off, and if the time-lag is too great this may prove difficult. From the point of view of genetic selection, by contrast, this is not a problem: the behaviour will be selected as long as its connection with the pay-off reliably influences survival and reproduction, however long the time-lag.

(iii) Intra-Modular Means-End Reasoning
So far I have been assuming that means-end reasoning, if it is to be found anywhere, will somehow mediate *between* perceptual inputs and behavioural outputs (or perhaps, as in (i) above, arise from the *interaction* between peripheral modules and input-output links). But what about the possibility that means-end reasoning might be found *within* peripheral modules, and in particular within behaviour-generating systems?

For example, consider the special navigation abilities, common to many animals, which enable them to find their way back home, or back to previously perceived food, even when these targets are hidden and distant. It is possible that some animals do this by combining given items of general (causal, conditional) information to derive new general conclusions. For example, they might start with the information 'If I go West from here, I'll get to A' and 'If I go North from A, I'll get to the food', and use this to infer 'If I go West until I get to A, and then North, I'll reach the food'.

There are two possible responses I could make here. One the one hand, I could appeal to the line I took in (i) above in order to exclude such intra-modular inferences from the category of means end-reasoning. Recall that I there specified that means-end reasoning should yield input-output links which are novel *relative to the animal's typology of behaviour*. Given this, then figuring out novel ways of 'going back home' will not count as means-end reasoning, whenever 'going back home' functions as a primitive behavioural unit relative to the structure of the animal's motivational and learning systems. (Thus different drives might in different circumstances each prompt the 'going back home' routine; again, 'going back home' may be a response that can be encouraged or extinguished as such by instrumental learning.) In support of this exclusionary line, note that intra-modular inferential mechanisms are likely to be highly content-specific, by comparison with means-end reasoning in mature human beings, which can work with pretty much any kind of information. A navigation system, for example, will deal only with spatial information, and will only select spatial routes as means.

On the other hand, all this seems a rather cheap way of denying means-end reasoning to animals. If animals piece together different bits of general information within the systems which govern their behavioural routines, and thereby figure out what to do, this will certainly be similar to the kind of behavioural flexibility I have been concerned with in this paper. After all, such animals will be able to extrapolate beyond specific behaviours which have proved advantageous in the past, and will do so by combining separate items of general information into inferences. Why downgrade this, just because it can be regarded as taking place within 'modules', rather than between them? And, again, why does it matter that these inferences will only operate on a specific subject matter? It isn't as if we could seriously have expected non-human animals to perform inferences across the same wide range of subjects as humans.

I do not propose to pursue this essentially classificatory issue any further. In the remainder on this paper I shall continue to focus on means-end reasoning which mediates between input and output systems in general, and which correspondingly has no inbuilt limitations on the kinds of content it deals with. But in doing so I do not want to suggest that it is unimportant that similar inferential

David Papineau

powers may be located within behavioural modules. Even if my focus in this paper lies elsewhere, this is clearly a significant question about animal cognition in its own right.

Before leaving this issue, let me comment briefly on the substantial issue of whether animal spatial navigation does in fact involve content-specific intra-modular means-end reasoning. This is not entirely straightforward. It is uncontroversial that many animals, including birds and insects, form non-egocentric spatial maps of their environments and behavioural targets, and that they can place and orientate themselves with respect to such maps using landmarks. However, this doesn't necessarily add up to means-end reasoning as I have been conceiving it. It depends on how they use the maps to generate behaviour.

Perhaps their brains simply execute the analogue of drawing a straight line from their present positions to their targets (perhaps iterating this strategy as they approach their targets, and in particular after any detours to circumvent obstacles). This wouldn't amount to anything like means-end reasoning as I am conceiving it.

It would be different, however, with animals who cognitively performed some analogue of tracing out a continuous obstacle-avoiding path from their starting positions to their targets, and then set themselves to follow these paths. This would seem clearly to qualify as intra-modular means-end reasoning in my sense. For it would be equivalent to combining separate items of causal information, in the way sketched above—'If I go West from here, I'll reach A, and then, if I go North from there, I'll reach the food'.

(iv) Classical Conditioning

So far the only kind of learning I have considered has been instrumental learning, in which the disposition to perform some response **R** given some **C** and **D** gets reinforced because so responding has led to some reinforcing outcome in the past. However, there is also another kind of learning, classical or Pavlovian learning, where an animal learns to associate one stimulus **B** with another stimulus **C** after observing their past association, and shows this by now responding to **B** as it previously responded to **C**. (Note that classical conditioning involves no feedback from previous 'rewards'; all it requires is that perceptual 'nodes' which were previously co-activated now come to activate each other.)

This now gives us another candidate for means-end reasoning. Take an animal who initially responds to **C** (and **D**) with **R**, and then after classical conditioning of **B** with **C** comes to respond similarly to **B**. I have previously agreed that the initial disposition here

166

can properly be understood as representing the information 'R in C (and D) will yield O' (where O is the relevant advantageous result). Given this, it is natural to regard the classical conditioning as yielding the extra information that 'All Bs are Cs', which is then combined with the prior information to generate 'R in B (and D) will yield O'.

Indeed there is nothing to stop such inferences being iterated. An animal could learn that 'All Bs are Cs' and then—separately—that 'All As are Bs', and consequently become disposed to behave on perceiving A in ways it originally behaved only on perceiving C. It is in an empirical question how far such inferential chains might stretch in any actual animals. But one would expect any mechanism underpinning classical conditioning to allow some such iteration.

These kinds of cases cannot be dismissed on the grounds that the extra general information lies *within* perceptual systems, as in (i) above. For the new items of general information which get combined with the prior behavioural dispositions are now embodied in links *between* outputs of perceptual systems, not in structures within such systems. (Note how this point will not be sensitive to any particular rationale for identifying 'perceptual modules'. However we decide to discriminate 'modules', a general mechanism for associative learning will build links between them.)

I can see no reason not to allow that associative learning will in this way give rise to means-end reasoning as so far defined. Note, however, that animals who can perform means-end reasoning only in this specific sense will still be cognitively extremely limited, by comparison with mature human reasoners. This is because they can only draw inferences about the *conditions* which render actions appropriate, and not about the *consequences* actions may have. They can use their general information to figure out that B provides just as good an opportunity for R-ing in pursuit of O as C does. But when it comes to figuring out what R-ing might be good for in the first place, they still lack any inferential powers. They are stuck with information of the form 'R will yield O', where R is some item from their behavioural repertoire, and O the outcome which in the past has instilled the disposition to R. In particular, they have no power to reason along such lines as: 'R will yield M' and 'M will yield O'— therefore, 'R will yield O'.

The point is that associative learning can allow animals to figure out that new conditions are suitable for old behavioural dispositions. But it can't generate any new behavioural dispositions. When it comes to information 'causally downstream' from behaviour, so to speak, the only means of representation available so far is embodi-

David Papineau

ment in behavioural dispositions. And the only mechanism for forming such dispositions is still phylogenetic or ontogenetic selection of some **R** which led to some **O** in the past. As yet we have seen no way to acquire the information of the form 'R will lead to O', except via such direct selection.

Both Gopnik, Glymour and Sobel (forthcoming) and Millikan (forthcoming) have compared this limitation to egocentricity in spatial mapping. An egocentric spatial map locates objects solely in terms of their relation to the subject's own position and orientation. Now, as I mentioned in the last section, many animals transcend this spatial egocentricity, and represent the spatial world in objective terms, in terms of maps in which they themselves are simply one item among many. However, animals who are spatially objective in this way may still be *causally egocentric*. In particular this will still be true of the Pavlovian animals we are currently considering. Despite their classical associative powers, they will lack any conception of objective 'causal space', as containing many objectively interacting items, of which their actions are just one special case. Instead all their causal information will necessarily be egocentric in form, with some piece of behaviour **R** at one end of the relation, and some reinforcing result **O** at the other.

So, at this stage, let me raise the stakes for full-fledged means-end reasoning once more, to include some degree of causal non-egocentricity. Let me now require that it involve, not just any use of general information to infer new general conclusions, but specifically that it allow animals to infer new causal facts of the form 'R will lead to O' from other causal facts. From now on, then, full-fledged means-end reasoning will use facts about objective causal relationships to figure out which behaviours will produce which requisite results.

(v) Dickinson's Rats
Now that this issue is in focus, the obvious question is whether there is any direct evidence for non-egocentric awareness of causal relations in non-human animals.

As it happens, the few studies which have attacked this question head-on suggest that even apes and other primates are very limited in their ability to appreciate objective causal connections. While apes can certainly learn to use tools in novel ways, they don't seem to represent causal connections in a way that can inform means-end reasoning. There is no direct evidence that non-human primates ever take the knowledge that some intermediary cause **M** produces end result **O**, combine this with knowledge that behaviour **R** leads to **M**, and use the two items of information together 'to devise novel ways of producing the intermediary and thus the end result'. (Tomasello and Call, 1997, p. 390. See also the rest of their chs 3 and 12.)

At the same time, however, there is also some very detailed work in the animal learning tradition, especially from Anthony Dickinson and his associates, which at first sight suggests that rats can perform exactly the kind of inference I am now asking for (Heyes and Dickinson, 1990, Dickinson and Balleine, 1999).

Consider this experiment. (This is just one of a range of related rat experiments, but it contains the essential points.) Rats are trained while hungry but not thirsty, in an environment where they gain dry food pellets from pressing a lever, and a sucrose solution from pulling a chain. Both the pellets and the sucrose solution satisfy hunger, but, as it happens, only the sucrose solution would satisfy thirst. Now make some of these rats thirsty, and give them the choice of pressing the lever or pulling the chain. With one important qualification to be entered shortly, the thirsty rats will straightaway display a preference for chain-pulling.

Since nothing during their training reinforced chain-pulling over lever-pressing, this experiment provides prima facie reason to suppose that the rats are explicitly storing the causal information that chain-pulling yields the sucrose solution, which they then combine with the fact that the solution quenches thirst, to derive the conclusion that chain-pulling will satisfy thirst.

It may seem as if there is a loophole in the argument. Even if the rats weren't thirsty during training, wouldn't their thirst-drive, low as it was, have been yet further reduced by the liquid-from-chain-pulling, but not by the pellets-from-lever-pressing? If the rats had a drive-specific learning mechanism (cf. the discussion of Level 4 above), then they may on this basis have acquired a preferential disposition to chain-pull when thirsty. (The idea here would be that certain behaviours—here chain-pulling—get attached to specific drives—thirst—not because they were generally rewarding in the past, but specifically because they *quenched thirst* in the past.)

However, this story is inconsistent with a further fact about the experiment. This is the rider I mentioned a moment ago. The trained rats won't chain-pull, even when thirsty, unless they are first given an opportunity to drink the sucrose solution *when they are thirsty*, and thereby discover that it quenches thirst. On the story just suggested, this further experience ought not to be necessary, for on that story the result of the initial training should already be to chain-pull *when thirsty*.

So it seems undeniable that the rats are somehow deriving from their training the information that chain-pulling leads specifically to sucrose solution, even though the difference between sucrose solution and food pellets is as yet of no motivational significance to them. Then, later on, the rats acquire the further information that sucrose solution quenches thirst. And at that point the rats combine the two pieces of information, to infer that chain-pulling as opposed to lever-pressing is a means to satisfying thirst. They thereby acquire a novel disposition to behaviour, a disposition that has never itself been reinforced for satisfying thirst.

So described, the rats would seem clearly to be capable of non-egocentric causal thinking, of the kind I am now requiring for full-fledged means-end reasoning. But perhaps there is another way of viewing their cognitive achievements, a way that will distance them less from simple animals. Suppose we regard their exposure to the sucrose solution when thirsty, not as giving them the factual information that sucrose solution quenches thirst, but rather as instilling in them a new 'acquired drive' for sucrose solution.

On this way of looking at things, the rats are not so different from simple animals after all. We can view the preferential chain-pulling behaviour as the upshot of (a) a drive to get sucrose solution and (b) a behavioural disposition to chain-pull in pursuit of sucrose solution when this drive is active. The rats will thus be prompted to act by just the same kind of practical syllogism as operates in other animals. Provided the 'acquired sucrose solution drive' is activated whenever the rats are thirsty, this model predicts just the same behaviour as a means-end reasoning model.

Of course, we will still need to acknowledge that the rats differ in very important ways from any simple animals discussed so far. Most obviously, we are now crediting them with an ability to *acquire* drives, where previously all drives were assumed to be innate. This is in fact a huge extension of cognitive power. Since there seems no reason why rats should not have the potential to acquire drives for any circumstance that they are capable of *recognizing*, we have here graduated from animals whose ends are limited to a few basic outcomes to animals that can embrace pretty much anything as an end. If we want to draw a sharp line between 'drives' and 'desires', this seems as good a place as any.

In addition, and even more interestingly, we must also acknowledge that the rats are capable of acquiring a disposition to do **R** (chain-pull) in pursuit of **O** (sucrose solution), *even though **R**'s so leading to **O** has never previously satisfied any drives*. The line I am now pushing is that the information '**R** leads to **O**' needn't be embodied anywhere except in a disposition to do **R** when a drive for **O** is activated. But it is striking, to say the least, that such a disposition can be acquired even before any internal representation of **O** has yet acquired the status of a drive.

It may seem, especially given this last point, that I am trying to build a distinction out of thin air. If I am admitting that somehow the **O**-productivity of **R** must be representable even when **R** isn't yet wired up to be triggered by a drive for **O**, then doesn't this already grant the rats the essential cognitive power at issue? However, a crucial limitation may still lie in the fact that this causal knowledge needs to be embodied in a disposition-ready way, so to speak. Before the rat has any drive directed at **O**, it is already able somehow to link behaviour **R** with an internal representation of **O**. But this link may consist in nothing more than that the rat would do **R** were its representation of **O** to acquire 'drive-active' status. If this is right, then the rats will still suffer from a form of causal ego-centricity. The only causal information available to them will still have an item of their own behaviour **R** at the front end.

If we do see the rats in this way, it will have the advantage of explaining why their powers of means-end reasoning are limited as they are.[7] In my terms, Dickinson's rats are certainly capable of novel actions. By combining their stored knowledge that **R** will lead to **O** with some newly acquired drive for **O**, they can be led to actions they have not previously performed. However, if their **R→O** information must always be stored in a 'dormant disposition', in the way just suggested, then the generative power of their overall cognitive system will be limited by their ability to acquire new drives. This is not the place to start considering details of the mechanisms by which animals acquire new drives (an issue which seems to me crucial, not just for understanding rats, but also for understanding humans). But if, as seems plausible, these mechanisms must work by some kind of direct association with pre-existing drives, then the causally egocentric rats will be capable of far less behavioural novelty than reasoners who are also able to derive **R→O** information from an unlimited range of non-egocentric causal links.

5. Reasoning by Accident

Overall, the previous section was a response to the thought that means-end reasoning is too easy to be a peculiarly human adapta-

---

[7] Moreover, it will also allow us to explain the above-mentioned limitations of apes and other primates. Since primates will presumably share any cognitive sophistications present in rats, we will be hard pressed to explain the poor primate performance, if we allow full-fledged means-end reasoning to rats.

David Papineau

tion, and so must be widespread through the animal kingdom. I now want to address the converse thought, that means-end reasoning is too hard to be a biological adaptation, and so has only become available to humans as a side-effect of other biological developments.

On this view, means-end reasoning would be like arithmetic or music. Proficiency at these practices may well have yielded a reproductive advantage in the period since they emerged, in the sense that adepts may have had more children on average. But this doesn't make them evolutionary adaptations. Other abilities, with independent evolutionary explanations, fully enable us to explain the emergence and preservation of arithmetic and music, once they get into our culture[8]. And in any case there probably hasn't been enough time since these practices started for any genes favouring them to be selected.

On this model, then, means-end reasoning rests on other abilities with a biological purpose, but has no such purpose itself. In the terminology made famous by Stephen Jay Gould and Richard Lewontin (1978), it would be a 'spandrel'. The idea that means-end reasoning is a spandrel is perhaps found more often in conversation than in print. But it is popular among a surprisingly wide range of theorists, from official 'evolutionary psychologists', through Dennettians, to neo-associationist experimentalists.

This general 'spandrel' suggestion can be combined with different hypotheses about the crucial prior ability. One fashionable candidate is 'understanding of mind'. Once our 'understanding of mind module' emerged, so this story goes, we would then have had the intellectual wherewithal for means-end reasoning, along with other cultural spin-offs like promising.

However, this particular suggestion seems to me to owe far more to intellectual fashion than serious analysis.[9] There is an obvious reason why means-end reasoning cannot have piggy-backed evolutionarily on understanding of mind. This is that the standard accounts of understanding of mind only make sense if we suppose that 'mind-readers' are *already* capable of means-end thinking. This applies to both the 'simulation-theory', which holds that understanding of mind rests largely on the ability to simulate the

[8] Which is not deny that these explanations themselves can be informed by biological facts. *Which* practices are preserved by 'culture' depends crucially on the which dispositions have been bequeathed to us by natural selection. Cf. Sperber, 1996.

[9] However, see Sperber, 1997 for some interesting specific suggestions about the connection between understanding of mind and logic in general.

decision-making of others, and the 'theory-theory', which holds that understanding of mind derives from an articulated theory of mind.

The point is perhaps most obvious in connection with the 'simulation-theory'. The central assumption of this theory is that 'mind-readers' proceed by simulating others' beliefs and desires and then mimicking their decision-making 'off-line'. But such 'decision-making' is nothing but the means-end reasoning we are trying to understand. Presumably an ability to perform such reasoning 'off-line' presupposes a prior ability to do it on-line. So this version of the story simply assumes what we want to explain.

The 'theory-theory' version of understanding of mind fares little better. On this version, 'mind-readers' anticipate others' reactions by drawing predictions from an articulated theory of mind. That is, they attribute beliefs and desires to others, feed these in as initial conditions to a set of general assumptions about the mind, and on this basis figure out their best strategies for dealing with others' behaviour. But this is then nothing but a special case of means-end reasoning as we have been considering it. Once more, the story simply begs the question.

A rather more plausible version of the 'spandrel' approach would be that means-end reasoning piggy-backs, not on understanding of mind, but on language. But here too there are difficulties. To start with, this story too seems to be in danger of assuming what needs to be explained. The worry here would be that the primary biological purpose of language is to increase each individual's stock of information. But such extra information wouldn't be any use to creatures who can't yet do means-end reasoning, since they wouldn't be able to use it to draw any extra conclusions about appropriate behaviour.

Perhaps this is a bit quick. Maybe language first evolved as a device for passing around pieces of *particular* information ('a tiger is coming', 'there are fruit in that tree', ...). Since even simple creatures are guided by particular information about their circumstances, the utility of this information doesn't yet call for any means-end reasoning. So maybe means-end reasoning only emerged after our ancestors had first developed a relatively sophisticated language for reporting particular facts. Building on this basis, perhaps language *then* biologically evolved to report and process general claims.

The problem now, however, is to explain this last bit—what exactly was the extra biological pressure which led to language reporting and processing general information? If the answer is that

David Papineau

language evolved this feature to facilitate means-end reasoning, then this will mean that means-end reasoning is not a spandrel after all. It may have been largely dependent on language, in the sense that its emergence had to wait on the biological selection of prior linguistic abilities. But insofar as certain genes were then selected specifically because they helped us to do means-end reasoning, means-end reasoning will qualify as an adaptation in its own right, not a spandrel.

On the other hand, if the answer is that language evolved the ability to represent and process general information for some independent reason, then the puzzle will be to understand how this ability was then parlayed, spandrel-like, into means end-reasoning. Suppose that our ancestors first became able to formulate general claims, and draw novel causal conclusions from them, for reasons quite independent of means-end reasoning. How exactly would these novel theoretical conclusions then have come to make a difference to their practical activities?

The point here is that means-end reasoning must exert some control over *behaviour*. However, pre-existing cognitive architectures, of the kind present in simple animals, have no place for anything to issue in behaviour except dispositions to behave in certain ways when triggered by perceptions and competing drives. Somehow the ability to process general representations has to be able to be able to *add* to this set of dispositions (either temporarily—'next time I see a post box I'll insert this letter', or permanently—'from now I'll eat fish instead of meat'). However, an ability to draw conclusions from general claims, even conclusions about means to ends, will not by itself ensure this. In addition, the outputs of such reasoning will have to intrude on the control of behaviour. Without being able to alter our behaviour-guiding programme in this way, means-end reasoning won't make any difference to what we *do*.

As it happens, this line of argument seems to me to present a difficulty, not just to the specific idea that means-end reasoning piggybacks on language, but to any version of the view that it is a non-adaptational spandrel. The problem is to understand how a new power to alter behaviour could arise without some basic biological alteration. It scarcely makes sense to suppose that a pure spandrel could intervene in some unprecedented way in the biological systems that direct action. Prior to means-end reasoning, behaviour is controlled by a set of dispositions that are laid down either by genes or by conditioning. Somehow means-end reasoning, however it is realized, must involve the power to create new such dispositions. It is hard to see how this could happen without some biological selection, some alteration of our biological design, which allowed the output of deliberative decisions to reset our dispositions to action.

Note that this is not yet an argument for supposing that this there is some quite separate mechanism in the human brain specifically devoted to means-end reasoning. There may well be such a mechanism, and I shall return to this possibility in my final remarks. But the argument I have just given supports only the far weaker conclusion that there must have been *some* biological selection for means-end reasoning. This could have been quite minimal, a matter of a few genetic alterations allowing some pre-existing cognitive activity to start exerting an influence on behaviour. The most obviously possibility would be the one suggested above: a linguistic ability to report and process general information evolved for some independent reason; once that was in place, then a further evolutionary step allowed its outputs to influence behaviour.

In the Introduction to this paper, I said that, if I had to choose, I would place means-end reasoning on the side of the 'modules', rather than with general-purpose cognitive mechanisms. I am now rather better placed to explain the thrust of this remark. My intention, in classifying means-end reasoning as modular, was not to claim that there is some dedicated processor in the brain which was built solely to perform means-end reasoning. As I have just said, this may be so, but it is not something I am insisting on. Rather, my concern was only to emphasize that means-end reasoning is a cognitive mechanism which is activated in specific circumstances to serve specific needs. It is not some meta-system which controls all human activity, constantly selecting whichever behavioural outputs are best suited to current perceptual inputs.

An implicit assumption of much philosophical thinking is that all human behaviour, apart perhaps from crude reflexes, is selected by just this kind of meta-systemic means-end thinking. However, this is not the picture that emerges from this paper. I see no reason to doubt that behaviour in humans is determined in the first instance in just the same way as it is in simple animals. We have a set of standing dispositions, which get triggered by current perceptual information and competing drives. The only difference is that we humans have an extra way, beyond genetic inheritance and conditioning, of adjusting those dispositions. Sometimes we take time out, to consider the pros and cons of various options, and we figure out that the best way to get **O** , under conditions **C** and **D**, is by **R**-ing. And then we *reset* our standing dispositions, so that we become disposed to do **R** next time **C** and **D** arise.

Looking at things this way, we can see that it would probably not

David Papineau

be a good idea for means-end reasoning to act as a constant media-
tor between perceptual inputs and behavioural outputs. Means-end
reasoning takes time, and action cannot always wait on deliberation.
If we always stopped to check whether we were doing the best thing,
the time for action would normally be gone. So for the most part we
simply allow our standing dispositions to guide us. But sometimes,
when the issues are weighty, and time does not press, we delay acting, and instead activate our powers of means-end reasoning.
(Think of this itself as a standing disposition, triggered by the
issues being weighty and by time not being pressing.) Then, after
means-end reasoning has done its job, we alter our current dispositions, and once more allow them to guide us.[10]

Let me finish this paper with some brief further reflections on
the evolutionary emergence of means-end reasoning. So far I have
maintained only that means-end reasoning must have played at least
some role in biological evolution.[11] As I argued a moment ago, even
if means-end reasoning was biologically posterior to language, there
must still have been some selection for means-end reasoning as
such, to account for its power to influence behaviour. Still, as I
observed, this is consistent with means-end reasoning being a small
biological add-on, as it were, to a language faculty that had evolved
for quite independent reasons.

However, it is also possible that means-end reasoning may have
played a more significant role in evolution. Even if we stick with the
idea that language is the sole medium of means-end reasoning[12],
there is the possibility that means-end reasoning is the primary
function of language, and that communication is the spandrel,
which spun off after language had initially evolved to facilitate
means-end reasoning. More plausibly, means-end reasoning and
communication might both be biological functions of language.
This idea is most naturally filled out in a co-evolutionary model:

[10] Note how this model, in which means-end reasoning 'resets' our dispositions to action, can easily accommodate *plans*, that is complicated
sequences of actions needed to achieve some end. This would only require
that the means-end system be able to produce multiple action settings, settings which will trigger a sequence of behaviours as a sequence of cues are
encountered (some of which might simply be the completion of previous
behaviours).

[11] At the same time, I take it to be uncontentious that, once means-end
reasoning had emerged biologically, it then came to play a major role in the
non-biological development of human civilization.

[12] I should perhaps make it clear that by 'language' I mean to include
mental processing of internalised sentences of public languages, as well the
overt expression of those sentences.

176

once the first small biological step along the linguistic path had been taken, to facilitate communication, say, then this would have made possible a further step, which facilitated means-end reasoning, which would have made possible a further step, which facilitated communication, and so on.

To complicate the picture still further, note that different aspects of language might call for different evolutionary models. Earlier I distinguished the language of particular facts from the language of general facts. Perhaps the language of particular facts evolved entirely for communicative purposes, as suggested earlier, while the language of general facts evolved primarily to serve means-end reasoning. Or perhaps the language of general facts evolved under the co-evolutionary pressure of means-end reasoning and communication. Or so on. It is not hard to think of further possibilities.

All these last suggestions assume, in one way or another, that means-end reasoning arrived only with language. And this is indeed an attractive assumption. For one thing, the combinatorial structure of language lends itself naturally to the kinds of inferences which are central to means-end reasoning. Moreover, this assumption explains immediately why means-end reasoning should be restricted to humans.

Still, it is also interesting to speculate on whether some forms of means-end reasoning might not initially have evolved independently of language. One obvious hypothesis would be that an initial stage of means-end reasoning made use of visual imagination. Our ancestors played out various scenarios in their 'mind's eye', and used this to choose between alternative courses of action.

This use of visual imagination is so familiar that it is often taken for granted in theoretical contexts. But this familiarity is deceptive. There are any number of theoretical puzzles here. Is means-end thinking the primary function of visual imagination? How does this kind of 'visual anticipation' relate to visual memory? Is the use of visual imagination for means-end reasoning a generalization of domain-specific uses like spatial manipulation of objects, or, indeed, of spatial navigation as discussed earlier? And, to return to a central theme of this section, how did the upshot of visual imaginings acquire the power to influence pre-existing structures of action control?

In response to this last point, here is another hypothesis. Perhaps a crucial evolutionary step came when our ancestors acquired the ability to copy complex sequences of actions from others. This would require them visually to 'parse' what their teachers were doing, and then translate this visual information into action. Once

David Papineau

this was possible, it may then have been a small evolutionary step to translating an imaginative visual representation of your own behaviour into action.

These are enough speculations to be getting on with. They already provide the agenda for a number of other papers. I hope that this paper has at least shown that means-end reasoning is a topic worth pursuing further.

Bibliography

Cosmides, L. and Tooby, J. 1992. 'The Psychological Foundations of Culture', in J. Barkow, L. Cosmides and J. Tooby (eds) (Oxford: Oxford University Press), pp. 19–136.

Barkow, J., Cosmides, L. and Tooby, J. (eds) 1992. *The Adapted Mind* (Oxford: Oxford University Press).

Dennett, D. 1978. *Brainstorms* (Cambridge, MA: MIT Press).

Dennett, D. 1987. *The Intentional Stance* (Cambridge, MA: MIT Press).

Dickinson, A. and Balleine, B. 1999. 'Causal Cognition and Goal-Directed Action', in C. Heyes and L. Huber (eds) (Cambridge, MA: MIT Press, 1999).

Heyes, C. and Huber, L. (eds) 1999. *The Evolution of Cognition* (Cambridge, MA: MIT Press).

Gould, S. and Lewontin, R. 1978. 'The Spandrels of San Marco and the Panglossian Paradigm: A Critique of the Adaptationist Program', *Proceedings of the Royal Society*, **B205**, 581–98.

Heyes C. and Dickinson, A. 1990. 'The Intentionality of Animal Action', *Mind and Language* **5**, 87–104.

Fodor, J. 1983. *The Modularity of Mind* (Cambridge, MA: MIT Press).

Gallistel, R. 1980. *The Organization of Behavior* (Hillside, NJ: Earlbaum).

Gopnik, A., Glymour, C. and Sobel, D. forthcoming: 'Causal maps and Bayes nets: A cognitive and computational account of theory-formation'.

Millikan, R. 1996. 'Pushmi-pullyu Representations,' in J. Tomberlin (ed.) *Philosophical Perspectives IX* (Atascadero, CA: Ridgeview Press), pp.

Millikan, R. forthcoming: 'Some Different Ways to Think'.

Sperber, D. 1996. *Explaining Culture* (Oxford: Basil Blackwell).

Sperber, D. 1997. 'Intuitive and Reflective Beliefs', *Mind and Language*, **12**, 67–83.

Tomasello, M. and Call, J. 1997. *Primate Cognition* (Oxford: Oxford University Press)

Rationality and Higher-Order Intentionality

ALAN MILLAR

I. Rationality and the Mental

According to *the rationality thesis*, the possession of propositional attitudes is inextricably tied to rationality. How in this context should we conceive of rationality? In one sense, being rational is contrasted with being non-rational, as when human beings are described as rational animals. In another sense, being rational is contrasted with being irrational. I shall call rationality in this latter sense *evaluative rationality*. Whatever else it might involve, evaluative rationality surely has to do with satisfying requirements of rationality such as, presumably, the following:

(1) That one avoid inconsistency in beliefs.
(2) That one not adopt new beliefs unless what one knows entails or is evidence for the truth of those beliefs.
(3) That one not have φing as a goal yet do nothing necessary for one to φ. (Means/end requirement.)

I take it that the usually intended reading of the rationality thesis interprets 'rationality' to mean *evaluative rationality*. The claim, then, is that if one has propositional attitudes then one must be, to some degree, evaluatively rational. In other words, there are limits to how far a subject of propositional attitudes can fall short of what evaluative rationality requires. What reason is there to think that the rationality thesis is true?

A crucial consideration concerns the individuation of content. Suppose that within the space of a short conversation Fred makes some utterances, in English, such that were we to take them at face value we would ascribe to him both the belief that Edinburgh is to the east of Glasgow and the belief that Glasgow is to the east of Edinburgh. A natural reaction, I think, would be that Fred had made some slip of the tongue. Perhaps instead of saying, 'Glasgow is to the east of Edinburgh' he really meant to say, 'Glasgow is to the west of Edinburgh' or maybe 'Hamburg is to the east of Edinburgh'. Or perhaps Fred is not a native speaker of English and has somehow associated the wrong concepts with the words 'east'

179

Alan Millar

and 'west'. We are led to take such possibilities seriously because the ascription of the beliefs in question is problematic. Fred would need to have some grasp of the concepts of east and west if he had the beliefs in question, but if he has a grasp of the concepts then, barring some specifial explanation, we expect him not to have both of the beliefs. That Edinburgh is to the east of Glasgow obviously implies that Glasgow is to the west of Edinburgh, which obviously implies that it is not the case that Glasgow is to the east of Edinburgh. Fred would be aware of such relationships if he adequately understood either what it is for a thing to be to the east of something else or what it is for something to be to the west of something else. In this case it is hard to see how he could be aware of the relationships yet believe what his utterances, taken at face value, suggest that he believes. The idea here is that there are some patterns of incoherence involving a specified belief which, barring special explanation, would be incompatible with having a grasp of the concepts implicated by the belief.[1] So there are limits to irrationality among one's beliefs, these limits being imposed by the requirement that one have a grasp of the relevant concepts.

Another consideration in support of the rationality thesis concerns how a subject must interact with its environment if it has propositional attitudes. Unless a subject sometimes correctly represented its environment, sometimes desired what it needed, and sometimes, guided by true beliefs, did what really was required to satisfy its desires, it is hard to see why we should think of it as having any propositional attitudes at all. We ascribe propositional attitudes to creatures only if they interact *intelligently* with their environment. Such creatures have information about their environment which they exploit in ways which meet their needs. Although having beliefs and desires carries with it the possibility of false belief and wayward desire, it is also inextricably linked with true belief, appropriate desire, and means/end rationality.

I take it that the rationality thesis is true. It cannot be too strongly

---

[1] The qualification about special explanations accommodates, possibly among other things, situations like that of Kripke's Pierre, who is blind to the fact that he believes two propositions one of which is the negation of the other, since he believes them under articulations in different languages. See Kripke, 1979. That a subject exhibits a pattern of incoherence one would not normally expect him to exhibit if he had a grasp of the relevant concepts may be explicable on the grounds that the subject is unaware of an incompatibility because unaware that two different expressions are expressions which designate the same object or express the same concept. In these cases there need be no failure to grasp relevant concepts.

emphasized, however, that the limits to irrationality imposed by the considerations just mentioned are not especially exacting. A creature can have propositional attitudes and fall seriously short of what evaluative rationality requires. Its beliefs may be riddled with incoherence.[2] Its behaviour can be intelligible though motivated by beliefs and desires which are highly irrational.

The rationality thesis is sometimes thought to provide an obstacle to reductionist, and thus naturalistic, accounts of the mental. The argument has two main steps. The first is that mentalistic concepts, like those of belief and desire, are normative concepts, since their application is constrained by considerations of evaluative rationality. The second is that the fact that mentalistic concepts are normative blocks the possibility of either definitional or nomological reduction of the mental to the physical.[3] Each step is open to dispute and would need careful examination in any appraisal of the argument. The focus of the present discussion lies elsewhere. Any account of the kind of mental life which we enjoy must do justice to the complexities of *our* mentality, while accommodating the fact that we have evolved from more primitive animals. A question which naturally arises in this connection is whether it is appropriate to attribute propositional attitudes, as we standardly conceive them, to non-human animals. After all, it is not difficult to see why it might be thought that non-human animals can satisfy rationality requirements such as (1)–(3) above. (See section II.) Further, if such animals can satisfy the rationality requirements then they would surely be rational animals at least in the sense that they are creatures of a sort which admit of evaluation in terms of the requirements. However, I shall argue that creatures who have propositional attitudes must be rational animals in a stronger sense. They must be the sorts of creatures who are capable of, what I shall call, *deliberative thinking*. In arguing for this claim in section III, I

[2] Some interpreters of Davidson take him to suppose that the ascription of any inconsistency to a subject is to some degree problematic—that the bare fact that an interpretation imputes an inconsistency counts at least to some extent against it. See, for example, Goldman, 1989. Some of Davidson's remarks may give the impression that he holds to this view, but I doubt that the underlying principles on which he relies commit him to it. I should say also that the rationality thesis as interpreted here seems to be compatible with the various empirical studies which attest to striking failures of rationality in human beings. For a convenient review of such failures, see Edward Stein, 1996.

[3] The points about normative concepts are explicit in Davidson's 1991. The line of thought is foreshadowed in Davidson, 1980.

explore links between having propositional attitudes and having the capacity to believe and act for reasons. In section IV I discuss intention and autobiographical memory.

II. Rationality, Higher-order Intentionality and Rational Agency

There is a widely accepted picture of what it is to be a rational animal on which a creature is a rational animal only if it is capable of believing and acting for reasons. This view goes along with the idea that the beliefs and actions of rational animals admit of rationalizing explanations. A rationalizing explanation for a subject's believing that p, or ψing, is simply an explanation of the subject's believing that p, or ψing, in terms of the subject's reason for believing that p, or for ψing. What is it to believe or act for a reason? An appealing view, which would hardly seem controversial were our focus entirely on human thought and action, is that we believe that p, or ψ, for a reason only if we are moved by a consideration which we at least tacitly believe to be a reason to believe that p, or to ψ , and are so moved *because* we at least tacitly believe the consideration to be a reason to believe that p, or to ψ. On this way of thinking, there is no being moved by reasons without a point of view on, and thus a capacity to think about, considerations and their normative (reason-giving) force.[4] The view might seem to threaten a regress. I am moved, say, to believe that Sally is coming by train in view of the consideration that either she is coming by train or she is coming by plane, and that she is not coming by plane. According to the story, I am so moved because I believe this consideration to be a reason to believe that Sally is coming by train. Does this mean that the content of my belief regarding the consideration has to be viewed as a further consideration which must be added to the original one, and do we then need to posit a further belief on my part as to the expanded consideration's being a reason to believe that Sally is coming by train, and so on? No. There is no regress because the consideration that the original consideration is a reason to believe that Sally is coming by train is not part of the justification for this latter belief. The original consideration is sufficient justification. The point is rather that my believing that the original consideration

---

[4] Julia Tanney floats the idea that rationalizing explanations of an agent's actions must reckon with *her* point of view in Tanney, 1999, especially, 55ff. This is a theme I pursue below in section III.

is a reason to believe that Sally is coming by train figures in the explanation of how the original consideration moves me to believe that Sally is coming by train. If the original consideration is truly my reason for believing that Sally is coming by train then it is one which I treat as a reason so to believe. That may amount to no more than that it is a consideration in view of which, and on account of which, I am persuaded so to believe. This way of thinking underpins the view that (most) non-human animals are non-rational. For however natural it is to credit, say, dogs, with beliefs and desires, we are rightly reluctant to suppose that they have attitudes which are about considerations, never mind attitudes about considerations conceived as being reasons for believing something or doing something. That is because we do not think of dogs as being *deliberative thinkers*. Deliberative thinking is evaluative thinking. In the theoretical sphere it is thinking about whether or not some proposition is true (or has some other status, like being convincing or plausible) in the light of any reasons for or against thinking it true (or has whatever other status is at issue). In the practical sphere it is evaluating some actual or possible action in the light of any reasons for or against performing the action. Perhaps dogs engage in reasoning. When a dog hears the clatter of its food dish and charges towards the kitchen, it comes naturally to us to suppose that it undergoes a transition from hearing that its food dish is clattering to believing that food is in its dish. We might think of the dog as reasoning because such a transition would mirror an evidential link between its being the case that the dish is clattering and its being the case that food is in the dish, and because the dog's undergoing this transition would be no accident, being explained by what it has learned.[5] But it is not engaged in deliberative thinking as I understand it, since, presumably, it is incapable of the kind of evaluative thinking which is characteristic of deliberative thinking. Hence the apparent tension between our willingness to credit dogs with beliefs and desires and our reluctance to regard them as rational animals. The tension is real if it is true that only beings who are deliberative thinkers, and who can be moved by reasons in the sense explained, can be rational animals. There is, however, a prima facie plausible case to the contrary.

To lead into the argument I need to invoke the idea that there are various orders of intentionality. First-order intentionality is the intentionality of attitudes like believing it is raining or wanting to eat. Such attitudes may be about all sorts of things, but what makes

---

[5] Even so, see further the discussion of section III.

Alan Millar

them first-order attitudes is, to a first approximation, that they are not themselves about attitudes. By contrast, believing that Sam wants to play cards would be a second-order attitude because it is about a desire of Sam, and believing that Sam wants me to believe he is joking would be a third-order attitude, because it is about a desire of Sam, which is itself about a belief, and so on. A feature of deliberative thinking is that it implicates an ability to think about contents *in abstraction* from any attitudes or speech acts of which they may be the contents. In the course of pondering whether it is true that p, in the light of certain considerations, you think about the proposition that p, and the considerations, in abstraction from any attitudes or speech acts of which they may be the contents. I shall take the notion of higher-order intentionality to encompass attitudes which are about contents considered in abstraction. That is why explaining higher-order intentionality in terms of attitudes about attitudes is only a first approximation.

Let us suppose that there are animals who have only first-order attitudes.[6] Think of such animals as walking the *low road*. Animals who, like ourselves, have the capacity for deliberative thinking are on the *high road*.[7] Suppose, that a dog, eager to fetch a stick which has been thrown, runs to catch it. We find it natural to attribute to the dog beliefs which track the location of the stick and a desire to catch it. By running to catch the stick the dog satisfies the requirement of means/end rationality not to have a goal, yet do nothing necessary to achieve the goal. In this case, it satisfies the requirement because its goal is maintained and it does what is necessary. Maybe on other occasions when the stick is thrown the dog loses track of it and then loses any desire to run to fetch it. Here too it satisfies the requirement, though this time it does so because the goal is abandoned, rather than because it does what is necessary to achieve it. The point of this sort of example is just this: It is surely no accident that the dog satisfies the means/end requirement in

[6] Davidson is committed to rejecting such a supposition by his view that anyone who has beliefs must have a concept of belief and thus beliefs regarding beliefs. See Davidson, 1984. Many would resist this view. However, see section III below.

[7] It is an open question whether some non-human animals might occupy the high road though I am inclined to think they do not. Relatedly, there is an interesting question whether there might be creatures who tread paths intermediate between the low and high roads, that is, creatures who exhibit higher-order intentionality, but lack a capacity for deliberative thinking. It is, at any rate, not obvious that being able to think about attitudes necessarily involves the ability to think evaluatively about contents in the way required for deliberative thinking.

those cases. It seems to be sensitive to the requirement at least to the extent that it has dispositions which tend to ensure that when it has a goal it either achieves it or abandons it. Similar considerations apply to the other requirements of rationality mentioned in the previous section. The general idea is that the dog is structured in such a way that it does not go too far out of line with what evaluative rationality requires, even though it lacks a capacity to think about the relevant requirements, or, for that matter, about the normative force of this or that consideration. It is this idea which makes sense of our evaluating the dog in terms of the rationality requirements and thus treating it as a rational animal in some thin sense. This way of thinking is not without problems. For one thing, we tell the story making attributions of content to the dog's beliefs which, if taken quite literally, would require attributing to it possession of the very concepts we would express by the words we use in making the attribution. If there is reason to hesitate about ascribing possession of these concepts, as there surely is, then the corresponding ascriptions of content should be read within inverted commas. I shall largely ignore this problem in the present discussion. The point I want to emphasize is that there is something to be said in favour of the idea that the condition for being a rational animal in the thin sense— admitting of evaluation in terms of the requirements of rationality—could be met even in the case of animals who lack the capacity for deliberative thinking. What, then, are we to make of the consideration which gave rise to the apparent tension between being a creature which lacks this capacity and being a rational animal?

There is a line of thought which is aimed at dissipating the tension. The key idea is that the particular kind of higher-order intentionality which places subjects on the high road is necessary, not for being a rational *animal*, but for being a rational *agent*. You are a rational agent only if you are capable of being moved to ψ, or to believe that p, by certain considerations on account of their being, as you think, reasons for, respectively, ψing or believing that p. If you are a rational agent then you must be a deliberative thinker, because only a deliberative thinker has a point of view on the considerations which move it. But a rational animal does not have to be a rational agent if our reflections about the dog are along the right lines. These reflections have a certain deflationary tendency in relation to the significance of higher-order intentionality. They might well be taken to suggest that, however important higher-order intentionality is for rational agency, and for important aspects of distinctively human psychology, it has no deep implications for our understanding of what is required for a propositional attitude

Alan Millar

psychology.[8] For it might be thought that the minimum requirement for a propositional attitude psychology is, simply, the possession of first-order motivational states (why not call them desires?),
first-order representational states (why not call them beliefs?) and,
as part of that package, abilities to exploit the motivational and representational states in ways which make rational sense. Thus far we
have seen no reason to suppose that animals on the low road could
not satisfy this requirement. In the next two sections, however, I
shall try to show that the situation is altogether more complicated.
The overarching theme is that our notions of belief and desire do
the work they do within a framework of thought about belief, action
and motivation, which has clear application only to animals on the
high road. I focus first on some issues concerning reasons for belief
or action, and then in the concluding section discuss intention and
autobiographical memory.

III. Acting and Believing for a Reason

The tension which was the theme of section II arose from the idea
that rational, as opposed to non-rational, animals are capable of
being moved by (what they take to be) reasons, and that only deliberative thinkers, who can think about considerations as reasons, are
capable of being so moved. The tension was to be dissipated by
showing that animals on the low road can be rational *animals*, while
at the same time acknowledging that only animals on the high road
can be rational *agents*. That led on to the deflationary reflections
which played down the significance of higher-order intentionality
for possession of propositional attitude psychology. I shall argue
that this tolerant strategy does not do full justice to the reflections

---

[8] It is a familiar idea that while higher-order intentionality is not a
requirement for having propositional attitudes generally, nevertheless it is
a requirement for important forms of mental life which we happen to
enjoy. It is evidently necessary for knowledge and understanding of mental states—a theme which has recently been explored in relation to the
analysis of autism and the possibility of mind-reading on the part of non-
human animals. On autism, see Baron-Cohen, 1995. On mindreading on
the part of animals, see Byrne, 1995; Whiten, 1996. Higher-order intentionality has also been claimed to be necessary for being a language-user
(Grice, 1957 & 1969), for being a person (Frankfurt, 1971; Dennett, 1981),
for being a thinker (Pettit, 1993), and for being a conscious subject
(Rosenthal, 1997; Carruthers 1996). Here the focus is on the specified conception of rational agency.

which underpin the view that only deliberators can be rational animals.

Beliefs and desires are essential components of any system of propositional attitudes. As we standardly conceive of them, beliefs and desires figure in rationalizing explanations of actions. These are explanations which show why the action *makes rational sense*, that is, makes sense in the light of the agent's reasons for performing those actions. Similar considerations apply to rationalizing explanations for the formation or retention of beliefs. Now, on the strategy of toleration under consideration, what are we to make of the idea of a subject's believing or acting *for reasons*?

It was belief and action for reasons which seemed to make being a deliberative thinker a necessary condition for being a rational animal. The idea was that to believe that p (or to ψ) for a reason is (i) to be moved by a consideration which one takes to be a reason to believe that p (or to ψ), and (ii) to be so moved because one takes the consideration to be a reason to believe that p (or to ψ). No very special sophistication, relative to normal human capacities, is required to be so moved. All that is required is that the consideration be one in view of which, and on account of which, the subject believes or does something. This amounts to saying that the consideration must be one which persuades the subject to believe or act as he does. Animals on the low road do not in the relevant sense believe or act for reasons because, lacking the capacity for deliberative thought, they do not have thoughts about considerations at all, and a fortiori do not treat considerations as reasons. To develop the point we need a distinction, familiar in the philosophy of practical reasoning, between motivating and normative reasons.[9] Normative reasons for a belief are considerations which justify having that belief. Normative reasons for an action are considerations which justify, or at least give point to, the agent's undertaking (or having undertaken) the action. Motivating reasons are reasons for which an agent actually believes something or actually does something. Note that whereas only true considerations can be normative reasons, motivating reasons may be false. A normative reason to ψ (or believe that p) is something like a (good) case for ψing (or believing that p). A case collapses if the consideration which makes the case includes as an essential component some consideration which is false.

Whereas normative reasons are always good reasons, the considerations which constitute an agent's motivating reasons may be bad reasons. Still, in line with the way of thinking about motivation by

[9] The distinction has an honourable history. Applied to actions, it figures prominently in Smith, 1993.

Alan Millar

reasons which I have been sketching, a consideration which constitutes a motivating reason for a belief or action must be one which the agent at least tacitly *believes to be* a normative reason for the belief or action. Indeed, to believe or act for a reason, on this way of thinking, just is to be moved to believe or act by a consideration which one takes to be a normative reason for the belief or action, and to be so moved because one takes the consideration to be a normative reason for the belief or action. I shall call this the *Motivation Principle*.

Animals on the low road do not believe or act for reasons in any sense governed by the Motivation Principle, since they lack a point of view on the reasons which move them. Nevertheless, there is a familiar theory about reasons which is meant to show how such animals may believe and act for reasons. According to this theory, motivating reasons are constituted not by considerations but by mental states, so I shall call it *the mental-state theory*. Motivating reasons for belief are constituted by other beliefs and motivating reasons for action are constituted by beliefs and desires. When a subject believes that p for a reason it must believe that p because it has certain other beliefs, and these other beliefs must make rational sense of its believing that p. When a subject ψs for a reason it must ψ because it has certain beliefs and desires and these beliefs and desires must make rational sense of its ψing. What is required for a belief or action to make rational sense is not always clearly spelled out, but one thing is clear; it does not require the subject to have a point of view on its own reasons. So the mental-state theory is clearly at odds with the Motivation Principle.

One of the reasons why philosophers think there is little if any problem about attributing a propositional attitude psychology to animals on the low road is that (as they see it) the behaviour of such animals admits of rationalizing explanation just as much as our behaviour does. This line of thought is sustained by thinking that the notion of an action's being done for a reason, or of a belief's being formed for a reason, applies indifferently to low road and high road creatures. But, as I shall now argue, the idea of belief or action for a reason lacks clear application once detached from a psychology which respects the Motivation Principle. To simplify the argument I shall focus on belief for reasons.

Suppose I am hypnotized into a state such that whatever belief I acquire next will induce me to believe that there are six apples on the table.[10] The next belief I acquire is that there is a group of two apples on the table and a distinct (non-overlapping) group of four

[10] The example is adapted from Kathleen Lennon, 1990, 38f.

188

apples on the table. I duly come to believe that there are six apples on the table. Intuitively, this is not a case of believing for a reason. I would have come to believe that there are six apples on the table whatever belief I first acquired after having been put into the hypnotic state. The problem is that though the content of the belief which prompts me to believe that there are six apples on the table constitutes a normative reason for believing that there are six apples on the table, the fact that the prompting belief has such a content is irrelevant to my having acquired the latter belief. Any plausible development of the theory will incorporate a condition to the effect that, when a subject believes that p for a reason, the *contents* of the beliefs which constitute the subject's reason for believing that p are not irrelevant to the causation of the belief that p. The following is such a condition:

> X's beliefs that q, r, s, ... constitute X's reason for believing that p only if [q, r, s, ... : p] instantiates a pattern P such that X's belief that p results from the exercise of a disposition on X's part to make belief-transitions in accordance with P.[11]

We are to think of P as an inference pattern the instances of which are constituted by a sequence of premises followed by a conclusion. The condition suffices to rule out the hypnotism example as a case of believing for a reason. For though, no doubt, I have a general disposition to believe that there are six apples on a table on coming to believe that there are two distinct groups of four and two apples on the table, in this case my believing that there are six apples on the table does not result from the exercise of such a disposition, nor any other disposition internalizing a pattern of inference. As it stands, however, the condition does not go far enough. I have said that we are to think of P as an inference pattern. Unfortunately, the account says nothing about how, for any instance of P, the premises should relate to the conclusion. For all that has been said, P might not be a pattern of reasonable inference, nor even a pattern of inferences such that believing the premises would make rational sense of believing the conclusion. We need to add a clause ((i) below) along the following lines:

Alternative Motivation Principle (Belief)

> X's beliefs that q, r, s, ... constitute X's reason for believing that p only if [q, r, s, ... : p] instantiates a pattern P such that:

[11] A similar condition figures in a proposal on inferring one belief from others given in Barbara Winters, 1983, p. 216.

Alan Millar

> (i) in any instance of P the premises are related to the conclusion in such a way that believing the conclusion on the basis of believing the premises would make rational sense, and
>
> (ii) X's belief that p results from the exercise of a disposition on X's part to make belief-transitions in accordance with P.

(By 'believing that p on the basis of believing that q, r, s, ...' I mean no more than that one believes that p because one believes that q, r, s, ...) The question now is how we should spell out condition (i). It might be suggested that P should be such that in any instance the premises would, if true, together constitute a normative reason to believe the conclusion.[12] That condition would clearly be too strong. The mental-state theory is meant to provide an account of motivating reasons for beliefs, where such reasons are taken to be constituted by further beliefs. A plausible development of the theory must accommodate the fact that motivating reasons can be *bad* reasons. The suggested condition can accommodate reasons which are bad due to falsity, since it does not require that the premises of inferences which instantiate P should actually be normative reasons for believing the conclusions of those inferences, only that they would, *if true*, be normative reasons for believing the conclusions. The trouble is that reasons can be bad on grounds other than falsity. Suppose that you believe that people in some class have a specified undesirable characteristic. You are moved to have this belief by the consideration that each person in this class which you have met, or have information about, has this undesirable characteristic. Suppose that this evidential consideration is true, but the sample of people you have encountered is small and not suitably varied for testing the distribution of the characteristic in the class. This is clearly a case of believing for a bad reason, where the badness of the reason is not due to falsity.[13] Sometimes our rationalizing explanations cite motivating reasons for beliefs which are bad reasons because even if true they would fail to justify the belief. How can such bad reasons be accommodated in the terms of the Alternative Motivation Principle (Belief)?

[12] This was the thought which underpinned the idea, discussed in section II, that the dog reasons to the conclusion that there is food its dish.

[13] This might be denied on the grounds that the subject tacitly relies on a false premise to the effect that the sample is suitably varied. But I see no reason to suppose that when subjects make inferences in the light of which their belief in the conclusion makes rational sense they always have as many premises as they need. I do not see in this case why we should suppose that the subject must have relied on a premise concerning the character of the sample.

190

Rationality and Higher-Order Intentionality

Let us first consider how motivating reasons which are bad on grounds other than falsity, might be accommodated from the perspective of our original Motivation Principle. Sticking with our example of bad inductive reasoning, how might your believing the generalization make rational sense? When bad reasoning makes sense of a belief it does so because the subject is one who, as it were, aspires to reason well but is somehow misled into treating a consideration as one which, if true, would justify the conclusion drawn from it. Bad reasoning, so conceived, is not simply a malfunction of a belief-forming mechanism the operation of which generally conforms to a pattern of good reasoning. It occurs when a subject, who is in the business of taking considerations to be (or not to be) reasons for belief or action, treats a bad reason as a good reason. If a belief formed because of such reasoning is to make sense, it must be intelligible that the subject should have been misled into falsely regarding a bad reason as a good reason. In the case in hand, it matters that the evidential consideration on which you based your generalization is inductively relevant to your conclusion. It is this fact coupled with its being explicable that you should be misled by the consideration, perhaps because of personal bias, which enables us to make rational sense of your believing the generalization.

The foregoing remarks are all in terms of the perspective of the Motivation Principle. As such they do little to advance the project of accommodating bad reasoning within the terms of a mental-state theory of motivating reasons designed to apply to animals on the low road. What is needed is some analogue for being a creature who aspires to reason well but wrongly takes a consideration to be one which if true would be a good reason for a belief. The best we can do here is to treat bad reasoning as a malfunction in a mechanism designed by evolution or learning to operate in accordance with good principles. Then, at least the mechanism might be thought to be aiming at good reasoning and the animal misled in virtue of a malfunction. The problem is that we are not entitled to suppose that animals on the low road have internalized patterns of good reasoning, *as opposed to patterns of cognitive-state transition, conformity to which often enough meets their needs.* Imagine a dog which, on hearing a noise in the driveway, believes its owner is about to enter the house. (Let us suppose that when it believes that its owner is about to enter it goes crazy as opposed merely to making a noise.) Suppose, further, that the dog is as often as not disappointed because the noises in response to which it expects its owner are caused by others. Assuming this to be a possible scenario compatible with canine psychology one might suggest that the dog's expectations

191

Alan Millar

make rational sense in much the way that the bad inductive reasoner's generalizations do. The fact that there are noises in the driveway on some occasion is evidentially relevant to the belief that the dog's owner is about to enter and, the story would go, we can explain why the dog is so often misled in terms of something like wishful thinking on its part. Apart from anything else, this overdescribes the situation. In practice we would probably gerrymander the ascription of beliefs so that the dog turns out to have beliefs the contents of which would, if true, constitute a normative reason for expecting its owner. So we might ascribe to the dog a false belief to the effect that usually when there is a noise of footsteps in the driveway it is succeeded, soon after, by its owner coming through the front door. I suspect, however, that there is no fact of the matter as to whether the dog reasons well from such a false belief, or, alternatively, reasons badly from true beliefs which might include, say, a belief to the effect that sometimes the sound of footsteps in the driveway is succeeded soon after by the entry of its owner. For want of a better description we may think of the dog as expecting its owner but we have little reason to think of it as having internalized principles of good reasoning. It seems perfectly conceivable that an animal should acquire habits of expectation-formation the exercise of which do it no harm, and often enough meet its needs, even though the patterns of transition which the habits embody are not patterns of good reasoning.[14]

The upshot is that it is doubtful that the very idea of a rationalizing explanation, conceived in terms of the notion of believing for a reason, has application to animals on the low road. Rationalizing explanation, and the notion of believing for a reason, make tolerably clear sense only in relation to a psychological economy such that the subject can misjudge the normative force of a consideration. Though I have not argued the point I think it can be shown that essentially the same issues arise in connection with action for reasons. Given these considerations and despite the discussion of section II, there really is a problem about regarding animals on the low road as being rational animals, in the sense currently in play, and as having propositional attitudes. The problem about their being rational animals is that they do not, in any clear sense, believe or act for reasons. The problem about their having propositional attitudes is posed by the idea that propositional attitude psychology goes with rationalizing explanation and thus the capacity to believe or act for

[14] Closely related considerations are pursued in Stein, 1996, ch.6 in the context of a critique of evolutionary arguments for the claim that humans are evaluatively rational.

reasons. I do not suggest that animals on the low road lack an intentional psychology, nor do I deny that they can intelligently exploit information about their environment. My point is only that they do not have propositional attitudes worthy of the name. If that is right, and they do indeed have an intentional psychology, then there is an incentive to explore in greater detail the possibility that their intentional states are integrated in a very different way from the way in which propositional attitudes are integrated.[15]

IV. Intention and Autobiographical Memory

It is obvious that there are categories of mental state which require higher-order intentionality. There is no feeling shame or regret, for example, without a point of view on one's own actions. But while shame or regret are crucial for moral agency they do not seem to be crucial for a propositional attitude psychology. Though a subject who lacked all capacity for shame or regret would be disturbing, we have no difficulty in conceiving of such a subject as having beliefs, desires, and a host of other attitudes. There are other categories of mental state which seem to be more fundamental. I have in mind intention and autobiographical memory. I want to suggest, rather than argue in detail, that intention and autobiographical memory implicate higher-order intentionality and that a propositional attitude psychology is as much bound up with intention and autobiographical memory, as with believing and acting for a reason.

Imagine that you keep a diary the entries of which describe past or anticipated events and actions. Some of the entries are future-directed. They describe things you have committed yourself to doing, like going to the dentist, or hosting a dinner party, or events which you might go along to, like a showing of a film. There is no unclarity as to which entries are future-directed and which past-descriptive. At each blank entry there is a future box and a past box. Commitments and options go in the future box and are clearly distinguished; descriptions of what you have done, and your personal impressions of events which have taken place, go in the past box. What role does the diary have in your life? Certainly both the future-directed and past-descriptive entries serve as reminders of what you have done, thought, or felt, and of what you intend to do, or might do. The diary is an extension of your mind, not merely an external expression of information you would keep in mind anyway.

[15] For a good exploration of aspects of this theme, see Bermúdez, 1995.

Alan Millar

It is a means whereby you are able to recall past experiences, as well as intentions and options. What enables it to be an extension of your mind is the fact that you have a practice of consulting and updating it. For it is only that practice which makes the contents of the diary the contents of your intentions, options and memories.

These reflections provide a further twist to the familiar idea that to account for our mental life it is necessary to take the mind to embrace more than is contained in the head of the individual. It may be that the only thing which makes it true of you now that you intend to visit the dentist on some specified date is that your diary, which figures in a practice of regular updating and consulting, indicates that you have an appointment on that date, marked as a commitment. And it may be that the only thing which makes it true of you now that a certain incident is retained in your memory, is that the diary, functioning as it does in your life, records that incident as having taken place. The claim about memory might seem problematic. Is it not a little odd to say that the claim that you remember visiting a certain gallery on holiday last year is true in virtue of the fact that there is an entry to that effect in the past-descriptive portion of your diary? Indeed, we can imagine your saying when asked if you visited the gallery, 'I don't remember; I need to consult my diary'. But, here, I think we need to distinguish between one's memories and one recollections. In saying, 'I don't remember' you are saying in effect that you don't recall straight off, which is not quite the same as saying that you have forgotten. Determining that you visited the gallery by using the diary, in the context of a regular practice of such use, is more akin to a form of recollection than it is to finding out by, say, coming across a ticket of admission or being informed by someone else. It is more akin to recollection because in recollection your own past experience is what lays down the record which you access at a later stage. In the diary case it just happens that the record is written down.

What does all this have to do with the current topic? I suggest that intention, even in the absence of the additional resource of the diary and its associated practice, should be understood on the *diary model*. To bring out the point of this, I need to highlight another feature of the use of the diary. When you consult the diary the entries it contains are for you objects of thought; they are objects of thought conceived, not as bare inscriptions, but as expressions of certain contents. (So we are in the area of higher-order intentionality.) The entries serve as reminders of what you intend to do and thus of the fact that you have the intentions in question. These reminders have a crucial role in prompting action aimed at carrying

194

out the intention. Something like this holds for intention generally. Whenever you intend to do something you have a belief concerning what you intend. In cases which approximate to the dental appointment scenario, in which the intention slips out of mind, the relevant belief may arise through some prompt to memory. In other cases, the belief as to what you intend is stored in the form of active knowledge of what you mean to do.

The upshot is that acting on intentions requires one to have a point of view on considerations which move one to action. This is because intentions are had only by subjects who can do things directed at carrying them out, and to do things directed at carrying out an intention you must be aware of the fact that you have the intention. When you, say, go to the Library by way of carrying out an intention to obtain some book, your reason for going is that you intend to borrow a book and can do so by going to the Library, a consideration which, by the Motivation Principle, you take to be a (normative) reason to go to the Library. Carrying out an intention, I claim, always involves having such considerations in view. This is so even in cases when the intention is not consciously formed prior to the action. Picking up a tin from a supermarket shelf can be something you intended to do even if you did not think to yourself in advance that you intended to do it. But even in such a case you have the intention in view in that you know what you mean to do and why you mean to do it. The diary model fits with this view, for it tells us that an intention leads to, or informs, an action aimed at carrying it out only in the presence of a belief as to what one intends. It also helps us to see the link between intention and deliberative thinking, since acting by way of carrying out an intention is always action in view of a consideration which one takes to be a reason for acting.

Somewhat similar considerations apply to auto-biographical memory. Memories of what one has done in the past come to mind in recollection. To be recollected they must become objects of thought. Recalling that one ψed is not simply an attitude with the content that one ψed, but a condition in which the consideration that one ψed is itself made an object of consideration, being thought of as something recalled. There is all the difference in the world between merely knowing that as a child you dropped a rather heavy toy on a friend's head and recalling that you did. In recollection, the fact that you dropped the toy presents itself to you as something you recall.

If all this is along the right lines then intentions and autobiographical memories require the kind of higher-order intentionality

Alan Millar

which distinguishes those who walk the high road. Autobiographical memories implicate a perspective on one's past and intentions implicate plans for, and thus, a perspective on, one's future.[16] The perspectives are intimately related. Memories feed into our plans for the future as well as enabling us to keep track of what we plan, what we need to do to implement our plans, and how far we have gone towards implementing them. In so far as intentions implicate plans they can be had only by creatures who can keep track of them as being *their* plans and who, therefore, have appropriate autobiographical memories. Conceived along these lines, autobiographical memory and intention are certainly crucial for the peculiar perspective we each have on our own past and on the future which we anticipate—a perspective from which we are not merely spectators, but think of our past and future, as it were, from the inside. But are they essential for a propositional attitude psychology? For all I have said in this section it might be that a propositional attitude psychology—one in which belief and desire have a central role—need involve neither intentions nor autobiographical memories. But if desires had a functional role which links them to intentions then there would be reason to think that a propositional attitude psychology must implicate intentions and as much autobiographical memory as is necessary to keep track of intentions. I think that a good case can be made to this effect though here I confine myself to the barest sketch.

No doubt when I open the window to let in fresh air, I want to let in fresh air. But there might be lots of things I want but do nothing to bring about, and when desires do prompt me to act I am not simply borne along by them. Desires are the sorts of states which lead us to action only if *endorsed* through the formation of a future-directed intention, or the performance of an intentional action, aimed at satisfying the desire. Creatures which lack higher-order intentionality can have goal-directed states. Such states are best conceived as being analogous, not to desires, but to intentions. Desires merely present certain ends as being attractive. It is through intentions that we set ourselves goals. Yet the goal-directed states, in creatures lacking higher-order intentionality, are not our familiar intentions—intentions in having which we always have a reason in view and thus know what we are about. It is right that we credit animals lacking higher-order intentionality with an ability to represent,

[16] That intentions involve plans has been a central theme of Michael Bratman's work. See Bratman, 1987 & 1999.
[17] Compare the challenge to the belief-desire model of motivation presented by Bratman in his 1987, especially pp. 18–27.

196

and to act appropriately in, their environment. All I am claiming is that central features of *our* psychology—intentions and autobiographical memories—involve higher-order intentionality, and that even what we ordinarily think of as desires are states which do their familiar work via their links with intentions.

Bibliography

Baron-Cohen, S. 1995. *Mindblindness: An Essay on Autism and Theory of Mind* (Cambridge, MA.: MIT Press).

Bermúdez, J. L. 1995. 'Nonconceptual content: From Perceptual Experience to Subpersonal Computational States', *Mind and Language*, **10**, 333–69.

Block, N., Flanagan, O. and Güzeldere, G. (eds.) 1997. *The Nature of Consciousness* (Cambridge, MA: MIT Press).

Bratman, M. 1987. *Intentions, Plans, and Practical Reason* (Cambridge, MA: Harvard University Press).

Bratman, M. 1999. *Faces of Intention; Selected Essays on Intention and Agency* (Cambridge: Cambridge University Press).

Byrne, R. 1995. *The Thinking Ape* (Oxford: Oxford University Press).

Carruthers, P. 1996. *Language, Thought, and Consciousness: An Essay in Philosophical Psychology* (Cambridge: Cambridge University Press).

Carruthers, P. and Smith, P. K. (eds) 1996. *Theories of Theories of Mind* (Cambridge: Cambridge University Press).

Davidson, D. 1980(a). 'Mental Events', in Davidson, D. 1980(b), pp. 207–27.

Davidson, D. 1980(b) *Essays on Actions and Events* (Oxford: Clarendon Press).

Davidson, D. 1984(a). 'Thought and Talk', in Davidson, D. 1984(b), pp. 155–70.

Davidson, D. 1984(b) *Inquiries into Truth and Interpretation* (Oxford: Clarendon Press).

Davidson, D. 1990. 'Representation and Interpretation', in Mohyeldin Said, K. A., Newton-Smith, W. H., Viale, R. and Wilkes, K. V. (eds) 1990, pp. 13–26.

Davidson, D. 1991. 'Three Varieties of Human Knowledge', in Phillips Griffiths, A. (ed.) 1999, pp. 153–66.

Dennett, D. C. 1981. 'Conditions of Personhood' in *Brainstorms* (Brighton, Sussex: The Harvester Press), pp. 267–85.

Goldman, A. 1989. 'Interpretation Psychologised', *Mind and Language*, **4**, 161–85.

Grice, H. P. 1957. 'Meaning' *Philosophical Review*, **66**, 337–88.

Grice, H. P. 1969. 'Utterer's meaning and Intentions', *Philosophical Review*, **78**, 147–77.

Kripke, S. 1979. 'A Puzzle About Belief', in Margalit, A. (ed.) 1979, pp. 239–83.

Alan Millar

Lennon, K. 1990. *Explaining Behaviour* (La Salle, Illinois: Open Court).

Margalit, A. (ed.) 1979. *Meaning and Use* (Dordrecht, Holland: Reidel).

Mohyeldin Said, K. A., Newton-Smith, W. H., Viale, R. and Wilkes, K. V., 1990. *Modelling the Mind* (Oxford: Clarendon Press).

Pettit, P. 1993. *The Common Mind* (New York: Oxford University Press).

Phillips Griffiths, A. (ed.) 1991. *A. J. Ayer Memorial Essays, Royal Institute of Philosophy Supplement:* **30** (Cambridge: Cambridge University Press).

Rosenthal, D. 1997. 'A Theory of Consciousness', in Block, N., Flanagan, O. and Güzeldere, G. (eds) (Cambridge, MA: MIT Press), pp. 729–53.

Smith, M. 1993. *The Moral Problem* (Oxford: Blackwell).

Stein, E. 1996. *Without Good Reason* (Oxford: Clarendon Press).

Tanney, J. 1999. 'Normativity and Judgement', *Proceedings of the Aristotelian Society, Supplementary Volume* **73**, 45–61.

Whiten, A. 1996. 'When does behaviour-reading become mind-reading?', in Carruthers, P. and Smith, P. K. (eds) 1996, pp. 277–92.

Winters, B. 1983. 'Inferring', *Philosophical Studies,* **44**, 201–20.

Theory of Mind in Non-Verbal Apes: conceptual issues and the critical experiments

ANDREW WHITEN

It is now over twenty years since Premack and Woodruff (1978) posed the question, 'Does the chimpanzee have a theory of mind?'—'by which we meant', explained Premack (1988) in a later reappraisal, 'does the ape do what humans do: attribute states of mind to the other one, and use these states to predict and explain the behaviour of the other one? For example, does the ape wonder, while looking quizzically at another individual, What does he really *want*? What does he *believe*? What are his *intentions*?'

That chimpanzees, and indeed other primates, might operate in this way came to be seen as a promising conjecture in the light of parallel studies of primate societies in the wild. It was never entirely clear why the laboratory scientists Premack and Woodruff asked their famous question, other than to express curiosity about one further respect in which an ape might be more like a human than had been acknowledged. But primate ethology offered a deeper rationale for suspecting the existence of something like a non-human theory of mind. Monkeys and apes were found naturally to interact with unsuspected sophistication. They were shown, for example, to build and exploit relationships with allies (Harcourt and de Waal, 1992); to deceive and counter-deceive (Whiten and Byrne, 1988a) and to repair beneficial relationships after over-enthusiastically denting them (de Waal, 1989; Castles and Whiten 1998a & 1998b). The emerging complexity of primate sociality was indicated by book titles like *Chimpanzee Politics* (de Waal, 1982) and *Machiavellian Intelligence* (Byrne and Whiten, 1988; Whiten and Byrne, 1997). This corpus of work showed that primate social life is often a fast-moving game in which the potential payoffs of reading the mind of potential opponents—asking the kinds of questions (above) that Premack put into the head of his hypothetical chimpanzee—and thus getting one step ahead in the political, sexual and reproductive stakes, seem all too apparent (Whiten, 1993 & 1997).

But does it happen? Are any primates mindreaders? How would one know? Philosophers have been actively involved in debates and

Andrew Whiten

discussions with behavioural scientists about the appropriate way to answer such questions from the start. Several philosophers provided influential peer commentaries in the *Behavioral and Brain Sciences* treatment of Premack and Woodruff's paper, suggesting that adequate criteria for demonstrating the attribution of states of mind had yet to be established, and proposing that tests for the attribution of false beliefs might provide the most convincing avenue of work.[1] A few years later, these ideas were taken up in a study of children's early theory of mind (Wimmer and Perner, 1983), that laid the foundations for a massive programme of research on this topic in the developmental psychology of the 1990s. As a result, we now know much about the child's theory of mind, which twenty years ago was an almost unexplored territory. Theory of Mind research has continued to witness productive interplay between philosophy and empirical scientific studies. The question of primate theory of mind arguably throws into stark perspective some particularly profound conceptual and theoretical questions that offer special challenges for philosophical analyses, ranging from those that have already received centuries of attention, like the problem of other minds, to many new ones thrown up by the ongoing research (Carruthers and Smith, 1996; Davies and Stone, 1996 and Sperber, 2000).

1. Chimpanzee theory of mind? The long road to strong inference

I borrow this header from Povinelli (1996), for the metaphor of a long hard road is apt. Developmental psychologists' account of children's burgeoning theory of mind, whilst replete with its own controversies, has in the last decade drawn a quite detailed and consensually agreed chart of the competencies in operation at each stage, particularly between the ages of two and five (Mitchell, 1996). This is based on literally hundreds of studies. By contrast, the number of studies on non-human primates has remained meagre and the nature—even the existence—of primate theory of mind is still unclear (Povinelli, 1996; Whiten, 1997 and Heyes 1998). In part this is because of practical and logistic constraints. Whilst children

---

[1] Bennett, 1978; Dennett 1978 and Harman 1978. This paper and the commentaries on it still offer some of the most illuminating thinking on the problems of what shall count as mindreading in non-verbal creatures, and how one might test for it.

are ubiquitous, generally biddable, and can be inducted into experiments with a few words of explanation, suitable primate subjects are typically rare, expensive to maintain in conducive conditions, dangerous to interact with directly, and have to be coaxed into experimental situations that are necessarily constrained to operate non-verbally. Our own experimental research in this area has been done in the USA, because there is simply no ape research facility in the UK. All the ape research has emanated from just a handful of such facilities.

Of more direct intellectual interest from the perspective of philosophy, I want to propose that progress is also hindered by a lack of adequate characterisation of what we really need to learn from the experiments we run. This is the topic of the present paper.

Here is the core of the problem as I see it. It is about what is really going to count as mindreading. Typically, to say that an individual is recognizing *a state of mind* in another is to make an implicit or explicit contrast with what seems on first pass the obvious non-mindreading alternative; that it is instead merely a public, observable *behaviour pattern* (or perhaps more generally an *observable situation*) that is being recognized. Consider, for example, the hypothetical attributions a mindreading chimpanzee might make, of the kind that Premack mused on: seeing another as in a state of *wanting*, or *intending*, for example. Such states are often described as internal and not directly observable, by their nature. In philosophy, mental state terms like *want* and *intend* have been recognized as demonstrating a distinctive quality of *referential* or *logical* opacity (Dennett, 1988), unlike behavioural terms such as *grab* or *leap*. Even young children show some appreciation of the attitudes adults take to these 'mental entities' as being 'internal, subjective, non-real and hypothetical' (Wellman, 1991)—and thus an entirely different kind of thing from observable behaviours and situations, that are external, and objectively verifiable.

The problem for our hypothetical mindreading chimpanzee is, how is she going to pick out such states of mind? We assume she is not a telepathist—she cannot magically see directly into the mind and perceive the state of *wanting*, any more than we can. Instead, she would have to read such a state in observable behaviour patterns or situations—'reading mind in behaviour', as Bennett (1991) once put it. The way her partner eyes her banana, perhaps, is the sign that *her partner wants the banana*. This is where we as investigators meet our first difficulty. If mind is in all cases read through such observables, what is going to be the difference between a chimpanzee who is a mindreader and one who is actually only reading

Andrew Whiten

behaviour? How shall we distinguish the chimpanzee who truly perceives the other as *wanting* the banana, from one who is simply sensitive to the external signs that her mindreading counterpart would presumably need to discriminate in any case?

2. Characterizing non-verbal mindreading

I have earlier discussed four different ways in which we might hope to discriminate non-verbal mindreading from 'mere' behaviour/ context reading (Whiten, 1993 & 1996). Here I shall re-examine these four and relate chimpanzee research findings garnered in the interim period to the two of them that I argue are the most powerful conceptualisations. The four approaches are, in outline, as follows[2].

A. *Counterdeception*

In an influential paper on the evolution of communication in animals, Dawkins and Krebs (1978) questioned the conventional wisdom of the time, that communication patterns evolve to *transmit information*. They pointed out that if this were the case, behaviour would be being shaped for the good of the receiver who is informed. However, behaviour is not selected for the good of others. To the contrary, one should really expect communication patterns to evolve so as to manipulate others, to the benefit of the communicator. At one extreme, such manipulation would be expected to involve deception. Where an animal threatening another can get away with a bluff that makes its threat apparently the more serious, we should expect it to be favoured by natural selection. This is the argument in outline. Dawkins and Krebs' exposition of the issue is, of course, a good deal fuller and more sophisticated.

So far, mindreading has not got into this picture. However, it is the next logical step, as Krebs and Dawkins (1984) suggested in a follow-up paper sub-titled 'mindreading and manipulation'. If selection pressures have favoured the evolution of certain communication strategies that involve manipulation and deception, leaving their victims at a selective disadvantage, a selection pressure then exists for those victims to detect the deception and ignore or counter it. In the case of our example of threat behaviour, there would be a pressure for the erstwhile victim to discriminate bluffs from the real

[2] Readers wishing for a fuller explanation and analysis are encouraged to consult Whiten (1996).

thing. Where this is successfully done, the receiver is in effect seeing through the surface behaviour (the bluff that advertises an apparent intent to attack) and recognizing instead the *true state of mind* of the bluffer (that there is really no intent to attack). According to this logic, the receiver is mindreading.

As it happens, collation of scientist's records of deception amongst primates did reveal cases where subjects perceptively recognized and countered deception, particularly in chimpanzees (Byrne and Whiten, 1990). However, it is not so clear that this sense of mindreading really cuts through the mindreading/behaviour-reading problem alluded to above. If we consider the basis on which any primate could detect that another's behaviour is deceptive, the most likely candidates are externally observable events. Whiten (1996) noted three possibilities, all of which appear to have representatives in the corpus of deceptive incidents collated by Whiten and Byrne. First, there is the history of previous interactions. An individual's signals might come to be recognized as untrustworthy if they are too often deceptive. For example, de Waal (1982) described one female chimpanzee who would often make a friendly overture, only to launch a sudden attack on her victims. Others came to treat such overtures more warily than they would normally. Second, there is what students of deception call 'leakage' of give-away information. Goodall (1986) described two young chimpanzees who were able to surreptitiously unscrew parts of a banana box and gain the contents before more mature males noticed— except that one youngster sometimes let his excitement 'leak' at the last minute, so his otherwise nonchalant cover was blown and the adults snatched his prize. Third, is contradiction, where cues discounting the deception remain available. Plooij (1993) described how his attempts to rid himself of the attentions of a young female chimpanzee by deceptively staring into the distance were apparently seen through; the female, having searched the space and found there was blatantly nothing there, returned, struck him and had nothing to do with him for the rest of the day.

Such observations are consistent with counter-deceptive mind-reading, in the sense that they imply an ability to tune into the would-be-deceivers' true intentions, discounting their surface behaviour. However, it is also the case that such discrimination must rest on other observable, surface evidence. Thus, we can also describe these phenomena in terms of an astute ability to discount the apparent significance of certain observable events on the basis of other observable information (history of prior behaviour, leakage, or contradiction). Accordingly, although recognizing and

Andrew Whiten

countering deception does offer one reputable rationale for a behaviour-reading/mind-reading distinction, the kind of evidence we have for primates inevitably slips back into the quagmire alluded to earlier, in which all putative mind reading translates to reading certain behavioural or contextual cues in any case.

That does not mean that examining such material is, after all, of no relevance. The evolution of mindreading, like its development, is likely to have been a stepwise process in which 'grades of mindreading' (Whiten, 1994) were achieved, each step representing a deeper sense of 'reading mind'. The reasons given above for discussing counterdeception as a certain kind of mindreading thus remain important. Animals who spend a significant part of their lives doing this may be attending to social phenomena in ways that could form important bridges to the deeper senses of mindreading that are considered below.

B. *Implicit Mind*

Gomez (1991) described the development of a young gorilla's social strategies for getting a high latch undone, in order to open a door. At an early stage, she would simply lead somebody to the door and then climb on them, using them in the same way as stacked boxes. Later, however, she developed a communicative strategy, that involved alternating her gaze between her human companion and the latch, apparently using her gaze to sign where she wanted the human to help (opening the latch), and also to monitor the human's own attention to her initiatives. 'Thus', remarked Gomez, 'she seemed to understand that in subjects, perceiving is causally related to acting. And here is where the mind appears, since the coordination between perceptions and actions is carried out by the mind.'

In more general terms the idea is that certain aspects of 'mind' will be implicit in certain complexes of action. In the example above described by Gomez, the aspect apparently recognized is the connection between perception and action. Other hypothetical cases of this line of reasoning would perhaps be that if an individual recognizing another as *searching in an incorrect location*, the state of mind *false belief* would be implicit; or alternatively if it was recognized that another was adopting an alternative pathway towards X after a first-attempted pathway was blocked, a state of *intending to get to* X would be implicitly recognized.

Like the case of recognizing counterdeception discussed earlier, this approach offers a valid rationale for a certain sense of mindreading, but also slides into our familiar quagmire, because we can directly re-describe each candidate case of mindreading in terms of the reading of a certain pattern of behaviour, albeit perhaps one with specific inherent complexities. Thus, like counterdeception, I conclude that we have here an interesting, yet weak, basis for diagnosing mindreading, over and above behaviour reading. However, as in the case of counterdeception we should acknowledge that a creature sensitive to the kinds of patterns Gomez described is achieving something on which deeper grades of mindreading might plausibly be built, whether in development or evolution.

C. *Recognizing 'intervening variables'*

Now we reach an approach that I have argued goes closer to the essence of what it is to read a state of mind (Whiten, 1993; 1994 & 1996). It exploits a notion of 'intervening variables' that arose in psychology in the mid-1900s, as some writers grappled with the need to go beyond behaviourism. The analogy is with a case such as that illustrated in Fig. 1, which concerns the drinking behaviour of experimental rats. A number of different 'outputs' (like how much the rat drinks, how much nasty quinine in the water will be tolerated) can each be shown to be affected by various 'inputs' (how long the rat has gone without water, for example, or the dryness of its food). We can represent these causal links by the nine arrows shown in Fig 1a. Alternatively, we can posit an intervening variable, as shown in Fig 1b, that is affected by each of the inputs, and the value of this variable then in turn can affect the outputs. This variable represents a single 'state' the rat can be in, a state that intervenes between the inputs and outputs. In the rat this state is presumably represented or coded by a particular pattern of neuronal activity, but we have an apt name for it in English: 'thirst'. In some sense this is a *psychological state* of the rat: indeed, a 'state of mind' if we define 'mind' as the psychological processes underlying the rat's actions.

Whether the reader finds this particular ascription of 'mental state' acceptable or not does not matter here, for I wish only to argue that Fig 1 provides a good *model* for what happens in the reading of mental states, rather than that the thirst scenario is in itself an example of this. Whiten (1996) portrayed hypothetical instances of what might count as the reading of states of *fearing, wanting*, and *knowing*, the latter illustrated in Fig 2. In all these cases, the mindreader might on different occasions see various actions and contexts, on the basis of which it classifies the actor as being in a certain state of mind; according to the circumstances that develop, it then uses

205

Andrew Whiten

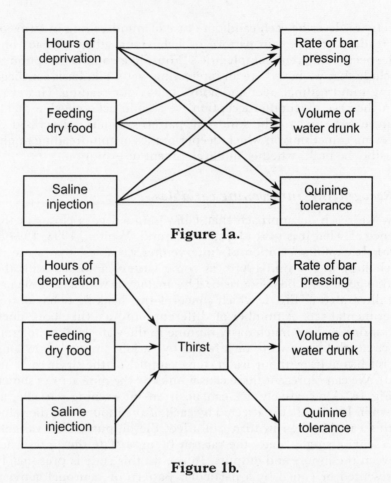

Figure 1a.

Figure 1b.

Figure 1. The idea of an intervening variable. (a) Causal relationships identified between three inputs and three outputs in rats' drinking behaviour; (b) Positing an intervening variable operating in the rat (here called 'thirst') permits a more economic representation of the causal linkages, in this case reduced from the nine shown in (a), to six (after Whiten, 1993, 1996; see also Sober, 1998).

this classification to predict what the actor will do next and perhaps what its own best response should be. Note that in doing this, the mindreader is being economical and efficient in its psychological analysis of the other. The gain in economy is illustrated in the shift from Fig 1a to Fig 1b. I earlier suggested this can be measured in the fewer number of causal arrows required (the gain from which will rise exponentially as the number of potential inputs and out-

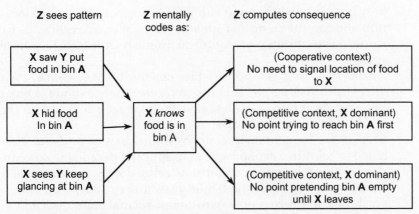

Figure 2. The recognition of a mental state as an intervening variable: knowledge. A hypothetical primate, Z, reads the mental state of knowledge in an individual X, coding this state as an intervening variable generated on different occasions by a variety of circumstances like those shown on the left, and in turn giving rise to various predictions appropriate to different circumstances such as those shown on the right. Such mentalising gains the same economy of representation expressed in Figure 1(b) contrasted with 1(a) (after Whiten, 1993, 1996).

puts to be modelled rises). Sober (1998) points out that it would be more appropriate to contrast the number of parameters in each model. Whichever measure is applied, a number of important implications arise from these ways of thinking about mental state attribution[3]:

1. *Power.* As outlined in the previous paragraph, the intervening variables conception suggests why we or other mentalist creatures might *be* mentalists (i.e. recognizing states of mind), in terms of that same cognitive power or efficiency obtained by any scientist crediting the rat with 'thirst'.
2. *Nature of mentalism.* It also proposes what it can *be* to be a mentalist, as opposed to a behaviourist who instead learned all the specific 'S–R' rules of others' behaviour patterns. In other words, it provides perhaps the most defensible definition of mentalism, compared to other approaches outlined above. However, mentalism is still a term which grades into behaviourism, because it is applied on the basis of *how complex* webs such as those shown in figs 1b and 2 are. If such a web had only one line of links (for example, if Fig 2 only included the link

[3] These are taken from Whiten (1996), pp. 285–88.

Andrew Whiten

between (on the left, input side) X putting something in a location and (on the right, output side) X's ability to recover it, we would have nothing we could distinguish from a behavioural rule).

3. *Abstraction*. Intervening variables constitute *states which others are classed as being in*: it is not *necessary* that they are seen as 'internal' to others, even less that they are seen as being 'in the head'. But see note 5, below.

4. *Cleverness*. If mentalism conceived in this way owes its existence to cognitive economy, it may appear a paradox if our current working hypothesis that it is refined only in particularly clever species is confirmed. The answer may depend on distinguishing the process of *acquisition* of mental state discrimination from the *application* of mentalism on subsequent particular occasions. The capacity to recognize in the first place the complex pattern which is covered by an intervening variable (see Figs 1–2) may require considerable neural resources. It is once this recognition has taken place that application in behavioural analysis can become efficient on any one occasion, facilitating fast and sophisticated tactics to be deployed (de Waal, 1982; Byrne and Whiten, 1988).

5. *Insight*. I have remarked before that the recognition phase may be likened to an insight into the underlying pattern (Whiten, 1993). This would suggest that experience could play an important part in the acquisition of a theory of mind, however much guided by innate preparedness. Although the idea of innateness rests on evolutionary theory, the fact of evolution itself presents a difficulty if innateness is thought of as a sort of preformation which solves the problem of recognizing certain complex patterns in the world, like language structure, or mental states: some recognition would have been necessary before natural selection could operate to shape a special-purpose mechanism to facilitate such recognition (a 'theory of mind module', Leslie and Thaiss, 1992). At a more specific level, I suggest it is plausible that mental states were recognized in ancestral populations before words (names) came to be designated for them, and thus before children were raised in an environment suffused with mental state names.

6. *Explicit mentalism*. Continuing this line of argument, there is a sense in which mental states as intervening variables could be said to be *explicitly* recognized by the mindreader, even if the mindreader is itself non-verbal. Explicit here means that in the brain of the mindreader, there is a state which uniquely codes

for the state (i.e. the intervening variable) of the mind that they are reading, this latter being an inclusion class which could be identical to the one which you and I name with a word like *knowing* or *wanting*[4]. If the nonverbal mindreader picks out this phenomenon in the same way we do, even though they cannot name it, they are doing something more than the implicit mindreading discussed earlier, where no such corresponding inclusion class is recognized.

7. *Methodology*. An implication of this analysis is that mentalism cannot be diagnosed using a one-shot test, like the standard Sally-Anne 'false-belief' task (Baron-Cohen, *et al.*, 1985), which could be solved by applying a single behavioural rule, such as that people search for things where they last watched them put. According to the analysis above, mindreading is diagnosed only when the mindreader classes different situations as leading to the same mental state, and puts this classification to different uses according to context. Few animal experiments approach this (Heyes 1993; Whiten 1993 & 1994), and we shall return to this issue in outlining new experimental work below. Ironically, it *may* be our ability to recognize this complex of evidence in large batches of everyday situations which permits us to assign children we know well to different levels of mindreading competence with some confidence, without performing any experiments at all. It is interesting that at this stage of our science, we do not know for sure how we *do* do this!

D. *Experience projection.*

In experience projection, the mindreader uses their own experience in a certain situation in the past to predict the state of mind of another individual they perceive currently to be in a sufficiently similar situation. Gallup (1982) gave a nice example of this, encapsulated in the outline of an appropriate experimental test. What Gallup suggested was that experimental animals might be given an experience novel to them: wearing a blindfold, perhaps, or opaque goggles: later, we would study their ability to take into account the effect on another individual of their wearing similar obstructions to vision. For example, if a primate with this kind of experience behind it was faced with a more dominant group-mate standing over inviting food, would they behave differently according to

[4] This argument echoes that of Bennett (1976).

Andrew Whiten

whether that animal had the blindfold on? (or, better, according to whether the blindfold was over its eyes, versus merely draped round its neck?)

This seems to be a quite powerful sense of mindreading, which escapes the collapse into behaviour-reading to which the three previous approaches considered are prone. If an animal behaves appropriately in situations like that suggested by Gallup, it can only be doing so by projecting onto the other the state it had earlier experienced, such as a state of visual ignorance. And this is surely a state of mind. Behaviour or context reading in and of itself will not allow the animal to succeed in this kind of situation.

Does this, then, offer us the prospect of a strong test for mindreading, that will at last give unambiguous answers with non-human, non-verbal, subjects? I have argued (1998b) that it does not necessarily do so, because there is an asymmetry in the implications of positive and negative results. A positive result is indeed strong evidence of mindreading, because of the logic discussed in the preceding paragraphs. Of course, important experimental conditions need to be met for this to be the case. One is that the experience learned about must be sufficiently novel; in the example above, the test would not be compelling if the animal already knew about the behavioural limits of its companions when they wear blindfolds. Also, as noted, appropriate control conditions would be necessary to identify the specific state being recognized; a condition with the blindfold on, but not obscuring vision, for example, as outlined above. The important point is that a positive result has the power, in principle, to identify mindreading in a quite clear sense.

A negative result, by contrast, does not allow us to reject the existence of mindreading in the species or subjects tested, for mindreading might be being done by other methods, such as recognizing intervening variables, rather than experience projection. For example, an individual might have become capable of recognizing mental states as intervening variables, not by experience projection, but by observing others for long enough to work out that such variables offer economic predictors of action. This alternative to experience projection leads us to consider a related dichotomy discussed in the theory of mind literature, 'theory-theory' versus simulationism.

3. 'Simulation' versus 'theory' models of mindreading

A dichotomy much discussed in both philosophy and psychology in recent years distinguishes the 'simulation' and 'theory' theories of how mindreading might operate. Gordon (1986)[5] refers to these as the 'hot' and 'cold' methods of mindreading respectively. The hot method of simulation uses the mindreader's own mind to simulate the mental processes of another individual. In this case the mindreader puts themselves 'in the shoes' of the other, and running their own mental operations 'off-line' (i.e. inhibiting the actions these operations would normally generate), discovers what mental states can be expected to be generated. Empathy, particularly when one identifies with another's emotions, seems by its very nature to illustrate such a 'hot' process.

The 'theory' theory, by contrast, often portrays the mindreader as a cold observer of the world, recognizing mental states in much the same way as other underlying factors like gravity, that allow prediction of how things in the world will behave. Such a mindreader does not rely on any kind of introspection or simulation any more than when they apply what they know of gravity to operate effectively in the world.

Carruthers and Smith's overview[6] of the history of the debate between these views cites a paper by Lewis (1966) as marking the beginning of a phase in which theory-theory became the dominant view, this 'orthodoxy' being challenged twenty years later in papers by Gordon and others, outlining simulationist alternatives. These rival ideas have continued to fuel debate, with further distinctions being added within each of the main branches (that mental theories are constructed by the child acting as a little scientist, versus the view that much of the theory is given innately, for example).

These complexities are beyond the scope of the current paper. The simulation/theory dichotomy is mentioned here because it appears, at least at first sight, to map rather directly to the intervening-variables/experience-projection distinction I have drawn. However, I suspect the mapping is not so neat.

Experience projection and simulation are perhaps the most closely tied. Any instance of experience projection is an example of simulation, for the mindreader will have to simulate the relevant experience themselves, in order to project it onto the other. Conversely, all simulation, to be effective, will eventuate in projecting the results of the simulation onto the other, attributing them with the corresponding state of mind. However, I am not intending that experience projection be just another label for the concept of simulation. Rather, I am presenting it as a minimal instance of simulation,

[5] Note that the idea of simulation was discussed earlier from the perspective of primatology by N. K. Humphrey (1980).
[6] Introduction to Carruthers and Smith (1996), pp. 1–8.

sufficient to provide worthy justification of the ascription of at least some basic grade of mindreading to a non-verbal creature, as exemplified by the kind of experiment suggested by Gallup, described earlier. In that experiment the subject would be projecting one very specific experience, that could perhaps be rendered as 'can't see the food'. By contrast, simulation is a concept developed as candidate machinery for the whole, complex, well-established business of human mindreading. As such, it must deal with much more than the projection of single and quite circumscribed experiences as envisaged in the Gallup experiment; in short it must eventually be able to run a model of the whole human mind, such as we are capable of reading in others. Thus, I am preserving 'simulation' as a potentially much bigger and more complex enterprise than the isolated instances of 'experience projection' that would encourage us to acknowledge an experimental subject to be demonstrating an act of mindreading.

Because of this, there may be reason to link recognition of intervening variables to simulation theories, as well as to theory-theories. The link to the latter seems quite obvious. In the version of theory-theory that sees the child as scientist, building theoretical models of the underlying principles of the social world she observes, then mental states as intervening variables are surely just the kind of explanatory construct that might be generated. Where innate foundations of such theories are advocated instead, there might be predispositions to interpret observed actions in terms of the principal kinds of mental states humans tune into, the predispositions extending to perceiving the webs of links that characterize the nature of intervening variables, as indicated in Fig. 2.

However, a fully-functioning simulation approach to mindreading would, it seems, also need to model the intervening-variable characteristics of mental states. For mindreading to operate as flexibly as it appears to do in the human case, and deal with relatively novel social scenarios, it needs to have the powers discussed earlier under the heading of intervening variables, attributing a state on the basis of one kind of input, to make a prediction on the output side that has not previously been directly associated with that input. That would go beyond the more limited projection of one specific experience to another individual faced with that situation. Thus, a fully elaborated simulation process might incorporate intervening variables; and these might have been generated by repeatedly running the self's mental processes off-line when attempting to predict others' actions, and discovering the intervening variables that lie at the appropriate junctures. To put this another way, whatever mental processes might have been thought to underlie the building of theories of other minds on the theory-theory approach, discovering in the process the key intervening variables, a similar kind of construction might be necessary to build an adequate simulator.

4. Experiments

With the approaches discussed above in mind, a suite of experiments has been conducted with chimpanzees as subjects. These chimpanzees, living at the Language Research Center of Georgia State University, run by D. Rumbaugh and S. Savage Rumbaugh, lead rich social lives, interacting daily both with other chimpanzees and with humans. Some of the experiments have involved chimpanzee subjects interacting with chimpanzees, others have been based on chimp-human interaction. The former is important because, if chimpanzees have any mindreading capacities, these are presumably adapted to the chimpanzee mind (Gomez, 1996). However, the use of humans as interactants—as surrogate chimpanzees—offers so many benefits in experimental control and design that this approach has been the most common. The experiments outlined here are of this kind. These abridged accounts are not intended to make a case here for or against particular conclusions about primate theory of mind, but instead to illustrate application of the criteria discussed above. Nor is my title intended to imply that one experiment will do the trick: many convergent attacks will be necessary. However, their design is indeed critical.

A. *Reading Attention*

The reading of visual attention is of interest for several reasons. First is our finding in an earlier study that the manipulation and monitoring of visual attention is a recurring feature in several of the main ways in which non-human primates in the wild have been recorded as deceiving each other (Whiten and Byrne, 1988b). In addition there are reasons to expect that reading attention might be an early step in mindreading: on the one hand attention can be directly 'observable' in its external manifestations (head and gaze direction, for example); on the other, attention links to more opaque psychological phenomena, like knowledge and interest.

The stimulus for the present experiment was a study by Baldwin and Moses (1994) that had shown 18-month-old children to reach a critical stage in language acquisition, when their parents merely gazing at a novel object and uttering a name for it can be shown to be sufficient for the child to acquire the name for the object. Baldwin and Moses pointed out that this is a candidate for early mindreading, because the child is seeing the parent's gaze as a kind of 'psychological spotlight', indicating what they 'have in mind'; the object gazed at is thus what they are talking about.

Working with chimpanzees that can use visual signs, called lexigrams, to 'name' objects (i.e. to both request objects, and to label these objects when asked to do so), (Savage-Rumbaugh, 1986) raised the prospect of investigating whether these apes also give evidence of treating others' attention as this kind of 'psychological spotlight'. Important background to this study is that typically, the apes are asked to name objects by holding up the object before them or touching it in some way. Thus, a novel experience was presented to each experimental subject, in which four objects were arranged in an archway above both their own head and that of a person who sat facing them. The person then looked up at one object and said, 'what's that?', a novel experience for the ape (Whiten, 1998a). What would they make of this? Would they appear puzzled, and wait for the experimenter to touch an object to be named? Would they respond with a random label? In the event (using a joystick and computer display to select a name), both of the chimpanzee subjects tested responded immediately and spontaneously with correct labels. The gaze of the experimenter immediately carried a certain meaning for them, making sense of the query, 'what's that?'. Thus these chimps appeared not merely to follow the gaze in a reflex fashion, in search of some object of interest, but instead to hold some expectation that the others' gaze is 'about' something out there, which they then use to disambiguate the question, that is asking for the name of an object.

Further experiments have explored the scope of this 'joint referential space' and shown that it extends to behind the ape (an extension also achieved by young children, but only by the age of about 18 months) and also behind the human. In the latter case, a human could turn their back on the ape, so only the back of their head can be seen. This, of course, is a very different visual array to that the chimpanzee sees when the human is facing them and can see their eyes and other facial features. But to the chimpanzees, it appears to 'mean the same thing' about attention—as indeed it does for us.

This latter finding ties this work to one of the criteria for discriminating mindreading from behaviour-reading, discussed earlier; that of intervening variables. If *attention* is being recognized as a state of mind in this sense, it should fit into a scheme of the kind

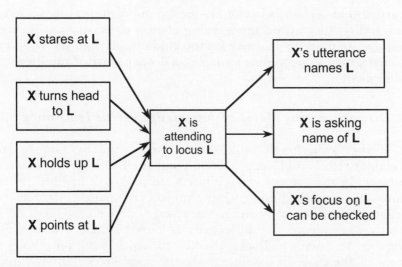

Figure 3. Recognizing another individual's state of attention as an intervening variable. Here Y reads X's state of visual attention, portrayed in according to the type of scheme developed in Figures 1–2.

illustrated in Fig. 3. The mindreader, Y, would code several different behaviours of X into the same class ('attending to') and from these, be able to generate a variety of responses, each appropriate to a particular context that has its own significance, given X's state of attention. Chimpanzees in this study treated the events on the left of Fig. 3 as equivalent, using them to generate an appropriate response for the context where X was asking for the name of the object. In addition, in some experimental conditions where the focus of X's attention was difficult for them to judge, they would sometimes gesture to one object, apparently in an effort to confirm if this is indeed the focus of attention. This is consistent with the kind of 'intervening variables' scheme in Fig 3.

Note that this goes one step beyond the interpretation discussed earlier for the finding that young children will use gaze to confirm the referent of a name the gazer utters. That was suggested to be a step towards mindreading because the linkage between perception and action (the 'psychological spotlight') was being recognized. Such an interpretation appears to be an application of the second of the four criteria for mindreading we discussed earlier, that I described as the reading of 'implicit mind', and judged weak because it so easily collapses to a behaviour re-description. For example in the present case, it might be argued that the child has

Andrew Whiten

learned that certain behaviours—gazing and uttering—have a certain utility; they afford the learning of new object-names. By contrast, as we move to evidence for the kind of portrayal shown in Fig 3., referring to intervening variables, a deeper sense of mindreading is implied.

B. *Discriminating states of knowledge versus ignorance*

A further experiment built on an earlier one by Gomez and Teixidor (1992 and Gomez, 1996), conducted with an orangutan as subject. In the present case (Whiten, (in press)), a baseline procedure was established, in which the subject chimpanzee, Panzee, was isolated from her companions in a large indoor cage, outside of which were placed two differently coloured boxes. The box lids were secured with padlocks, the key to which hung on a hook in front of the cage. In baseline trials, the apes' keeper entered, took the key, unlocked one box, baited it with attractive food, locked it, returned the key to its habitual position and left. A short while later another individual (the 'helper') entered the area and stood before the cage, awaiting communication from the chimp. Unsurprisingly, Panzee learned within a few trials that pointing towards the relevant box was sufficient to get the helper to take down the key, unlock that box and share the food with the ape. Before the study moved to the next phase of critical testing, Panzee experienced over twenty such baseline trials. One of the things this was designed to impress upon her was that the key was needed to open the box, and the location of the key could always be expected to be on the hook.

Panzee experienced 100 of these baseline trials spread over a two week period. After the first twenty of these, ten experimental trials were inserted at randomized points. In these, it was the helper who entered first and baited one of the boxes, as the keeper had done. The helper then left. A short while later the keeper entered, took the key from its usual location, and placed it in one of seven novel locations, around the back or side of the cage. The keeper then left. Finally, the helper reappeared and took their usual stance at the front of the cage, ready to receive and respond to any communications from the ape. Our question, of course, was whether Panzee would not indicate to the helper which box was baited, but would instead recognize that the helper would not know the key had been moved in their absence, and thus point first to the location of the key. In fact, that is what Panzee did in the first nine experimental trials.

Thus, Panzee discriminated between the ignorant and knowledgeable states of the helper with respect to the whereabouts of the key. The extent to which such states were being recognized as intervening variables was next explored by changing the circumstances creating the ignorance. Instead of the helper leaving the room before the keeper hid the key, the helper was distracted by various events, like a cup of juice being spilled, which caused them to look away. Now, in this circumstance, Panzee did not point out the new location of the key, that was moved whilst the helper was looking the wrong way. This suggests that in the earlier part of the experiment, Panzee was not recognizing a state of ignorance with the scope of an intervening variable, but instead operating according to some more restricted rule of a behavioural kind, referring to peoples' tendency not to retrieve objects moved from regular positions during their absence.

However, another recent experiment on chimpanzees' recognition of ignorance, conducted by Boysen (1998), suggests a somewhat different interpretation. In Boysen's study, the chimpanzee subject was in a position overlooking two adjacent yards. Into one of these came a 'predator'—a human with a dart gun, a real threat from the perspective of laboratory chimpanzees. This predator moved to a position so that, in one condition of the experiment, they would be obscured from the view of a second chimpanzee who was released into the other yard. This was the 'ignorant' condition, the second chimp being unaware of the predator. In a 'knowledgeable' condition, the second chimp was instead already in the yard when the predator appeared and the chimp could watch them as they moved into their 'ambush' position. Boysen found that the subject chimpanzee produced many more alarm calls when the other chimpanzee was ignorant than when it was knowledgeable. As in my own experiment, there was a basic discrimination of the states of knowledge, versus ignorance caused by absence.

Putting the two experiments alongside each other, we might argue there is more support for the idea that ignorance is being appreciated as a relatively abstract intervening variable. In Boysen's study the chimp is recognizing a situation in which it makes the appropriate chimpanzee-to-chimpanzee communication—an alarm call. One could hypothesize that this represents some innate response to the conjunction of a predator and another chimpanzee who was absent when the predator appeared. However, in my own experiment the subject was able to respond to a state of ignorance caused not by a predator but by moving an object from its familiar location, and the chimpanzee responded appropriately, using a human-like gesture it had acquired from humans (wild chimpanzees do not use pointing to draw attention to a locus, as Panzee had proficiently learned to do). Thus, the two experiments together could be taken to suggest that after all, 'ignorance' may be being recognized as the more abstract kind of entity required of an intervening variable, and the action appropriate to this circumstance then intelligently selected, at least in the case of chimp-human communication.

What seems in conflict with this generous interpretation is Panzee's failure to treat other situations of ignorance, caused by distraction, in the same way as sheer absence. However, there is other evidence that chimpanzees are remarkably poor, by human standards, at recognizing the niceties of what is involved in seeing or not seeing something—for example, whether the eyes are covered or not. One possibility we may need to entertain, then, is one that may seem somewhat paradoxical from a human perspective: that 'ignorance' is a very crude category for a chimpanzee, perhaps normally equated with sheer absence of the individual concerned at the time of the relevant event (absence was the source of ignorance in both Boysen's study and in Panzee's successful trials); yet this state, once perceived, may have the status of the kind of intervening variable that can be linked to a variety of different predictions and actions, according to context.

C. *Knowing versus Guessing: an opportunity for experience projection*

To my knowledge, no explicit test of experience projection has been published, although it has been advocated several times, from Gallup's early suggestion as outlined above (Gallup, 1988), to Heyes' recent appraisal of the state of primate theory of mind studies (Heyes, 1998). Panzee's failure to extend her discrimination of knowledge/ignorance to more refined contexts than presence/absence might have appeared to offer an opportunity to develop a test, but the specific design features of that rather complex experiment made it difficult to turn the tables and allow Panzee to gain the experience of being a distracted helper. This was more feasible in another experiment, however.

In the first phase of this study, a chimpanzee, Sherman, was faced by two human interactants and a single, lidded container. In each experimental trial, the container was taken out of the room, baited with one of a dozen types of food, and brought back. The experimenter asked both experimenters what they thought was in the container and each responded by saying the name of a food-type also pointing to a photograph portraying it. One did this after lifting the lid and overtly peering in to inspect the contents, so they made a correct choice. The other merely touched the box and made an incorrect choice. The chimpanzee subject was then itself allowed to guess the contents by picking one of 12 photographic portrayals. Although he could in principle have succeeded by taking the 'advice' of whichever human had peered in, Sherman failed to do significantly better than chance. He was then given 'personal experience' sessions, in which the human advisers were not present, but instead, before making his guess, he was sometimes allowed to peer in first (and thus succeeded), sometimes to merely touch the box (when his random guess always turned out to be wrong). The original type of trial, incorporating the human guesser and knower, was then presented again, but Sherman did not succeed any better. He appeared not to benefit from the opportunity to project onto these humans his own earlier experience of being knowledgeable or ignorant.

As Premack himself once lamented, negative results are frequently harder to interpret than positive ones; any number of excuses can be offered for why the subject might have the competence being investigated, yet failed to show it in the particular test applied. This particular test may have been too complex even for an ape enculturated to playing these kinds of experimental, communicative games with humans. Other tests are certainly required before an inability to experience-project would constitute a firm conclusion. I outline the approach here to illustrate that the experience projection hypothesis can be tackled quite directly in practice.

5. Concluding remarks

I have tried to show, first, that the question of what shall count as non-verbal mindreading is a profound one that has received insufficient conceptual and theoretical analysis. It therefore continues to offer much scope for input from professional philosophers, even though I would also argue that there is no substitute for those 'at the coalface' of empirical investigations grappling more deeply with the issues. In this paper, I discussed four different ways in which one might attempt to identify mindreading in a way that makes it interestingly different from abilities that are more readily described as 'mere behaviour reading'. Two of these—counterdeception and the reading of 'implicit mind'—I judged relatively weak, compared to approaches built on the ideas of intervening variables and experience projection.

Andrew Whiten

I then outlined recent experimental strategies that have generated some of the more positive findings on ape mindreading abilities, with the aim of showing how these relate to the considerations arising particularly from the stronger two of the approaches to identifying mindreading outlined earlier. Evidence for experience projection is either negative or non-existent (not tested for), yet my discussion suggests that positive results of such testing would be relatively unambiguous evidence for mindreading, and although difficult to set up, it has been shown to be practicable.

Some recent experiments on attention reading and attributing ignorance offer results more consistent with chimpanzee recognition of states that have some of the characteristics of intervening variables, but even here chimpanzees' responses have indicated constrained abilities compared with the achievements of human children. Some of these results suggest we need to be on our guard, however, against over anthropomorphic conceptions of what elementary steps in mindreading will be like. One interpretation of recent results is that chimpanzees do recognize states of mind like attention and ignorance, in the abstract sense consistent with the idea of intervening variables, yet remain naive about details that in the human case would be expected to be prior achievements, like appreciating the role of the eyes in seeing (Povinelli and Eddy, 1996). Alternatively it might be argued that the results of the ignorance-attribution studies indicate the chimp has at best a 'theory of absence' rather than a capacity that ought to be called theory of *mind*.

Time will tell. After Premack and Woodruff's famous paper, little follow-up happened for a decade, and for the practical reasons outlined earlier, ape research still seems destined to follow a slow hard road. However, we now appear to have passed into a phase where novel and interesting findings from new contributors are entering the field apace; accordingly, it is as important as ever to examine in depth the philosophical bases of the enterprise.

Bibliography

Baldwin, D. A. and Moses, L. J. 1994. 'Early understanding of referential intent and attentional focus: Evidence from language and emotion', in C. Lewis and P. Mitchell (eds) 1994a (Hillsdale, NJ: Erlbaum), 133–56.
Baron-Cohen, S., Leslie, A. M. and Frith, U. 1985. 'Does the autistic child have a "theory of mind"?', *Cognition* **21**, 37–46.
Baron-Cohen, S., Tager-Flusberg, H. and Cohen, D. J. (eds) 1993. *Understanding Other Minds* (Oxford: Oxford University Press).

Theory of Mind in Non-Verbal Apes

Bennett, J. 1976. *Linguistic Behaviour* (Cambridge: Cambridge University Press).

Bennett, J. 1978. 'Beliefs about beliefs', in *Behavioral and Brain Sciences*, 1, 557–8.

Bennett, J. 1991. 'How to read minds in behaviour: a suggestion from a philosopher', in A. Whiten, (ed.) (Oxford: Basil Blackwell), pp. 97–108.

Boysen, S. T. 1998. 'Attribution processes in chimpanzees: heresy, hearsay or heuristic?', paper presented at *The VIIth Congress of the International Primatological Society, Antananarivo*.

Byrne, R. W. and Whiten, A. (eds) 1988. *Machiavellian Intelligence: Social Expertise and the Evolution of Intellect in Monkeys' Apes and Humans*, R. W. Byrne and A. Whiten (eds) (Oxford: Oxford University Press).

Byrne, R. W. and Whiten, A. 1990. 'Tactical deception in primates: The 1990 database', *Primate Reports*, 27, 1–101.

Carruthers, P. and Smith, P. K. (eds) 1996. *Theories of Theories of Mind*. (Cambridge: Cambridge University Press).

Castles, D. L. and Whiten, A. 1998(a). 'Post-conflict behaviour of wild olive baboons. I. Reconciliation, redirection and consolation', *Ethology*, 104, 126–47.

Castles, D. L. and Whiten, A. 1998(b). 'Post-conflict behaviour of wild olive baboons. II. Stress and self-directed behaviour.' *Ethology*, 104, 148–60.

Davies, M. and Stone, T. (eds) 1995. *Folk Psychology: The Theory of Mind Debate* (Oxford: Basil Blackwell).

Davies, M. and Stone, T. (eds) 1996. *Mental Simulation: Evaluation and Applications*. (Oxford: Basil Blackwell).

Dawkins, R. and Krebs, J. R. 1978. 'Animal signals: information or manipulation?', in J. R. Krebs and N. B. Davies (eds) (Oxford: Blackwell), pp. 380–402.

Dennett, D. C. 1978. 'Beliefs about beliefs' in *Behavioral and Brain Sciences*, 1, 568–70.

Dennett, D. C. 1988. 'The intentional stance in theory and practice', in R. W. Byrne and A. Whiten, (eds) (Oxford: Oxford University Press), pp. 180–202.

de Waal, F. B. M. 1982. *Chimpanzee Politics* (London: Jonathan Cape).

de Waal, F. B. M. 1989. *Peacemaking Among Primates* (Cambridge, MA: Harvard University Press).

Gallup, G. G. 1982. 'Self-awareness and the emergence of mind in primates', *American Journal of Primatology*, 2, 237–48.

Gomez, J. C. 1991. 'Visual behaviour as a window for reading the mind of others in primates', in A. Whiten (ed.) (Oxford: Basil Blackwell), pp. 195–207.

Gomez, J. C. 1996. 'Nonhuman primate theories of (nonhuman primate) minds: some issues concerning the origins of mindreading', in P. Carruthers and P. K. Smith (eds) (Cambridge: Cambridge University Press), pp. 330–43.

221

Andrew Whiten

Gomez, J. C. and Teixidor, P. 1992. 'Theory of mind in an orangutan: a nonverbal test of false-belief appreciation?', *XIV Congress of the International Primatological Society, Strasbourg*.

Goodall, J. 1986. *The Chimpanzees of Gombe: Patterns of Behaviour* (Cambridge, MA: Harvard University Press).

Gordon, R. M. 1986. 'Folk psychology as simulation', in *Mind and Language*, **1**, 158–71.

Harcourt, A. H. and de Waal, F. B. M. (eds) 1992. *Coalitions and Alliances in Humans and Other Animals* (Oxford: Oxford University Press).

Harman, G. 1978. 'Studying the chimpanzee's theory of mind', in *Behavioral and Brain Sciences*, **1**, 576–77.

Heyes, C. M. 1993. 'Anecdotes, training, trapping and triangulating: do animals attribute mental states?', *Animal Behaviour*, **46**, 177–88

Heyes, C. M. 1998. 'Theory of mind in nonhuman primates', in *Behavioral and Brain Sciences*, **21**, 101–48.

Humphrey, N. K. 1980. 'Nature's psychologists', in B. Josephson and V. Ramachandran (eds), (Oxford: Pergamon), pp. 57–80.

Josephson, B. and Ramachandran, V. (eds) 1980. *Consciousness and the Physical World* (Oxford: Pergamon).

Krebs, J. R. and Davies, N. B. (eds) 1978/1984. *Behavioural Ecology: An Evolutionary Approach* (Oxford: Blackwell).

Krebs, J. R. and Dawkins, R. 1984. 'Animal signals: Mind reading and manipulation', in J. R. Krebs and N. B. Davies (eds) (Oxford: Blackwell), pp. 380–401.

Langer, J. and Killen, M. (eds) 1998. *Piaget. Evolution and Development* (Hove: Lawrence Erlbaum).

Leslie, A. M. and Thaiss, L. 1992. 'Domain specificity in conceptual development: Neuropsychological evidence from autism', *Cognition*, **43**, 225–51.

Lewis, C. and Mitchell, P. (eds) 1994a. *Children's Early Understanding of Mind* (Hillsdale, NJ: Erlbaum).

Lewis C. and Mitchell, P. (eds) 1994b. *Origins of an Understanding of Mind* (Hove: Lawrence Erlbaum).

Lewis, D. 1966. 'An argument for the identity theory', *Journal of Philosophy*, **63**, 17–25.

Mitchell, P. 1996. *Acquiring a Conception of Mind* (Hove: Psychology Press).

Plooij, F. X. 1993. 'Record No. 22', in R. W. Byrne, and A. Whiten (1993).

Povinelli, D. J. 1996. 'Chimpanzee theory of mind. the long road to strong inference', in P. Carruthers and P. K. Smith (eds) (Cambridge: Cambridge University Press).

Povinelli, D. J. and Eddy, T. J. 1996. 'What young chimpanzees know about seeing', *Monographs of the Society for Research in Child Development*, Serial No. 247, Vol. 61, No 3.

Premack, D. 1988. 'Does the chimpanzee have a theory of mind? revisited', in R. W. Byrne and A. Whiten (eds) (Oxford: Oxford University Press), pp. 160–79.

Premack, D. and Woodruff, G. 1978. 'Does the chimpanzee have a theory of mind?', in *Behavioral and Brain Sciences*, 1, 515–26.

Savage-Rumbaugh, E. S. 1986. *Ape Language: from Conditioned Response to Symbol* (New York: Columbia University Press).

Sober, E. 1998. 'Black box inference—when should intervening variables be postulated?', in *British Journal for the Philosophy of Science*, 49, 469–98.

Sperber, D. (ed.) 2000. *Meta-representations* (Oxford: Oxford University Press).

Wellman, H. M. 1991. 'From desires to beliefs: acquisition of a theory of mind', in A. Whiten, (ed.) (Oxford: Blackwell), pp. 19–38.

Whiten, A. (ed.) 1991: *Natural Theories of Mind: Evolution, Development and Simulation of Everyday Mindreading* (Oxford: Basil Blackwell).

Whiten, A. 1993. 'Evolving a theory of mind: The nature of non-verbal mentalism in other primates', in S. Baron-Cohen, H. Tager-Flusberg, and D. J. Cohen (eds) (Oxford: Oxford University Press), pp. 367–96.

Whiten, A. 1994. 'Grades of mindreading', in C. Lewis and P. Mitchell (eds.) 1994b (Hove: Lawrence Erlbaum), pp. 47–70.

Whiten, A. 1996. 'When does smart behaviour reading become mindreading', in P. Carruthers and P. K. Smith (eds), (Cambridge: Cambridge University Press), pp. 277–92.

Whiten, A. 1997. 'The Machiavellian mindreader', in A. Whiten and R.W. Byrne (eds), (Cambridge: Cambridge University Press), pp. 144–73.

Whiten, A. 1998a. 'Evolutionary and developmental origins of the mindreading system', in J. Langer and M. Killen (eds) (Hove: Lawrence Erlbaum), pp. 73–99.

Whiten, A. 1998b. 'How imitators represent the imitated: the vital experiments', Commentary on R. W. Byrne and A. E. Russon in *Behavioral and Brain Sciences*, 21, 707–8.

Whiten, A 2000. 'Chimpanzee cognition and the question of mental re-representation', in D. Sperber (ed.) (Oxford: Oxford University Press), pp?

Whiten, A. and Byrne, R. W. 1988a. 'Tactical deception in primates', in *Behavioural and Brain Sciences*, 11, 233–73.

Whiten, A. and Byrne, R. W. 1988b. 'The manipulation of attention in primate tactical deception', in R. W. Byrne and A. Whiten (eds) (Oxford: Oxford University Press), pp. 211–23.

Whiten, A and Byrne, R. W. 1997. *Machiavellian Intelligence II.: Evaluations and Extensions* (Cambridge: Cambridge University Press).

Wimmer, H. and Perner, J. 1983. 'Beliefs about beliefs: Representation and constraining function of wrong beliefs in young children's understanding of deception', in *Cognition*, 13, 103–28.

The Principle of Conservatism in Cognitive Ethology

ELLIOTT SOBER

Philosophy of mind is, and for a long while has been, 99% metaphysics and 1% epistemology. Attention is lavished on the question of the nature of mind, but questions concerning how we know about minds are discussed much less thoroughly. University courses in philosophy of mind routinely devote a lot of time to dualism, logical behaviourism, the mind/brain identity theory, and functionalism. But what gets said about the kinds of evidence that help one determine what mental states, if any, an individual occupies? Well, Skinner's puritanical disdain for postulating mental states gets raked over the coals, the problem of other minds gets solved by a perfunctory invocation of the principle of inference to the best explanation, and the Turing test gets discussed, mainly in order to emphasize that it can lead to mistaken answers.

An example of this bias toward metaphysics and away from epistemology may be found in the way philosophers often discuss Dennett's (1989) idea of *the intentional stance*. Dennett's principle is epistemological—it says that you should attribute mental states to a system when doing so helps you predict its behaviour. There is no point in treating relatively simple organisms and machines—like amoebas and hand calculators—as if they have minds; but more complicated systems—like primates and people and computers that play chess—make it almost irresistible for us to attribute mental states. The intentional stance is a piece of pragmatist epistemology. The problem with this idea is not that it is false, but that it is woefully short on details. In what circumstances does adopting the intentional stance enhance predictive accuracy? Dennett and others suggest that the intentional stance is appropriate when the behaviours observed are 'complicated,' but surely this remark is more a promissory note for a theory than a theory in itself. After all, there are plenty of complicated systems—like the turbulent flow of water coming out of a faucet and the waxing and waning of species diversity in an ecosystem—which do not tempt us to adopt the intentional stance. There is a vast and unknown continent of epistemological issues that needs to be explored here. Yet, the main discussion that the intentional stance has received in philosophy concerns Dennett's supposed 'anti-realism.' For Dennett, there is no separate fact of the matter as to whether a system really has a mind; there is only the question of whether or not it is useful to think that it does. Realism is a problem in metaphysics; discussion of the intentional stance has been sucked into this apparently irresistible black hole.

I don't want to suggest that this unequal emphasis of metaphysics over epistemology is wrong. But it does seem cockeyed, at least when it is seen from the point of view of the research programme that now goes by the name of 'cognitive ethology.' I'm not sure cognitive ethologists need much advice from philosophers about the nature of mind. They assume that mental states are internal causes of behaviour and that these inner states may be described in terms of their representational content. The fundamental question they face is epistemological—what counts as good evidence that a creature has a mind, and if the creature does have a mind, what further evidence is relevant to deciding which mental states one should attribute to it?

The usual answer that cognitive ethologists give to this epistemological question is that one's explanations should be 'conservative' (see, for example, Cheney and Seyfarth, 1990). If the behaviour of a system *can* be explained without attributing a mental state to it, that is how the behaviour *should* be explained. And even if the behaviour does require a mentalistic explanation, some such explanations are said to be more conservative than others.[1] In particular, if the behaviour can be explained just by attributing beliefs and desires about the nonmental world to the organism, then attribution of beliefs and desires that are about psychological states should be avoided. Better to say that a rat in a maze wants to find food than that it wants to obtain knowledge of food. Thus, the ethologist's principle of conservatism recommends a two-part plausibility ordering—*mindless* is preferable to *minded*, and *first-order intentionality* is preferable to *second-order intentionality*.[2]

The principle of conservatism serves a social function in cognitive ethology. Although most psychologists have long since thrown off the shackles of behaviourism, many remain concerned about the dangers of naive anthropomorphism. The common wisdom is that there is nothing wrong in principle with explanations that attribute mental states, but one has to be very careful about doing so uncritically,

[1] The principle of conservatism is a descendant of C. Lloyd Morgan's 'canon'. See Dennett, 1989 and Sober, 1998b for discussion.

[2] The terminology of 'first' and 'second' order intentionality is due to Dennett, 1989.

especially when the subjects are nonhuman organisms. The principle of conservatism is a prophylactic whose function is to reduce the risk of anthropomorphism. By using this protective device, ethologists avoid having other psychologists charge them with naiveté.

But why is there a special stigma here? One certainly should avoid falsely attributing mental states, but surely one also should avoid mistakenly withholding such attributions. Type-1 errors are errors, but type-2 errors are errors too:

	O lacks a mind	O has a mind
Deny that O has a mind		type-2 error
Attribute a mind to O	type-1 error	

The principle of conservatism cannot be justified simply by pointing out that it reduces the chance of type-1 error, any more than a mirror image 'principle of liberality' can be justified by pointing out that it reduces the chance of type-2 error. Within our scientific culture, anthropomorphism is regarded as a greater sin than its inverse, which does not even have a ready name; Block (1975) had to expropriate the term 'chauvinism' to label this second type of mistake. This asymmetry in our culture may provide individual scientists with a prudential justification for abiding by the principle of conservatism. But this is a fact about *people*, not about the *principle* itself. If the principle of conservatism makes sense, we need to look elsewhere for its justification.

Another suggestion is that the principle of conservatism is really a parsimony principle; perhaps mindless is *simpler* than minded, and first-order intentionality is *simpler* than second-order. It's not always easy to know how simplicity should be evaluated here. When a bowling ball falls to earth after it is released above the ground, what's wrong with saying that this occurs because the ball wants to move towards the earth's centre? The claim is implausible, but it is not so clear that the suggestion is flawed because it is complicated. In what sense is the explanation in terms of the law of gravitation simpler?

There is an additional reason to be sceptical about the claim that mindless is always simpler than minded. Sometimes, the reverse is true. Andrew Whiten (1993; 1994 & 1995) has pointed out that theories that postulate an intervening variable are sometimes simpler than theories that do not. As an example, he discusses the question of why we are entitled to attribute the intervening variable of 'thirst' to an organism (Figure 1). Postulating this internal state has the advantage of simplifying our account of how different stimuli

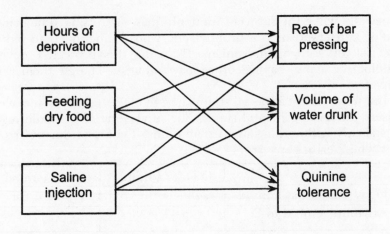

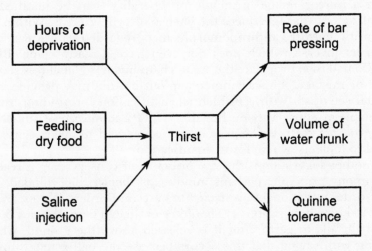

Figure 1.

are related to different responses. By invoking 'thirst' as an intervening variable, 'the multitude of S-R links no longer needs to be
coded. The observer needs only to know that the 'Ss' can each lead
to the state (thirst, in this case) and that for an organism in this
state, certain 'Rs' can be forecasted (Whiten, 1995, p. 284).'
Although it is better to measure simplicity by counting parameters
in a probability model than by counting arrows in a diagram (on
which, see Sober, 1998a), Whiten's example does show what he
claims—that postulating a mental state sometimes can be a move

towards simplification. It isn't always true that mindless is simpler than minded.

Does the same point apply to the relation of first-order and second-order intentionality? I think that it does. Sometimes hypotheses that attribute second-order intentionality to an organism are simpler than hypotheses that do not. To see why, let's consider an experiment that Povinelli *et al.* (1990) designed to address the question of whether chimps have a theory of mind. A chimp looks through a window at two trainers in a room. One trainer (the 'guesser') leaves, while the other (the 'knower') places food into one of four containers (the chimp can't see which). The guesser then re-enters the room. The knower points to the container where the food is hidden, the guesser points to a different container, and the chimp has to choose between the knower and the guesser. The chimp then gets to search the container singled out by the trainer that the chimp has chosen, and keep the contents. The chimps played this game for a number of rounds; each time the trainers decided at random who would be the knower and who the guesser. After a while, three of the four chimps in the experiment learned to point to the knower, not to the guesser. The hypothesis under test is that these chimps represented the knowledge states of the two trainers.

The chimps then went into a new experiment. Now the knower and the guesser both remain in the room while the food is hidden by a third party; the knower watches the food being hidden, while the guesser wears a bag over his head. The chimps have to choose between the knower and the guesser, as before. The chimps in this experiment initially acted as if they were learning from scratch— their success rates were merely at the level of chance (Povinelli, 1994)—but they subsequently learned to discriminate knower from guesser in this new set up, so that their mean success rate in the second experiment reached approximately the same level attained in the first experiment. Moreover, the chimps accomplished this with less training than was required in the first experiment. Povinelli (1994) and Heyes (1994 & 1998) conclude that the absence of immediate success in the second experiment means that these experiments fail to provide evidence that the chimps attributed mental states to the trainers. Evidently, the chimps learned faster in the second experiment than in the first and this is evidence that they learned *something* in the first experiment, which they carried forward; however, Povinelli and Heyes do not wish to explain this by attributing a theory of mind to the chimps.

I'll return to the issue of how the results of this experiment should be interpreted. Right now I want to describe two models and

Elliott Sober

First-order model

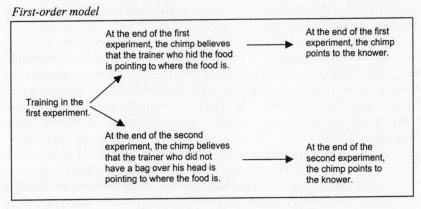

Second-order Model

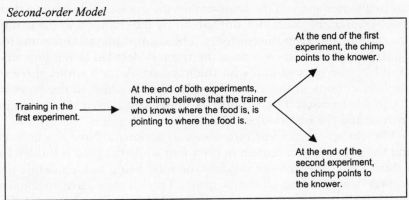

Figure 2.

assess how they differ in parsimony. These are depicted in Figure 2. The arrows represent causal relationships, which should be construed nondeterministically; causes raise the probabilities of their effects. The models agree that the training the chimps receive in the first experiment influences how they behave at the end of the first experiment and at the end of the second experiment. The models also agree that this influence is mediated by the formation of beliefs. They differ in that the first model claims that two different first-order beliefs get established, while the second model says that a single second-order belief does the work. I'm not making a claim about which model is more plausible. Rather, my present point is that the model that attributes a second-order belief is simpler because it postulates fewer intervening variables; it provides a unified explanation of the chimps' behaviour in the two experiments, whereas the first-order model explains the two behaviours by describing two

230

The Principle of Conservatism in Cognitive Ethology

different causal pathways. I conclude that first-order isn't always simpler than second-order.

I have argued that the principle of conservatism is not a parsimony principle. If this is right, what sort of justification does it have? My hunch is that *it doesn't*. To begin making a case for this claim, let me describe a remarkably similar principle that has been endorsed in evolutionary biology.

George C. Williams' (1966) book *Adaptation and Natural Selection* is one of the most influential books in 20th century evolutionary theory. In that book, Williams suggests that adaptation is an 'onerous principle,' which should be invoked only if necessary. A decade or so after Williams' book appeared, the debate about adaptationism was in full swing. Williams' principle was taken up by various critics of adaptationism, who suggested that if an adaptive hypothesis and a nonadaptive hypothesis can both explain the data, one should prefer the nonadaptive hypothesis. Here is an example of the kind of reasoning I have in mind:

> Why do most land vertebrates have four legs? The seemingly obvious answer is that this arrangement is the optimal design. This response would ignore, however, the fact that the fish that were ancestral to terrestrial animals also have four limbs, or fins. Four limbs may be very suitable for locomotion on dry land, but the real reason that terrestrial animals have this arrangement is because their evolutionary predecessors possessed the same pattern (Lewin, 1980, p. 886).

Lewin is suggesting that the better explanation is *ancestral influence*, or *phylogenetic inertia*. Selection (presumably *stabilizing* selection) also could explain why land vertebrates have four limbs, but, according to Lewin, this apparent symmetry should be broken by embracing the nonadaptive hypothesis. In a recent book, Williams (1998) describes the same example and draws the same conclusion. Williams' principle of conservatism, as it might be called, holds that nonadaptive is preferable to adaptive.

But Williams goes further. He adds that we should prefer lower-level selection hypotheses over higher-level ones. If a behaviour can be explained by the hypothesis of group selection, and it also can be explained by the hypothesis of individual selection, we should prefer the latter. For example, let's consider the question of why so many species of fish form schools. One hypothesis is that this is a group adaptation—in the species in question, groups that school go extinct less often and are more productive than groups that do not. A second hypothesis is that schooling is a 'statistical summation' of each individ-

Elliott Sober

ual's trying to get away from predators. It is advantageous for individuals to put a conspecific between themselves and danger; the net result is that individuals clump together. Williams' principle of conservatism says that we should reject the group selection hypothesis and accept the hypothesis that invokes individual selection. Thus, Williams' principle has two parts—nonadaptive is preferable to adaptive, and lower-level adaptations are preferable to higher-level adaptations.

I do not believe any of this. The simple principle that I would substitute for Williams' principle can be summed up in a single four-letter word: *DATA*. If you think that land vertebrates have four limbs because of ancestral influence and not because of stabilizing selection, please produce observational evidence that supports this hypothesis. If you cannot, you should adopt an agnostic attitude. Inertial hypotheses and adaptive hypotheses are both causal claims. To say that the state of an ancestor influenced the state of its descendant is to make a causal claim just as much as saying that a selection process in the lineage connecting ancestor to descendant influenced the state of the descendant. Neither is a 'null hypothesis.' In just the same way, the hypothesis that smoking causes lung cancer and the hypothesis that asbestos causes lung cancer both make causal claims. They are on an epistemic par. Neither takes precedence over the other; neither deserves to be regarded as innocent until proven guilty (Orzack and Sober, 2001).

The same point applies to the units of selection controversy. The individual selection hypothesis about schooling predicts that the fish in a school should be moving towards the school's interior. Do all schooling fish do this? The way to solve this problem is to develop detailed models about what schooling would look like if it were a group adaptation and what it would look like if it were an individual adaptation, and then subject the models to observational test. When this approach is applied to many traits in many lineages, it may turn out that some traits in some lineages have been influenced by group selection while others in others have not. Group selection can't be ruled out on the basis of general and *a prioristic* considerations (Sober and Wilson, 1998).

These brief remarks about the situation in evolutionary biology are only that. And even if they are right, it doesn't necessarily follow that the situation in cognitive ethology should be understood in the same way. Still, I hope they provide some indication of why I am suspicious of 'principles of conservatism.' What is needed is observational test, not the invocation of principles.

Returning to the epistemological issue in cognitive ethology, I have a few negative remarks and one positive suggestion. First, I do not think the proposition that 'S has a mind' can be tested directly. The same holds true for the hypothesis that 'trait T is an adaptation.' What gets tested are much more specific propositions. Specific claims about S's mental state will issue in observational predictions, and the same is true concerning specific claims about T's adaptive significance. It is these specific claims that, in the first instance, can be tested. After you've decided what S's mental state is, of course it follows that S has a mind. And after you've decided what trait T is an adaptation for, of course it follows that T is an adaptation. But the claim that S has a mind and that T is an adaptation are not sufficiently specific for them to be tested on their own.[3]

The same point applies to the theory of mind problem as it arises in connection with nonhuman primates or young children: You can't run a test of the bare hypothesis that an individual has second-order intentionality. Rather, what you can do is formulate a specific hypothesis that *involves* second-order intentionality—one that is specific enough to have implications about how probable the data are—and compare it with the predictions made by other specific hypotheses—for example, ones that attribute only first-order intentionality. The statement 'S has second-order intentionality,' I suspect, is rather like the statement 'T is a product of group selection.' It can't be tested directly. As the analogy with problems in evolutionary biology suggests, this isn't cause for dismay, but is a standard feature of scientific testing.

Now let's return to the two models depicted in Figure 2. The point I made earlier was that the model that attributes only first-order intentionality to the chimps is less parsimonious than the model that attributes second-order intentionality. I now want to describe an empirical procedure for testing these models against each other, one that has nothing to do with the question of which is more parsimonious. These models make different predictions about whether performance at the end of the first and second experiments will be *correlated*. According to the first-order model, they should be *probabilistically independent*. In contrast, the second-order model predicts a *positive association*.[4] At the end of the first experiment,

---

[3] The Duhemian point that hypotheses can be tested only when they are conjoined with auxiliary assumptions is not at issue here. Given independently attested auxiliary assumptions (Sober, 1999), some hypotheses issue in testable predictions, while others are not specific enough to do so.

[4] Here I am using Reichenbach's (1956) *principle of the common cause*. The claim that the models have these different predictions depends on making assumptions that are standard in causal modelling across the sciences. See Sober (1998a) for discussion.

Elliott Sober

the chimps point to the knower with a certain frequency; at the end of the second experiment, they point to the knower with a certain, possibly different, frequency. The hypothesis of first-order intentionality predicts that chimps who do better than average in the first experiment should not tend to do better in the second; the hypothesis of second-order intentionality says that chimps who do better than average on the first should tend to do better than average on the second. The data that Povinelli *et al.* (1990) gathered do not exhibit this positive association (Sober, 1998a). Thus, I agree with their assessment that the experiments do not favour the hypothesis that chimps have a theory of mind.

As I mentioned, Povinelli and Heyes both maintain that the chimps would have to exhibit 'immediate transfer' for these experiments to support the second-order model. This criterion differs from the one I am suggesting. What they mean is simply that the chimps have a success rate at the start of the second experiment that is better than chance. Now I agree that it is essential that the success rates in the first and second experiments each be better than chance. However, I don't require that the transfer be 'immediate'—delayed transfer would be fine. But I do impose a requirement that Povinelli and Heyes do not mention. Not only must the chimps do better than chance at the end of both experiments; in addition, there must be a correlation between performance in the first experiment and performance in the second.

Povinelli's use of the word 'transfer' is right on the money. If the theory of mind hypothesis is to gain support, what one wants is evidence that the chimps apply to the second experiment *the same conceptualization* that they learned to apply to the first. It isn't enough that their experience in the first experiment somehow helped them learn two unrelated things, with the first helping them in the first experiment and the second helping them in the second. This wouldn't be a transfer of anything. It is perfectly compatible with the first-order model that experience in the first experiment improved performance in both. The issue is how the experience did this, not whether it did so.

The methodology I am proposing suggests a certain strategy for designing experiments in the future. Most psychologists probably think that theory of mind is a *species-specific trait*. Either all chimps have a theory of mind, or none of them do. This assumption is suggested by the typological title of Premack and Woodruff's (1978) influential article, 'Does the chimpanzee have a theory of mind?' However, the methodology I am proposing suggests that evidence for the presence of a theory of mind cannot be obtained from experiments in which all subjects behave the same way. For example, if all the chimps had pointed to the knower in the first experiment, and all had done so in the second (even at the *beginning* of the second), no correlation would be found in the data, since (100%)(100%) = (100%). What is needed is an experiment in which some but not all chimps succeed in each task. If chimps who succeed in the first task also tend to succeed in the second, that is evidence for the existence of an intervening variable that is a *common cause* of the two behaviours.

Would an experiment that exhibits the correlation I have described automatically count against the claim that theory of mind is a species-wide trait? Well, it would not undermine the claim that the *capacity* for forming beliefs about the mental states of self and others is a universal. What it would disconfirm is the claim that all chimps *actually* formed a second-order representation in the experiments in question. However, if *some* of the chimps actually did so, perhaps one could maintain that this is a capacity that *all* chimps possess. This conclusion about a universal capacity would not be confirmed by the experimental outcome, but neither would it be refuted.

I want to end with a few comments concerning the implications of the epistemology I have described for naturalism in the philosophy of mind. As I mentioned at the outset, most philosophy of mind is metaphysics, and naturalistic philosophy of mind is no exception. Although self-proclaimed naturalists often have *anti*-reductionist views about the mind/body problem, naturalistic work on the theory of content is, in fact, *reductionistic*; the goal is to show how the semantic content of a representation can be reduced to its causal and/or functional characteristics (Shapiro, 1997). I hope this enterprise succeeds, but it remains to be seen whether it will. The naturalism embodied in what I have been saying is independent of this question concerning the nature of mental states. The naturalism on offer here is *methodological*, the idea being that the inferential methods needed in psychology are no different from the ones needed in the rest of the natural sciences. Just as metaphysical naturalism about semantic content has a positivist ring to it, the same is true of the methodological variety—it is one version of the thesis of *the unity of science*.

In this vein, it is worth noting that the reason the first-order and the second-order models make different predictions is that they are associated with different causal (and hence probabilistic) structures. Nothing would change if the subject matters of the two models were changed to something entirely nonmental. What is really being

Elliott Sober

tested is a model in which there is a single intervening variable that connects an observed cause and two observed effects, and a model in which there are two intervening variables, one for each linkage between the observed cause and an observed effect. It is the *form* of the models that matters, not their *content*.

There is another problem we might pose about Povinelli's experiments, one whose epistemology is very different. Suppose the observations discriminate between the two causal models I have described. The question we now wish to address is whether the intervening variables in the favoured model should be assigned a semantic content, and if so, what semantic content they should be assigned. This is a difficult question, which seems to require a well-grounded theory of content if it is to be answered. The problem I have addressed requires no such theory.

Povinelli *et al.* designed their pair of experiments with the intention that there should be no physical similarity between the knower in the first and the knower in the second. If both had been wearing purple suspenders, for example, it would be easy to invent a 'killjoy' explanation (Dennett, 1989) of whatever transfer occurred between the two experiments. However, if there are no such similarities—indeed, if the only similarity that connects the knowers in the two experiments is that both of them knew where the food was hidden—then the occurrence of transfer would be good evidence for the hypothesis that the chimps who made the transfer represented the two situations in terms of the knowledge the trainers possessed. This is why it makes sense to associate the first-order and the second-order models with different causal structures. However, once the competing models are formulated in this way, the semantic content of the states postulated by the two models plays no further role in testing the models[5].

Bibliography

Allen, C. and Cummins, D. (eds) 1998. *The Evolution of Mind* (Oxford: Oxford University Press).

Baron-Cohen, S., Tager-Flusberg, H. and Cohen, D. (eds) 1993. *Understanding Other Minds: Perspectives from Autism* (Oxford: Oxford University Press).

Block, N. 1975: 'Troubles with Functionalism', in W. Savage (ed.) (Minneapolis: University of Minnesota Press), pp. 261–325.

Carruthers, P. and Smith, P. (eds) 1995. *Theories of Theories of Mind.* (Cambridge: Cambridge University Press).

[5] My thanks to Berent Enç, Cecelia Heyes, David Over, and Andrew Whiten for comments on an earlier draft.

The Principle of Conservatism in Cognitive Ethology

Cheney, D. and Seyfarth, R. 1990. *How Monkeys See the World* (Chicago: University of Chicago Press).

Dennett, D. 1989. *The Intentional Stance* (Cambridge, MA: MIT Press).

Heyes, C. 1994. 'Cues, Convergence, and a Curmudgeon—a Reply to Povinelli', *Animal Behaviour*, **48**, 242–44.

Heyes, C. M. 1998. 'Theory of Mind in Nonhuman Primates', *Behavioral and Brain Sciences*, **21**, 101–48.

Lewin, R. 1980: 'Evolutionary Theory Under Fire', *Science*, **210**, 883–87.

Lewis, C. and Mitchell, P. (eds) 1994. *Understanding of Mind* (Hove, UK: LEA).

Orzack, S. and Sober, E. (eds) 2001. *Adaptationism and Optimality* (New York: Cambridge University Press).

Orzack, S. and Sober, E. 2001. 'Adaptation, Phylogenetic Inertia, and the Method of Controlled Comparisons', in S. Orzack and E. Sober (eds) (New York: Cambridge University Press).

Povinelli, D. 1994. 'Comparative Studies of Animal Mental State Attribution—a Reply to Heyes', *Animal Behaviour*, **48**, 239–41.

Povinelli, D., Nelson, K., and Boysen, S. 1990. 'Inferences about Guessing and Knowing by Chimpanzees', *Journal of Comparative Psychology*, **104**, 203–10.

Premack, D. and Woodruff, G. 1978: 'Does the Chimpanzee have a Theory of Mind?', *Behavior and Brain Sciences*, **4**, 515–26.

Reichenbach, H. 1956. *The Direction of Time* (Berkeley: University of California Press).

Savage, W. (ed.) 1975. *Perception and Cognition—Issues in the Foundations of Psychology. Minnesota Studies in the Philosophy of Science*, **9**, (Minneapolis: University of Minnesota Press).

Shapiro, L. 1997. 'The Nature of Nature—Rethinking Naturalistic Theories of Intentionality', *Philosophical Psychology*, **10**, 309–22.

Sober, E. 1998a. 'Black Box Inference—When Should an Intervening Variable be Postulated?', *British Journal for the Philosophy of Science*, **49**, 469–98.

Sober, E. 1998b. 'Morgan's Canon.' in C. Allen and D. Cummins (eds) *The Evolution of Mind* (Oxford: Oxford University Press), pp. 224–42.

Sober, E. 1999. 'Testability', *Proceedings and Addresses of the American Philosophical Association*. Also available at www: http://philosophy.wisc.edu/sober.

Sober, E. and Wilson, D. S. 1998. *Unto Others—The Evolution and Psychology of Unselfish Behavior* (Cambridge, MA: Harvard University Press).

Whiten, A. 1993. 'Evolving a Theory of Mind—the Nature of Non-Verbal Mentalism in Other Primates', in S. Baron-Cohen, H. Tager-Flusberg, and D. Cohen (eds) (Oxford: Oxford University Press), pp. 365–96.

Whiten, A. 1994. 'Grades of Mindreading', in C. Lewis and P. Mitchell (eds.) (Hove, UK: LEA), pp. 47–70.

Whiten, A. 1995. 'When does Smart Behaviour—Reading Become Mind-Reading?' in P. Carruthers and P. Smith (eds) (Cambridge: Cambridge University Press), pp. 277–92.

Elliott Sober

Williams, G. C. 1966. *Adaptation and Natural Selection* (Princeton: Princeton University Press).
Williams, G. C. 1998. *The Pony Fish's Glow* (New York: Basic Books).

Domains, Brains and Evolution

MICHAEL WHEELER AND ANTHONY ATKINSON

I. Introduction

According to Darwinian thinking, organisms are (for the most part) designed by natural selection, and so are (for the most part) integrated collections of adaptations, where an adaptation is a phenotypic trait that is a specialized response to a particular selection pressure. For animals that make their living in the Arctic, one adaptive problem is how to maintain body temperature above a certain minimum level necessary for survival. Polar bears' thick coats are a response to that selection pressure (surviving in extreme cold). A thick coat makes a positive difference to a polar bear's fitness, since polar bears with very thin coats left fewer offspring than those with thicker coats. The foundational idea of *evolutionary psychology* is that brains are no different from any other organ with an evolutionary function, insofar as brains too are systems shaped by natural selection to solve adaptive problems. Thus brains have a particular functional organization because their behavioural effects tend, or once tended, to help maintain or increase the fitness of organisms with those brains. Prominent evolutionary psychologists (for example: Cosmides and Tooby, 1987; Cosmides and Tooby, 1994 and Symons, 1992) have endorsed the view that the last time any significant modifications were made by natural selection to the human brain's functional architecture, we were hunter-gatherers, inhabiting a world quite different from that which we now inhabit. That world was the Pleistocene epoch, between about 2 million years ago and 10 thousand years ago. On this view, then, the Pleistocene constitutes what evolutionary psychologists often call our *environment of evolutionary adaptedness* (or *EEA*), and the information-processing structure and organization of our present-day cognitive architecture is no different from that of our recent hunter-gatherer ancestors.

Against this background, one claim that many evolutionary psychologists often make is that once a thoroughgoing Darwinian perspective is adopted, there emerge good reasons, of both an empirical and an in-principle kind, for thinking that the important work in explaining mind will be done by *domain-specific* (as opposed to domain-general) features of our cognitive architecture (see, e.g.,

Michael Wheeler and Anthony Atkinson

Tooby and Cosmides, 1992; Symons, 1992). This striking claim has attracted a good deal of recent critical fire (see, e.g., Samuels, 1998; Shapiro and Epstein, 1998). In this paper we shall engage with the arguments of the evolutionary psychologists in question, and those of their critics. However, our intention is not to give a 'final' answer to the question of whether our psychology is correctly explained in terms of domain-specific or domain-general features. (Taking on board the thought that some degree of functional specialization is to be expected in the human mind/brain, perhaps the right question is: how much of our evolved psychology is correctly explained in terms of domain-specific features, and how much in terms of domain-general features? We shall not give a 'final' answer to that question either.) Our aims are more modest. For while we are, in general, highly sympathetic to much of what the evolutionary psychologists say, it seems to us that this particular issue is clouded by the imprecise and indiscriminate use of the most basic terms in which the all-important claims and counter-claims in the dispute are expressed, terms such as 'domain', 'domain-specific' and 'domain-general'. This conceptual imprecision and promiscuity invites confusion and misinterpretation, and results in many supporters and critics talking past each other. Our principal intention in this paper, then, is to attempt some tidying up of the conceptual space encapsulated by the thorny and difficult matter of domain specificity, domain generality, and evolved cognition.[1]

II. Domains and Brains

One cannot hope to conduct a proper investigation of whether evolved psychological systems are domain-specific or domain-general in character without first saying what is meant by the term 'domain'. Unfortunately, principled definitions of what constitutes a domain are scarce in psychology. Examples and characterizations are more prevalent (Hirschfeld and Gelman, 1994b). The first task of this section is to say why evolutionary psychology provides us with a good candidate for the sort of principled definition that we need.

A useful starting point is Fodor's influential discussion of domain

[1] In what follows we shall often write as if evolutionary psychologists speak with one voice (roughly, that of Cosmides and Tooby). This is, of course, a distortion of what is a thriving research endeavour driven forward by internal disputes and differences of approach. At the very least, however, the position we describe is widely held within the field, and is championed vigorously by some of the discipline's leading theorists.

specificity. Fodor's thought is that certain psychological mechanisms are domain-specific in that they are specialized to operate with distinct and limited sets of inputs or information types. Or as Fodor himself puts it: 'only a relatively restricted class of stimulations can throw the switch that turns it [a mechanism] on' (Fodor, 1983, p. 48). According to this picture, then, a domain is a 'stimulus domain', that is, a type of stimulus for which humans have a special capacity to respond. Some stimulus types that are good candidates for stimulus domains are faces, non-face objects and language. Certain specific properties of stimuli, such as phonemes, colour, shape and three-dimensional form, are also candidates for stimulus domains, for there is much evidence that we are especially sensitive to these properties, as compared to other properties of the same types of stimuli (e.g., non-speech properties of sounds).

Despite the influential contribution of Fodor's discussion, the concept of a domain is sometimes used in a broader sense than that of a stimulus domain. Hirschfeld and Gelman, for example, outline what they 'take to be a fairly uncontroversial characterization' of the concept, as follows:

> A domain is a body of knowledge that identifies and interprets a class of phenomena assumed to share certain properties and to be of a distinct and general type. A domain functions as a stable response to a set of recurring and complex problems faced by the organism. This response involves ... perceptual, encoding, retrieval, and inferential processes dedicated to that solution. (Hirschfeld and Gelman, 1994b, p. 21).

In fact it seems there are at least five conceptions of a domain expressed or implied in this quotation.

(1) A specific body of information that constitutes the input to some perceptual mechanism or process, or to a mechanism or process that is more cognitive than perceptual, such as those involved in belief fixation, reasoning, or problem solving.
(2) An information-processing mechanism (or set of such mechanisms) dedicated to producing established responses to a problem (or set of problems) routinely faced by the organism.
(3) The output of an information-processing mechanism, where 'output' is taken to mean not behaviour, but rather an information-bearing representational state that is then delivered as input to some other, cognitively downstream information-processing mechanism.

Michael Wheeler and Anthony Atkinson

(4) The behavioural response, or set of responses.
(5) The problem, or set of problems.

Can any of these options be turned into the kind of principled definition of a domain that we are seeking? The answer, we think, is 'yes', and it is evolutionary psychology that shows us how. According to the fifth and final option on the list, a domain is a problem or set of problems routinely faced by an organism. To elaborate this idea into a proper definition, the first thing we need is a theoretically grounded method for determining what exactly constitutes a 'problem'. This is where Darwinian thinking makes its mark. The pivotal notion is that of an *adaptive problem*. Adaptive problems are problems that are specifiable in terms of evolutionary selection pressures, i.e., recurring environmental conditions that affect, or have affected, the reproductive success of individual organisms. So the evolutionary-psychological strategy is to require that the problems that delineate domains be adaptive problems. At a first pass, then, a domain may be a single adaptive problem or a set of adaptive problems. But this definition is immediately in need of attention. It is clearly important to find a way of ensuring that not any old, arbitrarily concocted, rag-bag of adaptive problems will count as a genuine domain. What one wants to say is that only a set of *suitably related* adaptive problems will do, which means saying something useful about what it means for a batch of adaptive problems to be suitably related. For the present we shall place this matter on hold. When we return to it later, we shall discover that it constitutes a pile of trouble.

Of course, there are all sorts of adaptive problems that selection has solved with means other than psychological mechanisms (e.g., we saw earlier that the adaptive problem of surviving extreme cold was solved, in the case of the polar bear, by selecting for a thick coat of fur). So, on the way of talking that we are about to import from evolutionary psychology, there exist non-psychological domains. But if psychological domains turn out to be a subset of domains in general, then we now need a way of drawing the distinction between the non-psychological and the psychological instances. Once one plugs in the fact that most evolutionary psychologists assume an information-processing theory of mind, the obvious move here presents itself. To be distinctively psychological, a domain must be defined by an adaptive problem (or a set of suitably related adaptive problems), posed in the creature's EEA, *for which an information-processing (as opposed to, say, a brutely anatomical) style of solution was appropriate*. For humans, such problems include how to throw in order to injure or kill one's dinner or enemy (Calvin, 1983), how to select a mate (Buss, 1992), how to speak and understand language (Pinker and Bloom, 1990), how to engage in and reason about social exchange (Cosmides and Tooby, 1989 & 1992) and how to explain and predict each other's behaviour (Baron-Cohen, 1995 and Leslie, 1994).

Having explicitly introduced the idea of a psychological domain, we shall, from now on, revert to speaking simply of domains. It should be clear enough in context whether we are concerned with psychological domains, non-psychological domains, or the generic notion of a domain that covers both sub-classes.

III. Information and Mechanisms

If domains are adaptive problems, then a feature of our cognitive architecture is maximally *domain-specific* just when that feature is dedicated to solving one particular adaptive problem (or one specific set of suitably related adaptive problems). On the other hand, a feature of our cognitive architecture is maximally *domain-general* just when that feature can contribute to the solution of any adaptive problem whatsoever. These definitions describe the end-points of a spectrum of imaginable cases. In many ways, in fact, it makes most sense to think of a system as being relatively domain-specific or relatively domain-general, compared with some other point on the spectrum. A desk-top computer is more domain-general than a pocket calculator, for example, which in turn is more domain-general than an abacus.

So what sort of inner elements might domain-specific or domain-general cognitive features be? As we have already seen, most evolutionary psychologists assume an information-processing theory of mind, such that the adaptationist logic that we have characterized is used to constrain and inform theorizing within that information-processing approach. As commonly understood, any information-processing psychology, Darwinian or otherwise, will buy into a distinction between data (bodies of information) and algorithms (processing mechanisms). Thus there are two ways in which a particular architectural feature might be domain-specific: it might be (a) a domain-specific body of information or (b) a domain-specific mechanism. And there are two ways in which a particular architectural feature might be domain-general: it might be (c) a domain-general body of information or (d) a domain-general mechanism.

Michael Wheeler and Anthony Atkinson

It is important to note right away that whilst we are not alone in bringing the data/algorithm distinction to the fore in discussions of domain specificity and evolutionary thinking (see, e.g., Elman *et al.*, 1996; Samuels, 1998 and Sterelny, 1995), the evolutionary psychologists do not themselves tend to make systematic use of that distinction in order to ask questions about the domain specificity or domain generality of information and mechanisms separately. There is often (although see later) simply an assumption at work that domain-specific mechanisms go hand-in-hand with domain-specific information, and that domain-general mechanisms go hand-in-hand with domain-general information. Thus consider the following, entirely typical quotations:

> [The] human psychological architecture contains many evolved mechanisms that are specialized for solving evolutionarily long-enduring adaptive problems and ... these mechanisms have content-specialized representational formats, procedures, cues, and so on. (Tooby and Cosmides, 1992, p. 34).

> To describe a system as domain-general or content-independent is to say not what it is but only what it lacks: It lacks any specific a priori knowledge about the recurrent structure of particular situations or problem-domains, either in declarative or procedural form, that might guide the system to a solution quickly. It lacks procedures that are specialized to detect and deal with particular kinds of problems, situations, relationships, or contents in ways that differ from any other kind of problems, situation, relationship, or content. (Tooby and Cosmides, 1992, pp. 103–4).

In order to view the full conceptual landscape here, we are going to have to proceed beyond this undifferentiated treatment of data and algorithm, and put some words into the collective evolutionary-psychological mouth. We can begin this process by wielding the conceptual distinction between information and mechanism in order to define a matrix of in-principle possibilities for the design of the human cognitive architecture.

information

mechanisms		domain-general	domain-specific
	domain-general	1. domain-general mechanisms coupled with domain-general information	2. domain-general mechanisms coupled with domain-specific information
	domain-specific	3. domain-specific mechanisms coupled with domain-general information	4. domain-specific mechanisms coupled with domain-specific information

At this point we need to tread carefully, because cognitive psychologists in general (and evolutionary psychologists in particular) employ a range of terminology in this area. For example, as well as the distinction between domain-specific and domain-general architectural features, a contrast is often drawn between *special-purpose* and *general-purpose* architectural features, as well as between *content-dependent* (*or content-specialized*) and *content-independent* (*or content-general*) architectural features. It would be an under-statement to say that there is no universal agreement in the psychological literature (evolutionary or otherwise) on exactly how to draw these distinctions, or of how, or even of whether, they line up with each other in systematic ways. Through our eyes, however, the terrain looks like this.

Something is *special-purpose* if it has a particular job to do. Pens are specialized for writing, coffee machines for making coffee, and kangaroo pouches for the carrying of joeys. On the other hand, something is *general-purpose* to the extent that it has many jobs that it can do. For example, there is a piece of folklore about the ingenuity of New Zealanders that involves the countless uses to which no. 8 fencing wire can be put. Although the fencing wire was originally designed solely for use in the construction of fences, in the context of the folklore, the wire is general-purpose. Since information surely cannot be described as 'having a job to do' (as opposed to 'being used by a task-performing mechanism'), in anything other than an artificially contrived sense, it seems natural to confine the terms 'special-purpose' and 'general-purpose' to considerations of mechanism. In addition, we can exploit the thought that 'having a job to do' is equivalent to 'solving a problem', and so (via the idea that domains are to be delineated in terms of adaptive problems) identify (i) the notion of a special-purpose mechanism

Michael Wheeler and Anthony Atkinson

with that of a domain-specific mechanism, and (ii) the notion of a general-purpose mechanism with that of a domain-general mechanism.

In the present context, of course, the mechanisms that are of particular interest to us will be drawn from the class of information-processing mechanisms. And it is here that the contrast between content dependence and content independence comes to the fore, since it allows us to explicate the particular ways in which specifically information-processing mechanisms might be either general-purpose or special-purpose. We can describe as *content-independent* those information-processing mechanisms that are able to operate upon representations regardless of the content of those representations; that is, to put it roughly, it does not matter what the information is about, the processor is able to deal with it. For example, a memory mechanism might store information with many different types of content. Content-independent information-processing mechanisms will be general-purpose (domain-general) in nature. Correspondingly, we can describe as *content-dependent* those information-processing mechanisms for which it does matter what its informational inputs are about; that is, content-dependent subsystems are only able to operate with a specific and limited set of information types or content. Content-dependent information-processing mechanisms will be special-purpose (domain-specific) in nature.

To avoid confusion, we should stress that saying that some mechanism is content-dependent is not the same thing as saying that it necessarily deals in domain-specific information. Similarly, saying that some mechanism is content-independent is not the same thing as saying that it necessarily deals in domain-general information. This is crucial, since we need to ensure that there remains conceptual room for the idea that a general-purpose (domain-general, content-independent) information-processing mechanism might perform its task by accessing and manipulating domain-specific information (possibility 2 in our matrix), and for the idea that a special-purpose (domain-specific, content-dependent) information-processing mechanism might perform its task by accessing and manipulating domain-general information (possibility 3). We can satisfy ourselves that this space remains intact by noting three things. First, where we are talking about content dependence and content independence, these content-related properties of interest are properties of some mechanism. By contrast, where we are talking about the domain specificity or domain generality of some body of information, we are, of course, specifying a property of that information. This indicates that the content-dependent/content-independent and the domain-specific/domain-general distinctions are conceptually distinct. Secondly, if there is such a thing as domain-general information, then that information will have a certain content. But that means that some target mechanism might be keyed into that content, and so will be content-dependent. Finally, since a content-independent mechanism (by definition) doesn't care what the information in which it deals is about, that mechanism might access and manipulate various bodies of information, each of which is specific to some particular domain.

In the interests of keeping things as clear as possible, let's now replay our matrix, using the terms 'special-purpose' and 'general-purpose' to replace 'domain-specific' and 'domain-general' in our characterization of mechanisms. (Since some of the discussion to come draws lessons from domains other than psychological ones, the notions of special-purpose and general-purpose are, for our purposes, preferable to those of content-dependent and content-independent, since the latter pair is restricted to the information-processing, and thus the psychological, cases.)

		Information	
		domain-general	**domain-specific**
mechanisms	**general-purpose**	1. general-purpose mechanisms coupled with domain-general information	2. general-purpose mechanisms coupled with domain-specific information
	special-purpose	3. special-purpose mechanisms coupled with domain-general information	4. special-purpose mechanisms coupled with domain-specific information

So which location in this matrix describes the design of the human cognitive architecture? Let's immediately narrow down the possibilities. As evolutionary psychologists often observe, the idea that cognition might be adaptive given only domain-general information is pretty much a non-starter. However, the point needs to be made with care. Tooby and Cosmides pour scorn on the thought that perfectly general information—information that would apply to every situation in all possible worlds—might have genuine adaptive utility (Tooby and Cosmides, 1992, p. 104). But a compelling case against the adaptive utility of domain-general

Michael Wheeler and Anthony Atkinson

information cannot be made on the basis of such an extreme take on the idea of domain generality. The first thing to say here is that the evolutionary strategy (as we have characterized it) is to define domains by reference to the adaptive problems confronting a given species. Thus any notion of perfectly domain-general information needs to be defined in a similarly species-relative way, as information that is about, or relevant to, all the adaptive problems facing the species in question. But now even this idea seems too extreme, since it seems likely that there simply is no item or body of information that really is relevant to *all* the adaptive problems faced by a given species. So, to avoid charges of straw opponents, any interesting argument against the adaptive utility of domain-general information would have to be levelled at some notion of *relatively* domain-general information, information that is relevant to some large number of (species-related) adaptive problems.

Having straightened that out, however, the prosecution-case remains strong. For even this revised notion of domain-general information, as species-specific and relativistic as it is, falls prey to the following principle: as one abstracts progressively further away from contextual detail, it becomes increasingly hard to see how the style of information that emerges could ever figure importantly in satisfying explanations of context-sensitive adaptive intelligence. Thus consider the relatively domain-general item of information that two physical objects cannot take up the same portion of space at the same time. This piece of information might, we suppose, help directly to solve the odd adaptive problem. Moreover, according to some philosophical or cognitive-scientific accounts (see e.g., Hayes, 1979), it might even be granted the status of a kind of tacit background assumption that is made in large numbers of action-related contexts. However, it seems implausible in the extreme that possessing the knowledge that two physical objects cannot take up the same portion of space at the same time is in any way decisive for a creature to achieve adaptive success at, say, foraging, hunting, escaping from predators, or mate-finding. It seems rather that the information that does the crucial work will almost inevitably be domain-specific (e.g., information about the typical behavioural characteristics of the creature's natural predators). These considerations effectively rule out options 1 and 3 in our matrix of design possibilities.[2]

[2] Although we have played along with a way of talking according to which certain general background assumptions, such as 'two physical objects cannot take up the same portion of space at the same time' and 'natural light always comes from above', are treated as items of informa-

Domains, Brains and Evolution

The next question is this: could there be a truly general-purpose problem-solving mechanism (in a suitably species-relative sense of general-purpose)? Symons thinks not:

> It is no more probable that some sort of general-purpose brain/mind mechanism could solve all the behavioural problems an organism faces (find food, choose a mate, select a habitat, etc.) than it is that some sort of general-purpose organ could perform all physiological functions (pump blood, digest food, nourish an embryo, etc.) or that some sort of general-purpose kitchen device could perform all food processing tasks (broil, freeze, chop, etc.). There is no such thing as a 'general problem solver' because there is no such thing as a general problem. (Symons, 1992, p. 142).

The fan of general-purpose mechanisms should, we think, simply concede that the notion of a *universal* problem solver simply doesn't make sense (cf. the equally troublesome concept of perfectly domain-general information that we ruled out above). However, what surely does make sense is the idea of a relatively general problem solver, a mechanism that works successfully in a large number of domains. So, from now on, we shall understand the term 'general-purpose mechanism' to capture precisely that idea.

IV. A Job for the Specialist?

With the clarifications of the previous section in place, the core interpretative question can now be posed. Do evolutionary psychologists expect our innate cognitive architecture to be a matter of special-purpose mechanisms coupled with domain-specific information, or of general-purpose mechanisms coupled with domain-specific information? There is much evidence in favour of the former. For example, Tooby and Cosmides claim that:

> the human mind consists of a set of evolved information-processing mechanisms ... many of these mechanisms are functionally specialized to produce behaviour that solves particular adaptive problems ... to be functionally specialized, many of these mechanisms must be richly structured in a content-specific way. (Tooby and Cosmides, 1992, p. 24).

tion that the system possesses, we are not remotely convinced that this is the best way to conceptualize matters. If such knowledge is not internally represented in a form which makes it accessible to and/or manipulable by the relevant psychological mechanisms, but rather is tacitly embedded in the basic operating principles of those mechanisms, then it is far from clear that it should be regarded as *information* that the system possesses at all.

And in a passage, the bulk of which we have reproduced once already, they state that:

> the human psychological architecture contains many evolved mechanisms that are specialized for solving evolutionarily long-enduring adaptive problems and ... these mechanisms have content-specialized representational formats, procedures, cues, and so on. ...[they are] richly content-sensitive evolved mechanisms. (Tooby and Cosmides 1992, p. 34).

How does such a view become plausible? There are certainly experimental studies which suggest that special-purpose mechanisms are indeed in operation in certain domains. Here is the flagship example: The Wason selection task requires subjects to detect violations of conditional rules, for which logically correct answers require the correct application of modus ponens and modus tollens. In the crucial experiments, the rules are presented either in abstract form (using letters and numbers), or with content that reflects a familiar context. It is a widely accepted interpretation of the robust results from studies of this task that subjects perform much better on the problem whose content reflects a familiar context, and is not presented merely in abstract form (for example: Bracewell and Hidi, 1974; Griggs and Cox, 1982 & 1983; Pollard, 1981). But this interpretation is problematic, because some familiar examples seem to cause as much difficulty as those with abstract symbols. In a series of studies, Cosmides, Tooby, and others have shown that subjects are good at the Wason selection task, if the example requires them to enforce a social contract (for example: Cosmides, 1989; Cosmides and Tooby, 1992; Gigerenzer and Hug, 1992). Spotting cheaters in social exchanges (those who accept a benefit without paying the required cost) is an ability which would have an obvious selective advantage in the human EEA, where many of the most serious adaptive challenges took place during social interactions with conspecifics. So far this looks like another good argument for the presence of domain-specific information (about social exchange) which, for all we know, may be manipulated by some sort of general-purpose reasoning algorithm. What tells against this interpretation, to some extent anyway, are experiments involving the 'switched social contract' task (Cosmides, 1989 and Cosmides and Tooby, 1992). In this task, the contractual information is presented in such a form that, if subjects apply our paradigm cases of general-purpose rules, modus ponens and modus tollens, they would give logically correct answers that violate the cost-benefit structure of social contracts. But if subjects apply rules of inference specialized for cheater detection, then they would give answers that fit the cost-benefit structure of social contracts, but which are logically incorrect. Overwhelmingly, subjects give answers consistent with the latter prediction, which indicates that special-purpose rules may well be involved (although it presumably remains possible that some presently unknown general-purpose rules other than those of the propositional calculus might be in operation).

By suggesting that special-purpose mechanisms are operative in particular contexts, experimental investigations such as the cheater detection studies are, of course, compelling and important. But one might wonder whether there are any good, in-principle evolutionary arguments for the claim that our cognitive architecture *must* consist in large numbers of special-purpose mechanisms rather than some small number of general-purpose mechanisms.

According to Shapiro and Epstein, the answer is 'no' (Shapiro and Epstein, 1998). They suggest that general-purpose mechanisms could well have evolved via what is, in effect, a process of *exaptation*. In Gould and Vrba's original explication of this concept, there are, strictly speaking, two varieties of exaptation (Gould and Vrba, 1982). In the first, an established biological feature that has no evolutionary function is later selected for by evolution to perform some adaptive task. In the second, an existing biological feature that has been selected for by evolution, and thus already has an evolutionary function, is later co-opted by selection to perform some new function. It is clear that to get the link between exaptation and the evolution of general-purpose mechanisms off the ground, one needs to focus on the second of these varieties of exaptation, and also add the rider that the previously evolved function must be maintained in addition to the newly acquired function; but with those qualifications in place, the following argument does have some prima facie appeal:

> Why develop new eyes with which to find kin when one can use old eyes that have served well in the detection of predators? Likewise, why develop a new process for recognizing kin when one has already in place a process that allows avoidance of kin when searching for mates? We should not be surprised if natural selection has recruited extant cognitive capacities for new purposes rather than going to the trouble of developing new capacities every time a novel problem comes along. (Shapiro and Epstein, 1998, p. 176).

This argument trades on an historical conception of domain gener-

Michael Wheeler and Anthony Atkinson

ality, according to which any mechanism that is selected as the solution to a particular adaptive problem counts initially as a special-purpose mechanism, but becomes increasingly general-purpose in character if and as it is exapted to perform other tasks. Of course, 'having been exapted' is not, on its own at least, a sufficient condition for a mechanism to count as general-purpose, since a mechanism that is selected for one task and then exapted for another is surely not yet general-purpose, in any interesting sense. So the idea must be that there is some (no doubt vague) point beyond which a repeatedly exapted mechanism will uncontroversially receive its general-purpose spurs. (Once one takes this fact on board, Shapiro and Epstein's once-exapted kin recognition mechanism still looks suspiciously special-purpose, relatively speaking, but we can let that pass.)

The problem is that, even with this tidied-up historical conception of domain generality in play, Shapiro and Epstein's argument misses its target, because when evolutionary psychologists use the term 'general-purpose mechanism' (or its equivalent), they simply do not mean 'suitably exapted mechanism'. They are appealing instead to another sense of general-purpose according to which any suitably (and so repeatedly) exapted mechanism that we might come across was, in fact, always general-purpose in character. On this view, the process of exaptation merely permits an intrinsically general-purpose mechanism to fulfill its potential. For this idea to make sense, what is needed is a strategy for characterizing what it means to be general-purpose that does not appeal to any actual history of evolutionary use. Such a strategy is precisely what we find in evolutionary psychology. Evolutionary psychologists typically illustrate the notion of a general-purpose mechanism by reference either to (a) what Tooby and Cosmides (1992) call the Standard Social Science Model (SSSM), or to (b) certain reasoning/learning architectures already established within cognitive science that are taken to be consonant with SSSM. Roughly, SSSM is the view that human beings are born with no innate psychological structure except for a small number of widely applicable learning devices that provide a capacity for absorbing culturally transmitted information and skills. Cognitive-scientific systems that evolutionary psychologists tend to cite as paradigmatic general-purpose mechanisms include the General Problem Solver (Newell and Simon, 1963) and mainstream connectionist networks. These are systems that can be applied to a wide class of information-processing problems, assuming that the problem-space in question can be defined within the particular representational format that is appropriate for the system

Domains, Brains and Evolution

being deployed.[3] So when evolutionary psychologists speak of general-purpose mechanisms, what they typically mean is the sort of intrinsically general-purpose mechanism that might be identified using (a) and (b). And what they typically say is that general-purpose mechanisms of this character are evolutionarily implausible *in principle* (and thus could not provide the raw material for exaptation).

At this point we need to make explicit certain explanatory constraints that are already implicitly at work in the arguments presented by evolutionary psychologists. By taking an evolutionary approach, the psychologist inherits two requirements on any proposed hypothesis about the design of our cognitive architecture (cf. Samuels, 1998). The first is what we shall call the *Minimal Requirement*. An estimated 99·9% of all species that have existed on Earth are now extinct (Lewontin, 1978; Raup, 1991), yet we as a species still exist. Thus we can confidently state that whatever design our cognitive architecture has, it must have been successful in solving the adaptive information-processing problems that our hunter-gatherer ancestors faced. From this it follows straightforwardly that for some postulated design even to be a reasonable candidate for the right story here, that design must, in principle, be able to solve all and each of those adaptive problems. The second requirement is what we shall call the *Darwinian Requirement*. The logic of Darwinism dictates that if a number of solutions to an adaptive problem (in this context, designs for cognitive systems) are present in the population, then selection will favour the superior performers. (What counts as superior will depend on the particular evolutionary scenario, but will typically involve criteria such as speed, efficiency, and reliability.) In the present context, the key implication of the Darwinian Requirement is that any information-processing system that is proposed as part of our evolved

[3] It is worth remarking that this picture requires that the various bodies of domain-specific information delivered to cognition-central be organized in a similar representational format, so that the same domain-general mechanism can operate on all the information. Although we shall not discuss this issue further here, we suspect that it is a veritable Pandora's Box of conceptual and practical difficulties. There are at least two general strategies that the fan of general-purpose central mechanisms might pursue, which, for the want of better terms, we might call the Gibsonian strategy and the Fodorian strategy. According to the Gibsonian strategy, the environment (somehow) structures the information. According to the Fodorian strategy, certain special-purpose input systems (somehow) structure the information. For a recent discussion that highlights some closely related issues, see Clark and Thornton, 1997.

253

Michael Wheeler and Anthony Atkinson

psychological architecture must have been superior to any competing system that was actually present in the human EEA (and which therefore could, potentially, have been the object of selection).

Evolutionary psychologists present a range of arguments designed to establish that general-purpose mechanisms will fail to meet the Minimal Requirement (see, e.g., Tooby and Cosmides, 1992, pp. 102–12). We shall concentrate on what is, we think, the strongest argument on offer, namely that there are many adaptive problems that could not, *in principle*, be solved by any general-purpose mechanism, because such a mechanism would be paralysed by a vicious combinatorial explosion.[4]

At the very core of the argument from combinatorial explosion is what, in artificial intelligence (AI), is called the frame problem (see, e.g., Pylyshyn, 1987).[5] As characterized by Fodor the frame problem is 'the problem of putting a "frame" around the set of beliefs that may need to be revised in the light of specified newly available information' (Fodor, 1983, pp. 112–13). Put another way, the difficulty is how to retrieve and revise just those beliefs or other representational states that are relevant in some particular context of action. Since a general-purpose reasoning system will have access to an entire system of beliefs etc., there is a real danger here of a kind of computational paralysis due to the enormity of the processing-load. It might seem that the obvious move is to deploy heuristics that decide which of a system's representations are relevant in a particular scenario. Unfortunately, this kite won't fly. The processing mechanisms would still face the problem of accessing just those relevancy heuristics that are relevant in the current context. And it is not merely that some sort of combinatorial explosion or infinite regress threatens here (which it does—how do we decide which relevancy heuristic is, in the present context, relevant?). The deeper concern is that we have no really good idea of how a computational process of relevance-based update might work. As Horgan and Tienson point out, the situation cannot be that the system first retrieves an inner structure (an item of information or a heuristic), and then decides whether or not it is relevant, as that would take us back to square one (Horgan and Tienson, 1994). But then how can the system assign relevance until the structure has been retrieved?

---

[4] For a clinical discussion of various other arguments, a discussion which finds those arguments wanting, see Samuels, 1998.

[5] For the evolutionary-psychological context, see Tooby and Cosmides, 1992, pp. 100–112.

Fodor argues that cognitive science has made progress in understanding input systems (e.g., perceptual systems) only because those systems are 'informationally encapsulated': they are systems for which the class of relevant information is restricted. In contrast, he argues, central cognitive systems, whose primary job is the fixation of beliefs, are unencapsulated, such that (i) information from anywhere in the agent's entire stock of beliefs is potentially relevant to fixing any specific belief, and (ii) the confirmation of an individual belief is relative to the structure of the whole belief system (Fodor, 1983). On Fodor's analysis the frame problem is symptomatic of this situation. But now a way to repel the frame problem seems to present itself. If central cognitive systems were like Fodorian input systems, and were thus informationally encapsulated rather than informationally unencapsulated, then they wouldn't succumb to the frame problem. And that, in part, is the picture of central cognitive systems that evolutionary psychologists have.

We say 'in part' because there is more to be said. It seems clear that the kind of system that Fodor identifies as unencapsulated must, by its very nature, contain general-purpose (i.e., content-independent) psychological mechanisms, so that any body of information present in the cognitive architecture as a whole might potentially be accessed and processed. However, it is far less clear that a commitment to informational encapsulation forces us to jump one way or the other on the issue of whether the psychological mechanisms concerned will be special-purpose or general-purpose. Any special-purpose (content-dependent) psychological mechanism will be encapsulated; but so, it seems, will an intrinsically general-purpose psychological mechanism that, through the opportunistic process of design by selection, has been allowed access only to a restricted body of information. If this analysis is right, then adopting the thought that central cognitive systems will need to be informationally encapsulated in order to defeat the frame problem (and thus, in this context, to satisfy the Minimal Requirement) does not yet decide the question of whether the mechanisms involved will need to be special-purpose or general-purpose, or, indeed, whether that is a question to which an *in-principle* answer can even be given. From what we have seen so far, the evolutionary psychologist will claim that distinctively special-purpose mechanisms, coupled with suitably organized bodies of domain-specific information, will be required. But if informational encapsulation really is the key here, then why, in principle, couldn't mechanisms which are intrinsically general-purpose in character, but which (as a matter of evolutionary fact) have access only to the appropriate body of domain-specific information, be capable of meeting the challenge?

As it happens, it is possible to be more positive. There already exists work in AI which suggests that if the designer can pre-define what is relevant in a particular scenario, then a system featuring a combination of informational encapsulation, general-purpose mechanisms, and domain-specific information will not be completely incapacitated by the frame problem. Consider Shakey (Nilsson, 1984), a famous AI-robot that inhabited an environment consisting of rooms populated by static blocks and wedges, in which it confronted a problem-domain defined by tasks of the form, 'move block A to some specified new location'. (We might treat this problem-domain as analogous to a simple adaptive domain in the natural world, although of course it is structured by the human designer rather than selection.) Shakey used visual input plus domain-specific 'innate' knowledge about its constrained world of rooms and static blocks, in order to build a model of that world in a set of first-order predicate calculus representations. These representations were then delivered to a central planning system based on the General Problem Solver (one of our paradigm cases of a general-purpose mechanism), which proceeded to determine a sequence of appropriate actions. The fact is that Shakey actually worked (albeit very slowly, more on which below); and so have many related AI-systems. It is true that these recorded successes might, in many ways, be attributable to the extreme simplicity and static nature of the relevant operating environments (for discussion, see Brooks, 1991). Nevertheless, such modest victories surely count as empirical evidence that general-purpose mechanisms are not always computationally paralysed by the frame problem, and thus that the Minimal Requirement might, at least sometimes, be met by general-purpose mechanisms using domain-specific information.

But now what about the Darwinian Requirement? For general-purpose mechanisms to meet this constraint, it would have to be the case that they are not, in general, outperformed in the efficiency stakes by special-purpose mechanisms. Tooby and Cosmides claim that special-purpose mechanisms will be the more efficient. As they put the point, 'domain-general, content-independent mechanisms are inefficient, handicapped, or inert compared to systems that also include specialized techniques for solving particular families of adaptive problems' (Tooby and Cosmides, 1992, p. 111). In response, Samuels complains (a) that no clear argument is provided for this specific claim, as opposed to the more general claim that systems with domain-specific features of some kind will be more efficient than those without, and (b) that 'it is far from clear that anyone knows how such an argument would go' (Samuels, 1998, p. 588). Samuels may be right; but perhaps something other than an argument will take us at least part of the way here. Some quite recent empirical work in AI-oriented robotics suggests that robots featuring architectures in which special-purpose mechanisms are employed alongside domain-specific information are typically faster and more robust than robots in which general-purpose mechanisms are used. For example, in the *subsumption architecture*, as pioneered by Brooks and his colleagues (see, e.g., Brooks, 1991), individual behaviour-producing mechanisms called 'layers' are designed to be individually capable of (and to be generally responsible for) connecting the robot's sensing and motor activity, in order to achieve some particular, ecologically relevant behaviour. Starting with layers that achieve simpler behaviours (such as 'avoid obstacles' and 'explore'), these special-purpose mechanisms are added, one at a time, to a debugged, working robot, so that overall behavioural competence increases incrementally. In a 'pure' subsumption architecture, no detailed messages are passed between the parallel-running multiple layers. Indeed, each layer is completely oblivious of the layers above it, although it can suppress or *subsume* the activity of the layers below it. In practice, however, the layers are often only semi-independent.

Although, from a certain perspective, the tasks performed by subsumption-based robots remain quite simple [e.g., navigating to a light source without bumping into obstacles (Franceschini *et al.*, 1992), or collecting soft-drink cans from around the MIT labs (Connell, 1989)], the approach has scored notable successes in achieving real-time behaviour in everyday, unconstrained, dynamic environments. It is thus a potentially important observation that whilst Shakey was not completely incapacitated by the frame problem, it was painfully slow, and its environment was (unlike the environments of most animals) essentially static. So to the extent that it is permissible, in the present context, to generalize from the achievements of these relatively simple robots, there is some empirical support for the following claim: even though general-purpose mechanisms might have been able to solve the adaptive problems faced in the human EEA, they will have been less efficient and robust than any competing special-purpose mechanisms that were available to evolution at the time, and thus will have been selected against.

Michael Wheeler and Anthony Atkinson

V. Contradictions, Crabs, and a Crisis

So far we have characterized evolutionary psychology as being committed to the view that the human cognitive architecture is essentially a collection of special-purpose mechanisms operating on domain-specific information. However, it is time to complicate matters, and record the fact that statements of a less dogmatic kind can often be found nestled in the evolutionary-psychological literature, statements which suggest that special-purpose and general-purpose mechanisms might peacefully co-exist, and which at least allow for the possibility that adaptive success might sometimes be explained by general-purpose mechanisms operating on domain-specific information. For example, in a recent paper, Tooby and Cosmides remind us that, in previous work, they have

> made some serious and extended arguments about why many more cognitive mechanisms [than those underpinning vision and language] will turn out to include domain-specific features alongside whatever domain-general principles of operation they have. (Tooby and Cosmides, 1998, p. 198).

And in an earlier paper, Cosmides and Tooby summarize their view by saying that our minds consist primarily of a 'constellation of specialized mechanisms that have domain-specific procedures, or operate over domain-specific representations, or both' (Cosmides and Tooby, 1994, p. 94). So it seems that evolutionary psychologists do (sometimes at least) treat the human cognitive architecture as containing a mix of general-purpose and special-purpose mechanisms. But one surely has to wonder whether the evolutionary psychologists we have been considering have the warrant to occupy such a position. After all, we have seen them launch *in-principle* arguments against the evolutionary plausibility of general-purpose mechanisms, so it is difficult to avoid the thought that they are in real danger of simply contradicting themselves here by conceding the evolutionary plausibility of such mechanisms. At first sight, however, we are rather better placed than these evolutionary psychologists to take the mixed mechanism option seriously. We found the best in-principle argument against the evolutionary plausibility of general-purpose mechanisms to be somewhat less then compelling, and ended up by confining the case 'merely' to empirical evidence from research in AI which suggests that general-purpose mechanisms will not meet the Darwinian Requirement. Moreover, perhaps we have been too hasty in suggesting (implicitly) that the results of that empirical research can be generalized across all evolutionary niches. It is time, then, to explore the possibility that there exist styles of evolutionary niche which are distinctive in that they provide conditions in which the Darwinian Requirement may be met by recognizably general-purpose mechanisms. The phenomenon of diffuse co-evolution (Janzen, 1980) generates a prime example of the kind of conditions we have in mind.

Diffuse co-evolution occurs when a group of traits in one population (which may contain several species) drives evolutionary change in a trait in a second population, via the imposition of selection pressures that act in parallel. For example, the hard shells of many crustaceans are an evolutionary response to a range of shell-breaking mechanisms deployed by a number of different predatory species. If each individual shell-breaking strategy (the deployment of pincers, crushing techniques, and so on) can be treated as a distinct adaptive domain (more on this soon), one may conclude that the crustacean shell is a relatively general-purpose response that works in a variety of different adaptive domains.

As a first pass, then, one might think that general-purpose mechanisms may result from the operation of multiple simultaneous selection pressures. But this idea is in immediate need of tightening up. Just about every organism faces multiple, simultaneous selection pressures, but only a (probably quite small) subset of these would likely have led to the development of general-purpose mechanisms. To introduce a selective force in favour of a general-purpose mechanism, the selection pressures concerned would have to be *related* in some *systematic* way. It's not easy to give a principled definition of 'systematically related', but its meaning is at least intuitively clear. On the one hand, it is rather unlikely that a mechanism would have evolved that was capable of, say, protecting the crab from attack *and* controlling its leg muscles or pumping blood around its body. But on the other hand, it seems clear that (a) attacks by one type of weapon can count as one selection pressure, and (b) attacks by different types of weapons can count as multiple selection pressures which are systematically related.

The proposal we wish to extract from the example of diffuse co-evolution has now emerged: where multiple, simultaneous, systematically related selection pressures are in operation, the adaptive response may well be a general-purpose mechanism. (Although diffuse co-evolution provides a paradigmatic case of this process, the *co*-evolutionary nature of the scenario is not strictly crucial to out point.)[6] Our further suggestion (which owes much to a discussion of diffuse co-evolution by Bullock, 1998) is that there might well be analogous selective forces in favour of general-purpose cognitive mechanisms. These forces may occur, we suggest, just where an organism confronts multiple, simultaneous, systematically related selection pressures that require an information-processing style of solution. Note that the general-purpose character of these mechanisms would not approach that of the mechanisms evolutionary psychologists typically rally against, that is, mechanisms identified by reference either to the SSSM or to reasoning/learning architectures such as the General Problem Solver and mainstream connectionist networks (see section IV). Perhaps a good term for what might be achieved is *cross-domain adaptation.*[7]

As mentioned above, one constraint on the evolution of such relatively general-purpose, cross-domain adaptive mechanisms is that they must meet the Darwinian Requirement. But, at first sight, this seems to introduce a difficulty with the present proposal, namely that in any one of its domains of application, we might expect a cross-domain adaptive mechanism to have been out-performed by any suitably aimed special-purpose mechanism that was present in the relevant EEA. With respect to that particular domain, therefore, the cross-domain adaptive mechanism would fail to meet the Darwinian Requirement. In fact, what is at fault here is not the argument for cross-domain adaptation, but the idea that the Darwinian Requirement must be met for each individual selection pressure (e.g., each predatory strategy). After all, while pincer cutting machinery may out-score a hard shell in the context of attack by pincers, it will do much worse than the hard shell against some

---

[6] In cases of exaptation (as described earlier in this paper), the multiple selection pressures at issue will certainly be systematically related, and, in some instances of the phenomenon, may even end up acting in parallel. However, by hypothesis, those selection pressures will be introduced in a sequential or additive fashion. At first, selection will generate a trait as a response to a single adaptive problem. Given the Darwinian Requirement, we would typically expect the nature of the evolutionary response to be tailored in highly specific ways to the nature of the adaptive problem. Subsequently, selection may tinker with that already-established trait, in order to meet later adaptive challenges. But, in our view, it is to the extent that the selection pressures in question operate in parallel *from the beginning* of the relevant period of evolutionary design-history that we should expect to see some sort of intrinsically general-purpose mechanism as the outcome.

[7] Our thanks to Gary Brase for suggesting this alternative term.

Domains, Brains and Evolution

crushing strategy. It is no good running rings round the pincer monster if you get flattened by the crushing beast five minutes later. Thus it is surely plausible that where the relevant selection pressures are multiple, simultaneous, and systematically related, the selective advantages bestowed by relative efficiency, relative reliability, and so on, will accrue at the level of the whole set of selection pressures.

Unfortunately we have just stepped on to a very slippery slope indeed. We have suggested that if a group of multiple, simultaneous selection pressures (such as the different predatory strategies facing the crab) are systematically related, then an accurate account of what structures and traits have evolved, and why, would seem to require that selective advantage be specified at the level of the entire set of selection pressures. But if that is so, then why isn't the set of selection pressures in question itself just a bona fide adaptive domain, making the mechanism that evolved in response (the crab's shell, for example) special-purpose? In this context, recall our earlier observation that a domain may be a single adaptive problem, or it may be a set of *suitably related* adaptive problems. This observation was accompanied by the warning that once we sorted out what 'suitably related' might mean, there would be trouble. We are now in a position to see why. It is surely plausible that at least one way in which a collection of adaptive problems might be suitably related to each other, so as to constitute a domain, is by meeting the dual requirements of operating in parallel and being systematically related. But that means that the set of different predatory strategies facing the crab constitutes an adaptive domain, and thus that the crab's shell is a special-purpose mechanism. Indeed one might conceivably go further: if certain multiple simultaneous selection pressures are indeed systematically related in the way we have described, why doesn't that make their joint operation precisely a kind of single, although higher-order and complex, selection pressure in its own right, one to which the crab's shell is a special-purpose response?

At this juncture you might well be thinking, 'So much the worse for Wheeler and Atkinson's attempt to identify a style of evolutionary niche in which the Darwinian Requirement may be met by a recognizably general-purpose style of mechanism'. If that were the extent of the trouble here, then, indeed, not much would be at stake. But now consider this. It is certainly beginning to look as if the specification of what counts as a domain, and therefore any subsequent judgment of domain specificity or domain generality, will be relative to our description of the evolutionary scenario. In

Michael Wheeler and Anthony Atkinson

one sense, this may come as no great surprise. As any survey of the appropriate academic literature will indicate, it is common for cognitive and brain scientists to be somewhat promiscuous in their deployment of the term 'domain', in line, we suppose, with its pretheoretical, everyday usage. Perceptual and cognitive tasks at various levels of description are said to be domains (and therefore cognitive/neural mechanisms at various levels of description are said to be domain-specific or special-purpose). For example, language, vision and audition are often delineated as domains. But so are more fine-grained tasks, such as word recognition, object recognition and face recognition. And sometimes even finer-grained psychological problems seem to count, problems such as phoneme segmentation and line orientation. What our investigation here suggests is that, from an evolutionary perspective, the promiscuity present in the scientific literature may well be warranted; which is just fine, unless, that is, one feels that there ought to be room for a genuine debate over whether the features of our evolved psychological architecture should be categorized as domain-specific or as domain-general. The fact that such judgements are, if we are right, relative to some adopted level of description suggests that the best one can say in this debate is that once a level of description has been agreed, a particular mechanism, or a particular body of information, will turn out to be in one category or the other. Nevertheless, there always remains the possibility of switching to another level of description, at which we may well get an entirely different result.

The consequence just highlighted might not seem so bad, if one concentrates on cases where there exist plausible criteria for deciding, in a principled fashion, between competing levels of description. But what do we say about cases where no such criteria exist? Think again about the crab's shell. On the face of it, there doesn't seem to be anything to choose between our two competing interpretations of this evolutionary scenario. The interpretation that finds the target mechanism to be special-purpose doesn't seem to be any worse than the one that finds that mechanism to be general-purpose. But it certainly doesn't seem to be any better either. In other words, it seems as if a dangerous kind of *arbitrariness* may often infect the whole enterprise of fixing the all-important level of description from which decisions concerning the domain-specific or domain-general status of some architectural feature might be made. To the extent that this is so, and to the extent that such troublesome cases are widespread, the idea that there is a robust and principled distinction between domain-specific and domain-general features of an evolved cognitive architecture threatens simply to evaporate, and with it, we are afraid, the debate that has exercised us in this paper.[8]

VI. Conclusions

The definition of domains in terms of adaptive problems, implicit in evolutionary psychology, was at the heart of our attempt to do some conceptual spring-cleaning. Adopting this definition allowed us to make the conceptual space surrounding notions such as domain, domain specificity, and domain generality a lot tidier. But it also led us, eventually, to see that this cleaner conceptual space is much less rigid and immutable than is seemingly required by those who think there exists an absolute answer to the question of whether any given architectural feature is domain-specific or domain-general in character. The rather unnerving implication of our investigation here is that for at least some evolved characters, this question may have no definitive answer[9].

[8] There are without doubt some close connections between the problem that we have aired here (roughly, that choosing between levels of evolutionary description may sometimes be arbitrary), and what Sterelny and Griffiths have identified recently as evolutionary psychology's 'grain problem'; see Sterelny and Griffiths, 1999. (As these authors explain it, the grain problem is that it is very difficult, and in many cases perhaps impossible, to match distinct adaptive problems with distinct phenotypic features that have evolved to solve them.) In the end, it may even be that our two problems are in fact equivalent. If so, then what one line of thought in the present paper has achieved is the mapping out of a significantly different route to, and a significantly different elaboration of, that single problem.

[9] This work grew out of discussions on evolutionary psychology between the two of us while we were both based in the Department of Experimental Psychology, University of Oxford. During this time, AA was partly supported by St. Edmund Hall, Oxford, and MW was supported by a Junior Research Fellowship at Christ Church, Oxford, with additional assistance from the McDonnell-Pew Centre for Cognitive Neuroscience. Our thanks to all these institutes for their support. AA also wishes to thank the Department of Psychology, University of York, where he was an Honorary Visiting Fellow while this work was completed. For their helpful comments, questions and advice at various stages, we thank Gary Brase, Seth Bullock, Julie Coultas, Martin Davies, Matthew Elton, David Over, David Papineau and Henry Plotkin.

Michael Wheeler and Anthony Atkinson

Bibliography

Barkow, J. H., Cosmides, L. and Tooby, J. (eds) 1992. *The Adapted Mind: Evolutionary Psychology and the Generation of Culture* (New York: Oxford University Press).

Baron-Cohen, S. 1995. *Mindblindness: An Essay on Autism and Theory of Mind* (Cambridge, MA: MIT Press/Bradford Books).

Bracewell, R. J. and Hidi, S. E. 1974. 'The Solution of an Inferential Problem as a Function of the Stimulus Materials', *Quarterly Journal of Experimental Psychology*, **26**, 480–88.

Brooks, R. A. 1991. 'Intelligence Without Reason', in *Proceedings of the Twelfth International Joint Conference on Artificial Intelligence San Mateo, California* (Morgan Kauffman), pp. 569–95.

Bullock, S. 1998. *Evolutionary Simulation Models: On Their Character and Application to Problems Concerning the Evolution of Natural Signalling Systems*. D-Phil Thesis, University of Sussex.

Buss, D. M. 1992. 'Mate Preference Mechanisms: Consequences for Partner Choice and Intrasexual Competition', in J. H. Barkow, L. Cosmides, and J. Tooby (eds) (New York: Oxford University Press), pp. 249–66.

Calvin, W. 1983. *The Throwing Madonna: Essays on the Brain* (New York: McGraw-Hill).

Clark, A. and Thornton, C. 1997. 'Trading Spaces: Computation, Representation and the Limits of Uninformed Learning', *Behavioral and Brain Sciences*, **20**, 57–90.

Connell, J. H. 1989. 'A Colony Architecture for an Artificial Creature', *MIT AI Lab Memo* 1151.

Cosmides, L. and Tooby, J. 1987. 'From Evolution to Behavior: Evolutionary Psychology as the Missing Link', in J. Dupre (ed.) (Cambridge, MA: MIT Press, 1987), pp. 227–306.

Cosmides, L. 1989. 'The Logic of Social Exchange: Has Natural Selection Shaped How Humans Reason? Studies with the Wason Selection Task', *Cognition*, **31**, 187–276.

Cosmides, L. and Tooby, J. 1989. 'Evolutionary Psychology and the Generation of Culture, Part II. Case Study: A Computational Theory of Social Exchange', *Ethology and Sociobiology*, **10**, 51–97

Cosmides, L. and Tooby, J. 1992. 'Cognitive Adaptations for Social Exchange', in J. H. Barkow, L. Cosmides, and J. Tooby (eds) (New York: Oxford University Press), pp. 163–228.

Cosmides, L. and Tooby, J. 1994. 'Beyond Intuition and Instinct Blindness: Toward an Evolutionary Rigorous Cognitive Science', *Cognition*, **50**, 41–77.

Dupre, J. (ed.) 1987. *The Latest on the Best: Essays on Evolution and Optimality* (Cambridge, MA: MIT Press).

Elman, J. L., Bates, E. A., Johnson, M. H., Karmiloff-Smith, A., Parisi, D. and Plunkett, K. 1996. *Rethinking Innateness: A Connectionist*

Domains, Brains and Evolution

Perspective on Development (Cambridge, MA: MIT Press/Bradford Books)

Feigenbaum, E. A. and Feldman, J. (eds) 1963. *Computers and Thought* (New York: McGraw-Hill)

Fodor, J. A. 1983. *The Modularity of Mind* (Cambridge, MA: MIT Press).

Franceschini, N., Pichon, J. M. and Blanes, C. 1992. 'From Insect Vision to Robot Vision', *Philosophical Transactions of the Royal Society B* 337, 283–94.

Gigerenzer, G. and Hug, K. 1992: 'Domain-Specific Reasoning: Social Contracts, Cheating, and Perspective Change', *Cognition,* **43**, 127–71.

Gould, S. J. and Vrba, E. S. 1982: 'Exaptation: A Missing Term in the Science of Form', *Paleobiology,* **1.8**, 4–15.

Griggs, R. A. and Cox, J. R. 1982. 'The Elusive Thematic-Materials Effect in Wason's Selection Task', *British Journal of Psychology,* **73**, 407–20.

Griggs, R. A. and Cox, J. R. 1983. 'The Effects of Problem Content and Negation on Wason's Selection Task', *Quarterly Journal of Experimental Psychology,* **35A**, 519–33.

Hayes, P. J. 1979. 'The Naive Physics Manifesto', in D. Michie (ed.) (Edinburgh: Edinburgh University Press), pp. 242–70.

Hirschfeld, L.A. and Gelman, S. A. (eds.) 1994a: *Mapping the Mind: Domain Specificity in Cognition and Culture.* (Cambridge and New York: Cambridge University Press).

Hirschfeld, L. A. and Gelman, S. A. 1994b. 'Toward a Topography of Mind: An Introduction to Domain Specificity', in L. A. Hirschfeld and S. A. Gelman (eds) (Cambridge and New York: Cambridge University Press, 1994), pp. 3–35.

Horgan, T. and Tienson, J. 1994. 'A Nonclassical Framework for Cognitive Science', *Synthese,* **101**, 305–45.

Janzen, D. H. 1980. 'When is it Co-Evolution?', *Evolution,* **34**, 611–12.

Leslie, A. M. 1994. 'ToMM, ToBy, and Agency: Core Architecture and Domain Specificity', in L. A. Hirschfeld and S. A. Gelman (eds) (Cambridge and New York: Cambridge University Press), pp. 119–48.

Lewontin, R.C. 1978. 'Adaptation', *Scientific American,* **239.3**, 156–69.

Michie, D. (ed.) 1979. *Expert Systems in the Micro-Electronic Age* (Edinburgh: Edinburgh University Press).

Newell, A. and Simon, H. A. 1963. 'GPS—A Program that Simulates Human Thought', in E. A. Feigenbaum and J. Feldman (eds) (New York: McGraw-Hill), pp. 279–96.

Nilsson, N. J. 1984. 'Shakey the Robot', *S.R.I. AI Centre Tech. Report. no. 323.*

Pinker, S. and Bloom, P. 1990. 'Natural Language and Natural Selection', *Behavioral and Brain Sciences,* **13**, 707–27.

Pollard, P. 1981. 'The Effect of Thematic Content on the "Wason selection task"', *Current Psychological Research,* **1**, 21–29.

Pylyshyn, Z. (ed.) 1987. *The Robot's Dilemma: The Frame Problem in Artificial Intelligence* (New Jersey: Ablex).

265

Michael Wheeler and Anthony Atkinson

Raup, D. M. 1991. *Extinction: Bad Genes or Bad Luck?* (New York: W. W. Norton).

Samuels, R. 1998. 'Evolutionary Psychology and the Massive Modularity Hypothesis', *British Journal for the Philosophy of Science*, **49**, 575–602.

Shapiro, L. and Epstein, W. 1998: 'Evolutionary Theory Meets Cognitive Psychology: A More Selective Perspective', *Mind and Language*, **13**, 171–94.

Sterelny, K. 1995. 'Review of The Adapted Mind', *Biology and Philosophy*, **10**, 255–85.

Sterelny, K. and Griffiths, P. E. 1999. *Sex and Death: An Introduction to Philosophy of Biology* (Chicago: University of Chicago Press).

Symons, D. 1992. 'On the Use and Misuse of Darwinism in the Study of Human Behavior', in J. H. Barkow, L. Cosmides, and J. Tooby (eds) (New York: Oxford University Press), pp. 137–59.

Tooby, J. and Cosmides, L. 1992. 'The Psychological Foundations of Culture', in J. H. Barkow, L. Cosmides, and J. Tooby (eds) (New York: Oxford University Press), pp. 19–136.

Tooby, J. and Cosmides, L. 1998: 'Evolutionizing the Cognitive Sciences: A Reply to Shapiro and Epstein', *Mind and Language*, **13**, 195–204.

Evolution and the Human Mind: how far can we go?[1]

HENRY PLOTKIN

A disjunction that needs explaining.

There is a close coincidence in time between the appearance of psychology as a science and the rise of evolutionary theory. The first laboratory of experimental psychology was established in Germany by Wilhelm Wundt just as Darwin's writings were beginning to have their enormous impact, especially as they might be applied to understanding the human mind (Darwin, 1871). Psychology is an important discipline because it straddles the boundary between the biological sciences and the social or human sciences (defined as those sciences that study exclusively human characteristics) of anthropology, sociology and economics. Given that importance, and given that new sciences lack the conceptual history within which older, established sciences might be mired, it might have been expected that psychology would have embraced in a way that established sciences did not the equally new, sensational and central theorem of biology which spoke to the origins of species as well as the origins of their traits and, crucially, the functions of those traits. Yet for over a century evolutionary theory had virtually no presence in psychology, despite having powerful friends like William James at court (James, 1880).

One reason for psychology's failure to incorporate evolution into its thinking was that its founders as a science, people like Wundt, Helmholtz and both J. and G. E. Muller, were physiologists by training whose methodology was rooted in the search for proximate causes by way of experimentation. Biology now incorporates a number of different causal frameworks, (Mayr, 1961; Tinbergen, 1963) but the distal or ultimate causes of ecology, phylogeny and functional utility were not the staple diet of 19th century physiology—indeed, they were not the staple diet of any 19th century natural science. The scientific 'reflexes' of the founding fathers of psychology were those of physiologists. Any chance that evolution might have had of breaking into psychology following the

[1] This is a precis of the public lecture given as part of the Royal Institute of Philosophy conference in July 1999.

Henry Plotkin

construction of the modern synthesis from around 1920 was destroyed by the rise of behaviourism, whose effect on psychological science for almost half a century is hard to overstate. In effect, behaviourism forbade theoretical recourse to unobservable causes. Since much of evolution's causal mechanisms as they apply to the mind are embodied in psychological states such as predispositions or constrained cognitive devices, brain structures, and genes, none of them visible to the naked eye which is what behaviourism demanded of its causes, evolution was forbidden entry to scientific psychology. The real significance of the rise of cognitivism in the 1960s was that cognitive psychology readmitted unobservable causes to its explanatory toolbox. At almost the same time there was an upwelling of new interest in evolution both within the sciences at large and within the wider culture because of a number of new theories challenging the supremacy of NeoDarwinism. This further coincidence between a resurgent evolutionary theory (or theories) and a new kind of psychological science did not have a result quite as negative as that original coincidence of 120 years before, but neither was it overwhelming. Evolution has now gained a small presence in academic psychology, but it remains the case that by any measure (for examples, journals or journal pages given over to evolutionary material, textbook pages, taught courses at both undergraduate and graduate levels, numbers of PhD theses, research funding, or numbers of academic posts) evolution and evolutionary theory is very under-represented within psychology. This, of course, is at variance with the considerable interest in the evolution of mind amongst academic colleagues from other disciplines, notably philosophy, as well as the wider public.

This continuing disjunction between the interests of psychologists themselves and those who stand outside of the discipline is significant, but not easy to explain, especially as the hostility is strongest amongst those most influential in the cognitive revolution, the most famous example being Chomsky. Partly it remains, one assumes, a matter of history. We are all of us children of our times and our teachers of the 1960s and 1970s were not teaching us evolution. Partly, and this is without doubt, it is because many psychologists find distasteful what they see as simple-minded nativism that blocks further study (Elman *et al.*, 1996; Mandler, 1997). This dislike is combined with a further distaste for claims about issues like sex-differences and the causes of human warfare that are sometimes cliches, sometimes manifestly wrong, and sometimes highly offensive. They also judge these claims, if they are couched in terms of past selection pressures, unscientific in their

Evolution and the Human Mind: how far can we go?

explanations which are cast in terms of an empirically unreachable 'environment of evolutionary adaptiveness'. Indeed, some evolutionary psychology is judged to be simple-minded and unacceptable in its unverifiable speculation by other evolutionary psychologists.

What is evolutionary psychology?

In the period immediately following the cognitive revolution a tiny minority of psychologists, often influenced by ethologists, began to take an interest in evolution across a broad range of problems, notably animal behaviour as it bears on that of humans, (Eibl-Eibesfeldt, 1967) evolutionary epistemology, (Campbell, 1959) cognitive development, (Piaget, 1971) and learning theory (Razran, 1971). It was only following the publication of Barkow *et al.*'s *The Adapted Mind* (1992) that evolutionary psychology assumes any real identity within the subject. Yet even that is illusory because there are many ways of practicing evolutionary psychology, and some are seriously at odds with one another.

The fundamental tenet of all evolutionary psychology is that the human mind is a product of evolution, and has characteristics consistent with its evolutionary origins. There is also agreement on all sides on the broader perspective of human psychological evolution. If the agricultural revolution is put at about ten thousand years before the present and the origins of *Homo sapiens* at around two hundred thousand years ago, then modern humans occupy just 5% of the time our species has existed; and if the genus *Homo* first appeared about two million years ago, then modern humans cover a mere 0·5% in the evolution of our genus. The general assumption is that modern humans are not different in terms of basic psychological processes and mechanisms from humans who predated the appearance of agriculture. Beyond that there is little agreement. For example, whilst the origins of language are unknown, its appearance has been put as early as two million years before the present, (Tobias, 1995) or in the period following the first appearance of our species, which places its origins no earlier than two hundred thousand years ago. The same depth of disagreement applies to the extent to which language is a specifically evolved organ of mind (Pinker, 1994; Deacon, 1997). There are also over half a dozen separate and different methods of studying evolutionary psychology, including approaches based on selfish-gene theory, behavioural ecology, game theory, sexual selection theory, Darwinian algorithms, child development, behavioural genetics, and the evolution of culture. Methodological variety is not uncommon in science, but in evolutionary psychology the antagonism between the proponents of different approaches makes it unusual science. Social Darwinism always lurks just beyond the horizon of evolutionary psychology and is, of course, the source of this dissension.

Limitations of space allows brief discussion of just two of these approaches. They have been chosen because they represent two very different lines of study of the same thing, namely the evolution of the human mind. Yet each demonstrates that evolutionary psychology has the potential for going very far indeed in giving us an understanding of the human mind.

Evolution in the family.

Darwin considered the existence of sterile insect castes to represent a challenge to his theory. He resolved the problem by appealing to 'the good of the community', a shift from individual to group selection. A century later sterile insect castes were explained, as was all biological altruism, by inclusive fitness and kin selection, (Hamilton, 1964; Williams, 1966) that is, selfish-gene theory. Selfish-gene theory was used in turn to provide a model for parent-offspring conflict (Trivers, 1974). This model of parent-offspring conflict and sibling rivalry was then exploited by Sulloway (1996) in a massive study of family dynamics, birth-order effects and human personality. Sulloway's work is notable for the way he has extended the boundaries of evolutionary psychology, and for the massive quantity of data that he has accumulated.

Sulloway's starting point is that siblings raised together are as different in personality from one another as they are from people from different families. From this he deduces that the family is an environment made up of many niches, the latter deriving from the relationships that children bear both to their parents and their siblings. He also adopts the ecological principle of competitive exclusion to assume that no niche can be occupied by more than one child. In the interests of their inclusive fitness benefits, children employ different strategies to maximize parental investment in themselves. As children compete for the limited resource of parental care they diverge into different psychological niches within the family which determines personality characteristics. The most readily available and rewarding of these niches, which include close identification with parental values, are occupied by older children. The niches left to younger siblings result in less conventional personality types.

Evolution and the Human Mind: how far can we go?

Using the theory of the school of personality theorists who assume the existence of a small set of basic personality dimensions, (Digman, 1990) Sulloway investigated how factors in family life, notably birth order, affects where individuals end up on these basic dimensions of extroversion, neuroticism, agreeableness, conscientiousness, and openness to experience. In general, firstborns are more dominating, assertive, status-conscious and defensive. Younger sibs are less self-assured, more open to ideas, questioning, flexible and easy-going. Using a meta-analysis of published studies of birth-order effects he finds openness to experience and agreeableness to be present to a significantly higher degree in later-born children, whereas conscientiousness is very much a characteristic of firstborns.

Sulloway also established a database of some six thousand people, including about 3,900 scientists, who lived over the last six centuries. Amongst many findings he shows that laterborns are overwhelmingly more likely to support new ideas than are firstborns. For example, between 1700 and 1875, laterborns were four times more likely to be proponents of evolution than firstborns of the same age. He extends a similar analysis to the political allegiances of brothers who were deputies to the National Convention of France during the revolution and the voting patterns of Supreme Court judges of the United States, amongst other sources of data.

Whatever reservations one might have about this work, and these include prominent counter-examples (Newton, Kepler, Galileo, Lavoisier, Einstein, Freud, and Martin Luther), gender effects, applicability to modern families with much reduced sibship sizes, and the need for cross-cultural studies to assess the universality of his main findings, Sulloway's scholarship is a wonderfully impressive contribution to evolutionary psychology. In the unusual focus upon family dynamics and personality, he is able to show just how far one can go in illuminating fundamental and important features of the human mind with the application of evolutionary theory.

The problem of culture.

The human capacity to create and enter into culture, defined as shared knowledge and beliefs, (Goodenough, 1957) is perhaps the single wholly unique attribute of humans. An awesomely complex phenomenon, culture is often held up like a talisman by social scientists to ward off the advances of a rampant biology. The extent to which evolutionary thinking can establish a better understanding of culture and how the human mind can enter a collective of beliefs and knowledge, is as sensitive a measure one can get of how far such thinking can go in understanding the mind.

There is, however, a puzzle at the heart of any evolutionary analysis of culture. This is that culture, the supreme manifestation of the flexibility of the human mind, arises out of discrete psychological mechanisms. Some of these mechanisms, perhaps all of them, are products of evolution, having been selected for the specific adaptive functions they have for individuals and for the increases in fitness bestowed on individuals. But culture itself, or, more correctly, the capacity for enculturation, is not some single psychological trait. It is, rather, a 'supertrait'. That is, it is an attribute that has not itself been selected for, but which is a consequence of constituent evolved traits. Thus defined, it is not clear that any other species demonstrate supertraits of any kind, or whether our own species has any supertraits other than enculturation. It is certainly possible that other features of the mind, like language or other complex cognitive capacities, are supertraits.

Our continuing ignorance of the psychological and neurological mechanisms that drive human cognition condemn us for the present only to speculation, though it is speculation which psychology and neuroscience can eventually invest with empirical certainties. In any event, neural plasticity probably evolved soon after the appearance of nervous systems in multicellular animals. Five hundred million years of evolutionary tinkering and moulding upon the basic mechanism of plasticity constitutes a form of pre-adaptation on a grand scale. If neuroscience is able to demonstrate that all neural plasticity is driven by a single set of biochemical events acting within a single neural microstructure, then this must mean that known differences in different forms of cognition are the result of macrostructural differences in the way that the basic microstructural units are configured. It will also mean that the architecture of the mind will strain the conceptual resources of evolutionists.

In short, it is being argued that culture is a supertrait which has not been specifically selected for, but is a consequence of cognitive mechanisms which have been selected for, and which in turn evolved as pre-adaptations or exaptations (Gould, 1991; Skoyles, 1997) as a result of repeated co-opting to function of previously evolved neural network structures on a scale unlike any other encountered by biologists. This might, coincidentally, account for the rapid expansion in brain size during the evolution of the hominid lineage leading to humans which has had no other equal in the evolution of nervous systems.

Evolution and the Human Mind: how far can we go?

The application of evolutionary theory to the psychology and neuroscience of culture is likely to be the most complex task that evolutionists are ever asked to undertake. Given that culture is the most complex phenomenon on Earth, a collective of minds by definition being more complex than any one of its constituent minds, this should surprise no-one.

Biologists wielding evolutionary theory are often accused of being simple-minded in their approach to human complexity, in particular threatening reductionist explanations, especially some form of genetic reductionism (Rose *et al.* 1984). Proper reduction, of course, is a complex and precise exercise, seldom achieved and never simple-minded. However that may be, in the matter of the human mind, its very flexibility precludes genetic reductionist analysis. This is because intelligence evolved precisely because of the inability of the main biological programme, evolution as normally understood, to deal with significant fluctuations in the conditions of the world. It was the adaptive value of being able to track conserved, co-varying relationships in the world, which are too fine-grained to be detected by evolution itself, that led to the evolution of learning and intelligence (Plotkin, 1994). Put in other terms, the evolution of intelligence constituted the partial resiting of behavioural causation away from genes and in to neural networks. This fundamental shift in the causes of behaviour simply negates the claims of its critics that an evolutionary account of the mind is reductionist in impulse.

There is, though, one approach to the evolution of culture for which the criticism of simple-mindedness might be justified. This is the view built on the assumption that culture comprises units, memes, which are the analogues of genes, and which are based upon imitation. There may well be identifiable units of culture, and calling them memes does no harm. But equating memes with imitation is either to reduce culture to an outrageous simplification of copied behaviours because that is what imitation properly refers to, or to inflate the meaning of imitation to the point where the word has no meaning. There is a real difference between analysing culture as shared beliefs and knowledge, and analysing culture as shared actions. One of the most important tasks for those seeking to understand the evolution of culture is to identify the psychological mechanisms essential for enculturation. Resting the case on the mechanisms of imitation is to impoverish an evolutionary explanation of culture and confirm the worst fears of social scientists.

Developing a natural science account of culture requires, then, an understanding of mechanisms that are consonant with the

Henry Plotkin

complexity of culture. How far this can be done will determine how far we can go in understanding the evolution of the mind.

Bibliography

Barkow, J. H., Cosmides, L. and Tooby, J. 1992. *The Adapted Mind: Evolutionary Psychology and the Generation of Culture* (New York: Oxford University Press).

Campbell, D. T. 1959. 'Methodological suggestions from a comparative psychology of knowledge processes', *Inquiry*, **2**, 152–82.

Darwin, C. 1871. *The Descent of Man* (London: Murray).

Deacon, T. 1997. *The Symbolic Species* (London: Norton).

Digman, J. M. 1990. 'Personality structure: emergence of the 5-factor model', *Annual Review of Psychology*, **41**, 417–40.

Eibl-Eibesfeldt, I. 1967. 'Concepts of ethology and their significance in the study of human behaviour', in H. W. Stevenson, E. H. Hess and H. L. Rheingold (eds) (New York: Wiley).

Elman, J. L., Bates, E. A., Johnson, M. H., Karmiloff-Smith, A., Parisi, D. and Plunkett, K. 1996. *Rethinking Innateness* (Cambridge, MA: MIT Press).

Goodenough, W. H. 1957. 'Cultural anthropology and linguistics', in P. Garim (ed.) *Report of the 7th Annual Round Table Meeting on Linguistics and Language Study. Georgetown University Monograph Series on Language and Linguistics*, **9**, 167–73.

Gould, S. J. 1991. 'Exaptation: a crucial tool for evolutionary psychology', *Journal of Social Issues*, **47**, 43–65.

Hamilton, W. D. 1964. 'The genetical evolution of social behaviour', *Journal of Theoretical Biology*, **7**, 1–52.

James, W. 1880. 'Great men, great thoughts, and the environment', *Atlantic Monthly*, **46**, 441–59.

Mandler, G. 1997. *Human Nature Explained* (Oxford: Oxford University Press).

Mayr, E. 1961. 'Cause and effect in biology', *Science*, **134**, 1501–06.

Stevenson, H. W., Hess, E. H. and Rheingold, H. L. (eds) 1967. *Early Behaviour* (New York: Wiley).

Piaget, J. 1971. *Biology and Knowledge* (Edinburgh: Edinburgh University Press).

Pinker, S. 1994. *The Language Instinct* (London: Penguin).

Plotkin, H. 1994. *The Nature of Knowledge* (London: Allen Lane).

Plotkin, H. 1997. *Evolution in Mind* (London: Allen Lane).

Razran, G. 1971. *Mind in Evolution* (Boston: Houghton Mifflin).

Rose, S., Kamin, L. J. and Lewontin, R. C. 1984. *Not in our Genes* (London: Penguin).

Skoyles, J. R. 1997. 'Evolution's missing link: a hypothesis upon neural plasticity, prefrontal working memory and the origins of modern cognition', *Medical Hypotheses*, **48**, 499–509.

Evolution and the Human Mind: how far can we go?

Sulloway, F. J. 1996. *Born to Rebel: Birth Order, Family Dynamics and Creative Lives* (New York: Pantheon Books).

Tinbergen, N. 1963. 'On the aims and methods of ethology', *Zeitschrift fur Tierpsychologie,* **20**, 410–33.

Tobias, P. V. 1995. *The Communication of the Dead: Earliest Vestiges of the Origin of Articulate Language.* 17th Kroon-Voordracht Lecture. Amsterdam, Nederlands Museum.

Trivers, R. L. 1974. 'Parent-offspring conflict', *American Zoologist,* **14**, 249–64.

Williams, G. C. 1966. *Adaptation and Natural Selection* (Princeton: Princeton University Press).

Index

Index

Index

Index